Staying Healthy with SIGNET Books

EAT
TO
WIN

THE
SPORTS
NUTRITION
BIBLE

Dr. Robert Haas

Recipes by
Hilarie Porter

A SIGNET BOOK

NEW AMERICAN LIBRARY

This or any other diet should be followed
only under a doctor's supervision.

To my parents

NAL BOOKS ARE AVAILABLE AT QUANTITY DISCOUNTS
WHEN USED TO PROMOTE PRODUCTS OR SERVICES.
FOR INFORMATION PLEASE WRITE TO PREMIUM MARKETING DIVISION,
NEW AMERICAN LIBRARY, 1633 BROADWAY,
NEW YORK, NEW YORK 10019.

SIGNET TRADEMARK REG. U.S. PAT. OFF. AND FOREIGN COUNTRIES
REGISTERED TRADEMARK—MARCA REGISTRADA
HECHO EN CHICAGO, U.S.A.

SIGNET, SIGNET CLASSIC, MENTOR, PLUME, MERIDIAN AND
NAL BOOKS are published by New American Library,
1633 Broadway, New York, New York 10019

First Signet Printing, February, 1985

1   2   3   4   5   6   7   8   9

PRINTED IN THE UNITED STATES OF AMERICA

Contents

SECTION II
THE EAT TO WIN RECIPE BOOK

Acknowledgments

I gratefully acknowledge my debt to the following scientists, whose help, wisdom, and support greatly contributed to my scientific success: Robert W. Wissler, M.D.; Jeremiah Stamler, M.D.; David M. Berkson, M.D.; David C. White, M.D., Ph.D.

I also wish to extend my gratitude and deep appreciation to the following members of my research institute: Hilarie Porter, M.S.; Steven Diamond, B.S.; Stanley Silverblatt, M.D.

And special thanks go to June Nusser for her editorial efforts, and to Eleanor Rawson for her critical comments, excellent suggestions, and general guidance during the writing of this book.

Foreword

I have discovered the secret of achieving peak performance and endurance in training and competition. The seemingly endless energy and stamina levels that helped me so much through the recent professional season spring from the unique and revolutionary nutrition program I've embraced.

When I first entered professional competition, I ate like all the other tennis players and never gave much thought to the idea that food and food supplements could improve my athletic performance or endurance. Most of us knew nothing about the relatively new and highly specialized science of sports nutrition. We ate what we thought was a "balanced" diet, choosing foods from the four food groups. Some of us, including me, occasionally took vitamin-mineral supplements without really knowing what benefits, if any, they provided. There were no experts to help us choose the right foods or supplements. My own good sense told me that diet and nutrition played an important part in how I felt and performed, yet I really didn't have the time or knowledge to evaluate scientifically the effects of nutrition on sports performance and endurance. Then I discovered Robert Haas.

I had heard of his work with other tennis champions and athletes but I did not actually meet him until after I suffered a bout with toxoplasmosis—a rare disease that attacks and injures virtually every organ in the body, as well as the muscles. I had just lost in the quarterfinal round of the 1982 U.S. Open—a tournament that meant a great deal to me—but I was fighting an unseen and greater opponent than I had ever faced across the court. The toxoplasmosis had robbed me of my strength and stamina, and I could barely climb a flight of stairs without feeling weak and exhausted. I began working closely with Dr. Haas just when I most needed to regain my lost stamina, energy, and strength. Today, I have surpassed even my greatest expectations of athletic performance, endurance, and good health by following the Haas Peak Performance Program.

I do not endorse or recommend anything unless I truly believe that it is the best in the world—from tennis racquets and tennis shoes to my own personal peak performance program. I believe that the Haas Peak Performance Program can truly help you to be the best you can be in any activity—from tennis to typing! Peak energy, stamina, endurance, strength, and good health are the very foundation of performance in every aspect of your active life.

Most professional athletes do not know how or what to eat for peak performance. Many of my friends in sports other than tennis still do not realize that what they eat determines how they will perform. Athletes at the top of their professions could be even better than they already are by following the revolutionary peak performance program I have embraced. Most amateur and weekend athletes could make tremendous gains in their stamina, strength, endurance, and performance by adopting the individualized and sport-specific programs Dr. Haas recommends.

I strongly urge all active people, from weekend warriors to potential Olympic decathalon champions, to examine the important new nutritional information in *Eat to Win* before they take another bite of their favorite foods. As an American, I sincerely hope that our Olympic athletes will heed Dr. Haas's advice and adopt his program before the 1984 summer Olympics in Los Angeles. Indeed, every active American stands to benefit from it.

America is currently experiencing a fitness and health revolution that I believe will eventually lead it to dominate world athletics and help all Americans to achieve optimal health and fitness. Dr. Haas, Nancy Lieberman, my fitness advisor, and I, along with a number of sports-care professionals and athletes, are at the fore-front of this sports nutrition, health, and fitness revolution. We are, in a sense, pioneers in a new field of knowledge that I believe will make sports history.

I, personally, intend to make sports history by winning tennis tournaments well past the age when most players have retired. The Haas Peak Performance Program has made me feel younger (a recent blood chemistry analysis revealed that my blood profile resembles that of a ten-year-old girl), and I see no reason why I won't feel the same way ten years from now. In fact, recent nutritional research has shown that the kind of diet and nutritional supplements recommended in this book provide a scientifi-cally sound way to retard the effects of aging that eventually end all athletic careers.

I have found the Haas Peak Performance Pro-gram easy to follow at home or on the road. I can enjoy my favorite restaurant cuisine while dining out 12,000 miles from home, or by fol-lowing the delicious recipes Dr. Haas has cre-ated for me in my own kitchen—the same ones you'll find in the recipe section of this book. People who knew me in my heavier days are amazed to watch me dining on piles of pasta, potatoes, rice, and bread while still maintaining my exceptionally low 10% body fat (the average body fat range for American women is 22% to 28% body fat).

Once you have adopted the Haas Peak Performance Program, I believe you will share my enthusiasm for this unique and effective nutritional plan. You'll discover how I've been able to reach new heights of energy, stamina, and endurance. Now I enjoy the very foods I used to avoid—foods that *you* can enjoy while achieving your new peak performance levels of energy and endurance, on the job or on the court.

Bon appétit!

Martina Navratilova

SECTION I

EAT
TO
WIN

Before You Begin
This Book

At the very moment you are reading this sentence, there is a world revolution going on. No governments will topple, no declarations of war will be signed; no bombs will burst and not a single shot will be fired.

I'm speaking of the sports nutrition revolution—the one you are about to join; in fact, by purchasing this book you already have joined it. But don't worry—you're on the right side, the *winning* side.

And that's what the sports nutrition revolution is all about—winning!

Eat to Win is the official manifesto of this revolution, and you are now part of a team of the world's foremost athletes who have learned how to eat to win. In a sense, *Eat to Win* has already become a "Bible" of high-energy, peak performance eating for champions such as Martina Navratilova, Gene and Sandy Mayer,

Stan Smith, Nancy Lieberman, and the other world-class competitors who have joined my revolutionary team. I welcome you as the newest member of our team, and here's what I'll do to help you become the best you can be.

First, I'll show you how to increase your energy, endurance, and sports performance to peak levels, far beyond what you could hope to achieve by following the traditional steak-and-eggs high-protein diets that have long been recommended by the established order: coaches, trainers, dietitians, and team physicians.

Next, I will help you relearn the right stuff: how to stay younger longer and slow down the "normal" effects of aging that eventually end all athletic careers. I'll show you how to de-age your blood—results that you (and your physician) will be able to see and evaluate through a simple and inexpensive blood chemistry analysis.

Then, I will explain my unique and highly individualized sport-specific eating plans that will show you how to experience the thrill of peak performance—at your job, on the playing field, or even in the bedroom. I'll also tell you how Martina Navratilova stays at the top of women's tennis; why Nancy Lieberman is the fittest and fiercest female basketball player in the world; how James and Jonathan DiDonato break one long-distance swimming record after another; how Gene Mayer, who climbed from low to high on the world professional tennis

4

ladder (number 148 to 4), keeps his endurance and sports performance at peak levels; why Sylviane and Patricia Puntous, the famous triathalon twins, dominate this physically demanding event, and why Stan Smith and Fred Stolle still have the stamina and endurance to defeat opponents many years younger.

Finally, I'll tell you about how the champions *win through chemistry*—the safe and legal way—without the use of drugs or other dangerous substances that make losers out of winners.

When I started my one-man sports nutrition revolution nearly a decade ago, few athletes and coaches took notice. At that time, most sports professionals I talked to believed that diet and nutritional supplements could do little to boost athletic performance and endurance. They said it couldn't be done; that made me want to do it all the more. And I did!

My revolutionary research with professional and amateur athletes reveals that *anyone*, regardless of age, sex, or ability, can enormously benefit from the nutritional discoveries you'll learn about in the following chapters. As an international sports nutrition consultant, I have traveled worldwide, advising members of the Association of Tennis Professionals, the U.S. Ski Team, the U.S. Davis Cup Team, the United States Professional Tennis Association, the Women's Tennis Association, the Japan Tennis Association, and other sports organizations. By following my revolutionary sports nutrition programs, professional athletes have set world records and won world championships.

Weekend athletes, even those with heart disease, diabetes, high blood pressure, and arthritis, have improved their speed, strength, endurance, and health to overcome serious health problems and win local sports competitions. These diseases no longer mean a life of inactivity and disease.

My peak performance program will work for *you* because it is based on *your own* individual blood chemistry and sport-specific requirements. I'll help you create a special peak performance plan that will meet your unique metabolic and nutritional needs, the same way I do for Martina and the other world-class members of my peak performance team.

Eat to Win: The Sports Nutrition Bible provides all active people with the sports diet program of the future, *today*. Throughout its pages, you will find my sports nutrition revolution does not take the middle road between food faddism and traditional dietetics that most athletes, coaches, and trainers mistakenly recommend. The proper route is a new one, traveled only by the champions I counsel, yet paved with scientific truths. *Eat to Win* will take all who follow these truths down that route.

ONE

Sports Nutrition
My Way

Think about the best game you ever had in your life, the rare one, when *everything* went right. That was you at your level of *peak performance*, with maximum energy, stamina, and endurance.

I am going to show you how to *permanently* improve the quality of your active life so that you will be the best you can be in your favorite sport, at your job, and in your life. Sports nutrition—my way—holds the secret of peak performance. You literally *can* eat to win!

The nutritional advice that helped put Jimmy Connors back on the top, enabled the DiDonato twins to break one long-distance swimming record after another, got Nancy Lieberman in shape for her pro-basketball tour, gave Sylviane and Patricia Puntous the endless energy to win triathalon after triathalon, and is currently keeping Martina Navratilova the world's number-one woman in tennis will work for *you*.

I'll show you how to get in shape, how to eat to win, and how to eat to *keep on winning*—long after most professional athletes retire from competition.

What is your favorite sport? Do you jog, ski, bike, swim, play tennis, squash, racquetball, work out with weights or weight machines, or enjoy aerobic dancing? These sports and activities require varying levels of stamina, endurance, and energy, and their players have different nutritional requirements. I have developed special, *individualized* programs for every popular sport to help you reach your level of peak performance in whatever activity you enjoy.

Although much of my current work is with world-class athletes, I also counsel weekend athletes and people who are interested in living longer and *healthier*. In 1981, the Haas Peak Performance Program was tested by the study "MR FIT" (an acronym that stands for Multiple Risk Factor Intervention Trial).

You'll find the Haas Peak Performance Program easy to follow. There are no exotic foods—you can buy everything in your favorite supermarket. Although you'll find tips on cooking techniques and easy, delicious, competition-tested recipes that have helped professional athletes eat to win, you can enjoy my peak performance program when dining out, *even at fast-food restaurants*. After all, professional athletes on tour can be half the world away from home cooking, grabbing quick meals at the nearest restaurant or fast-food emporium.

Before we get down to specifics—why the peak performance program works, how it works, and how it will work for *you*—you are going to have to rethink a lot of things you've been taught about sports nutrition.

Forget the "Balanced" Diet

For years, nutritionists have recommended a balanced diet chosen from four food groups for people concerned with physical fitness. The diet we know as the ordinary American diet is actually *unbalanced*: too much protein and fat and too little carbohydrate! You can achieve peak performance only by radically changing the amounts of protein, fat, and carbohydrate in your meals and snacks. In the following chapters, you'll find just how easy this is.

Forget What You've Heard About High-Energy Foods

Athletes need lots of steak and eggs, right? *Wrong.* Even two-time Wimbledon tennis champion Jimmy Connors was surprised when I told him that protein supplied his body with little energy during his Wimbledon victories. Don't be misled by the high-protein fad diets that

have been in and out of vogue for the past
hundred years. You actually can boost your
stored energy levels by an amazing 300% or
more by following my peak performance program. You will learn how to eat enough protein without sacrificing the vitally important complex carbohydrates (such as potatoes and spaghetti) that are key foods for high-level fitness
and health.

Forget What You've Been Told About Vitamin and Mineral Supplements

Most coaches, trainers, and even professional
athletes know very little about boosting athletic
endurance and sports performance through the
use of vitamin-mineral supplements and food
concentrates.

The scientific and effective use of many of
these ergogenic (energy-boosting) aids is a new
and important area in sports nutrition research.
When I studied nutrition in graduate school,
my professors taught that vitamin-mineral supplements and other naturally occurring food compounds could not improve athletic performance
and endurance. My research in nutritional supplementation with world champions and weekend athletes has demonstrated that active people
can improve their stamina, sports performance,
and health through the scientific use of food

supplements and concentrates. Recent nutritional research has shown that active people require specific nutrients in amounts that cannot be replenished *by diet alone*. Women, especially active women, have some very important nutritional needs that sports-care professionals long have overlooked. You'll learn much more about these uniquely female needs in Chapter 8.

Forget What You've Been Told About How to Lose Weight

I will show you the most efficient way to burn body fat while sparing muscle. Actually, you will get stronger faster as you become slimmer! World-champion swimmers, tennis players, and athletes in a variety of sports who follow my peak performance program to trim excess body fat that can cripple their performance find that when they use the program, their strength and speed also increase dramatically. As you learn the chemistry of peak performance foods, you will discover that by eating such enjoyable foods as potatoes, spaghetti, rice, and bread, you actually can develop super strength and a super body! You were probably told that all those foods would make you fat, right? *Wrong*!

Forget What You've Been Told About Diet and Health

Food is more than mere sustenance. It can provide pleasure as well as nourishment—but it can also be dangerous. Food substances such as fat and cholesterol can clog arteries, raise blood pressure, prematurely age our bodies; other chemicals in food can harm our unborn children and even contribute to some forms of cancer. How can something so vital be so harmful?

When the Chicago Heart Association invited me to train their staff members to administer my diet program to a group of volunteers at high risk of cardiovascular disease (heart attack and stroke), I became part of a seven-year national study designed to lower the rate of cardiovascular disease in middle-aged American men. "MR FIT" was conducted at a dozen research centers across the country. One MR FIT research center in Chicago, directed by Dr. David M. Berkson, studied those men at high risk of heart disease who had already received regular medical and nutritional care for six years before following my program. Dr. Berkson, who is also chief of cardiology at St. Joseph's Hospital in Chicago, reported that volunteers who followed my program decreased their serum cholesterol by 20% after just 28 days. In fact, one man achieved a 50% reduction in his cholesterol level! Weight loss was equally impressive.

12

This test of the Haas Peak Performance Program in a small group of highly motivated men at increased risk of heart disease and stroke demonstrated a rate of weight loss and serum cholesterol reduction not ordinarily achieved on most nutritional programs.

A Sports Nutrition Revolution Is Long Overdue

Nothing is more depressing than to watch dedicated world-class and weekend athletes sweat, toil, grimace, and endure the rigors of training—only to cripple their sports performance because of poor nutritional advice and unsound dietary practices. When it comes to nutrition, many athletes are their own worst enemies. Their opponents don't defeat them and the clock doesn't beat them; they defeat themselves at their own training tables!

Tennis champion Martina Navratilova knows only too well that poor diet can mean poor performance. Twenty-five pounds and a few hundred cheese cakes ago, Martina was losing to opponents who weren't even in her class. Her endurance and performance were erratic; the most talented female tennis player in history suffered unexplainable losses from time to time, because she hampered her athletic performance and endurance with poor nutritional habits. It was Martina's extraordinary skill with

13

knife and fork, not lack of skill with her racket, that lost her many a match.

But no more. Today, I provide Martina with the most scientifically advanced approach to achieving peak performance—through the use of sophisticated blood chemistry analysis, state-of-the-art computer technology, and by working with athletes in a variety of sports and levels of skill. Martina is at the top of her profession and will remain there for many years to come because she is the most *scientifically* trained world-class athlete in sports today. These nutritional and medical tests and measurements provide me with the data that I use to boost her athletic performance through the science of sports nutrition.

The Haas Peak Performance Program Is Flexible

There is no fixed formula that works for everyone. The nutritional advice I gave to Nancy Lieberman, national women's basketball star, was quite different from the counsel I gave tennis champion Gene Mayer. Each has different dietary requirements (especially because of sex and sport differences), body chemistry, and favorite foods. Yes, personal taste is involved in this program. You don't have to eat foods you don't enjoy, because there is plenty of opportunity for substitution.

The Haas Peak Performance Program Has Three Levels and One of Them Is Right For You

Any successful diet and nutrition program must be individualized, not generalized. You will discover just how easily you can tailor my peak performance program to your individual needs and tastes and how you can eat to be your personal best.

I Urge You to Work With Your Physician

When it comes to an individualized plan of diet and exercise, your physician can be your best coach. Even though medical schools still sadly neglect the nutritional education of their students, your physician knows your health profile and is the best judge of what you should and should not attempt to do with respect to diet and exercise.

A Blood Chemistry Analysis Is Your Body's Health Blueprint

I strongly recommend that you and your physician track your initial progress on my Peak Performance Program through a quick and inexpensive blood chemistry profile (a test physicians commonly call an SMA, including HDL cholesterol). This test, which analyzes the blood concentration of dozens of substances carried in your blood, is a mirror of your body's health. It is also one way that you can use to determine the entry level into your new diet. The test, which you'll take just before and four weeks after you begin your personalized program, is also an important way to chart your progress toward peak performance. I have included a special section in Chapter 4 that will give you an easy way to inerpret your own blood chemistry. So even if you failed high school chemistry, you will easily be able to earn an "A" in blood chemistry this time, when it *really* counts!

One Last Word

To my surprise (and delight), I discovered that my Peak Performance Program will benefit you in more than one playing area. Many men and women report an exciting improvement in their sex lives! It all fits together: peak sexual performance, like peak performance in sports and on the job, requires optimal fitness and health— all generated by the right nutrition.

Beds are also for sleeping. Despite job tensions and worries that tend to make insomniacs out of the calmest among us, Haas dieters consistently report greatly improved sleeping patterns. They seem to enjoy deeper, more restful sleep—as well as a slight reduction in total sleeping time. This can mean more energy and clearer thinking throughout the work day, even in high-stress situations.

Improve Your Active Life Today!

The Peak Performance Program is a new way of eating best suited to your *unique* needs, tastes, and favorite sports or activies. It can lead to a lifelong commitment of health, energy, and *winning*—in all areas of your active life.

TWO

How I Discovered the Secrets of Peak Performance Nutrition

I originally developed the Haas Peak Performance Program in order to save my own life. This sounds pretty dramatic, but it is no more than the simple truth.

I was quite athletic in college. Weight lifting was an important part of my total fitness regimen, but I also jogged and played tennis. At 5'11" I weighed about 190 pounds and most of it was solid muscle.

After graduation, I had a date with my draft board—and it was at my preinduction physical that I got the news that was to change *and* save my life. The doctors told me I had extremely high blood pressure—170 over 110—a most unusual and very dangerous reading for a twenty year old.

My own physician told me that my serum cholesterol was dangerously high. Elevated blood pressure and serum cholesterol were two indications that I was a high-risk candidate for heart attack or stroke at the tender age of twenty!

My physician told me that I would have to take one or more medications for the rest of my life to control these abnormally high risk factors for cardiovascular disease. The drugs that help lower blood pressure and serum cholesterol *all* have side effects, some of which seemed to be more uncomfortable than the diseases they were used to prevent! In seeking an alternative, I pondered what *I was doing to myself to cause such an abnormally high disease risk profile at such a young age.*

Instinct led me to the local bookstore. The disciples of natural foods, high-protein diets, and Far Eastern eating regimens were interesting enough, but my background in chemistry told me that their recommendations often side-stepped real science.

It became increasingly clear that nutrition was the only pharmaceutical-free alternative to my health problems—and that I had to learn all I could about chemistry, biochemistry, biology, physiology, and even medical pharmacology (the study of pharmaceuticals, the very things I was trying to avoid), before trying to explore the relationship between nutrition and health.

Back to college I went to master the basic and advanced sciences I needed for personal survival.

Sadly, however, I never really learned about nutrition until I graduated. Most professors I encountered in the department of nutrition did not acknowledge the role of dietary cholesterol in promoting heart disease, or the importance of environmental factors and food in promoting some types of cancer and the role of free-radicals in damaging healthy body tissue in the aging process.

I began, like so many research scientists, to use myself as a guinea pig, recording laboratory data on the changes in blood chemistry, following various diets and swallowing a variety of food concentrates and food supplements. The complex interrelationships between diet chemistry and body chemistry were logged into a computer.

As if by magic, my blood pressure dropped into the low normal range (110 over 60), as did my serum cholesterol (125) without resorting to harsh, stringent, and tasteless diet regimens. My body settled at its ideal weight—140 pounds— and I eagerly embraced long-distance running because my physical endurance increased far beyond my wildest expectations. Something unique and important had been discovered.

I opened my own clinical nutritional practice in association with a group of physicians at a regional medical center in Florida, and today I am a nutritional consultant in private practice.

Several years ago, some of the world's most famous tennis players began seeking my counsel, and I have been counseling tennis professionals ever since. Jimmy Connors, Stan Smith, Harold Solomon, Gene and Sandy Mayer, Fred Stolle, and Martina Navratilova are just a few of the world champions with whom I work. Tennis is a sport that demands *both* aerobic and anaerobic metabolism, and tennis players require a nutritional program that ensures them endurance as well as explosive energy. This combination tests the Peak Performance Program even more rigorously than sports that primarily demand quick power for a short period of time, such as weight lifting.

The Haas Peak Performance Program is currently used by more world-class tennis players than any other sports nutrition program. As a matter of fact, this probably is the first time in sports history that a whole class of pros in this sport has followed the nutritional advice of one scientist.

The Peak Performance Program has worked for skiers such as U.S. Olympic and U.S. Ski Team member Viki Fleckenstein; swimmers such as James and Jonathan DiDonato, co-world-record holders in long-distance swimming; U.S. and Canadian triathalon champions Sylviane and Patricia Puntous; and top-ranked basketball players such as Nancy Lieberman, as well as a host of collegiate athletes in most major sports.

But right now, I want to start working with *you.*

THREE

The Wrong Stuff

Everybody who has spent time in sports has heard lots of advice about sports nutrition. See how many of these ideas you agree with.

	Right	Wrong
Athletes need extra protein to improve strength and endurance.	____	____
You must take salt tablets when you are training and competing in hot weather.	____	____
Commercial "sports drinks" improve endurance because they get into the blood faster than water.	____	____
Controlled fasting will improve endurance.	____	____
You should drink beer after competition to replace lost fluid.	____	____

Right *Wrong*

You must burn 3,500 kilocalories to lose one pound of body weight.   ____ ____

The best way to relieve hypoglycemia (low blood sugar) is to eat high-protein foods such as cheese, peanut butter, and eggs.   ____ ____

All of these sacred cows of sports nutrition are the purest hot air—and I'm going to tell you why.

The Protein Myth

The myth that athletes need extra protein goes back to the dawn of recorded history. The ancient Greeks, who elevated sport into art, had their coaches and sports nutrition consultants. Writings survive with specific instructions—eat antelope to run fast; feast on goat to jump high; for strength, let a wrestler devour the flesh of a bull.

We can smile at this advice—but how different is it from the steak-and-eggs diet that my high school and college coaches insisted on?

Protein is the primary structural material for our bodies—but it is a poor source of immediate energy for active people. Many athletes, even the pros, consume four to eight times more protein than they need each day!

23

You only need 40 to 80 grams of protein each day. This is two to five times less than you probably are eating today. This isn't surprising when you realize that one 6½-ounce can of water-packed tuna provides 45 grams of protein—almost 100% of your daily protein requirement!

Let's see what happens when you eat too much protein (more than your body can use each day).

Before protein can be absorbed into the blood, internal enzymes and acids digest protein into its components—amino acids and short chains of amino acids called peptides. The body uses these small building blocks of protein for many functions, including maintaining and repairing cells and tissue, making more enzymes to help digest more protein, keeping the immune system strong, building new tissue whenever and wherever the body demands, and many, many more life-sustaining processes. Protein left over after the body's housekeeping is done is converted to fat and sugar, then stored in various parts of the body. In other words, excess protein builds *fatter* bodies—not bigger muscles!

Protein metabolism releases toxic waste products (such as ammonia) which contribute to the final product of protein metabolism, urea, also a toxic substance. If you eat more protein than your body can use (more than 40 to 80 grams each day), your kidneys and liver must work harder to detoxify and remove these potential poisons. Since the body forms more urine to dispose of the increased ammonia and urea, vital minerals such as potassium, calcium, and magnesium are lost along with waste as your body dehydrates. Potassium helps control muscle temperature, blood flow, and nerve conduction; calcium means strong bones and proper muscle function; magnesium helps regulate muscle contraction and the conversion of carbohydrates into energy. Eating excess protein (above 80 grams each day, in most cases) can clearly hamper athletic performance and endurance through *dehydration* and *essential mineral losses*.

The Salt Myth

Sodium is the most abundant mineral in the blood and every active person needs it—approximately 1/2 gram each day. You probably get far more than this from the foods you eat—without once reaching for the saltshaker. The average American consumes about ten times the minimum sodium requirement he or she needs every day (not, however, on the Haas Peak Performance Program).

Professional coaches, trainers, and team physicians, who should know better but who still advise athletes to swallow salt tablets before, during, and after competition, defeat more athletes than their opponents do .

Salt tablets (which may contain sodium chloride, potassium chloride, and other substances normally lost in very small amounts in sweat) are precisely what sweating athletes need *least*.

Athletes, indeed all people who regularly exercise, lose very little sodium and even less potassium in their sweat during exercise. Their bodies have been "trained" to retain a healthful and adequate amount of salts to meet the demands of hard physical activity.

What active people lose in sweat and really do need to replace is *water*. When a sweating athlete swallows salt tablets, two very harmful things can happen. Water is pulled away from the working muscles where it is needed most, as well as from other parts of the body, in order to dilute the high salt concentration in the stomach. This internal dehydration builds dangerously high salt concentrations in the blood, which can lead to kidney problems.

The Sports Drink Myth

When a conscientious and enterprising renal physiologist originally developed a sports drink he named after a university football team, the formula contained saccharin, an artificial sweetener, glucose, salts, and water. It was supposed to get into the bloodstream faster than water to provide athletes with quick calories.

Carefully controlled scientific studies have demonstrated just the opposite. This country's most famous sports drink (and all of its imitators) actually gets into the blood *much more slowly* than does pure water!

The American College of Sports Medicine recently gave these sugar-laced and salt-loaded sport drinks low marks as fluid and salt replacement beverages for active people. Most athletes I have polled still believe that sport drinks offer them a competitive edge. You can have the edge over these misguided athletes if you stick to what every active person needs—water, water, and still more water.

The Fasting Myth

Abstaining from food for ritualistic reasons may have its place in some religions, but fasting cripples athletic performance and endurance. Fasting has no rational role in modern sports nutrition.

Today, many athletes still believe that eating no solid food before competing or performing somehow cleanses their bodies of poisons or toxins and contributes to high performance and increased endurance. *Nothing could be further from the truth*.

Fasting robs athletes of endurance because lack of food disrupts normal storage of energy (in the form of glycogen, the energy storage carbohydrate) and energy metabolism itself, which requires a specific balance of protein, fat, carbohydrate, and the vitamins and minerals they provide. If you fast for more than 12 to 24 hours your body will begin to *eat itself* and you will lose vital muscle tissue, glycogen, vitamins, and minerals.

Do not be misled by claims any sports superstars may make. Fasting for athletes is unnecessary and potentially dangerous. It can defeat even the champions themselves.

The Beer Myth

Several years ago, a popular runner, writer, and physician publicly recommended that athletes drink beer after competition to replace fluid lost during physical activity.

Unfortunately, this confirmed what many athletes thought. From football field to baseball diamond and tennis court, athletes pour down the beer after competition. Yet all of the available scientific evidence—enough to fill a small library—demostrates that beer and all other alcoholic beverages hurt athletic endurance.

"But," the athlete will say, "I need the minerals and carbohydrates in beer. Besides, you don't buy beer, you just rent it! I'll just sweat out the alcohol and play on with no ill effects."

Absolutely, positively, one hundred percent wrong. Alcohol is a dehydrating substance. It blocks the release of the anti-diuretic hormone (ADH), which helps regulate the amount of water lost in the urine. The less ADH released by the pituitary gland, the more water lost. And, as we saw in the dehydrating action of excess protein, along with that water go important minerals that muscles require for peak performance.

Alcohol also destroys vitamins (especially thiamin, vitamin B-1, a key factor in energy metabolism) and has a direct, toxic effect on many organs, including the liver and kidneys.

The best beverage you can drink to replace fluid after exhaustive exercise is and always has been water—cool, clear water.

The 3,500 Kilocalories Myth

While I was a graduate student in nutrition, my college professors taught that people must eat 3,500 kilocalories (nutritionists refer to the common calorie that we all count from time to time by its correct scientific name, the kilocalorie) to gain one pound of fat; logically, then, people must either "burn" or decrease their food intake by the same amount of kilocalories. Yet, when I tested this "rule" in the real world on real people, it just didn't work! Some people cannot lose a significant amount of weight on as little as 1,200 kilocalories a day: some cannot gain on as much as 3,000 a day.

This problem interested me so much that I began a methodical and thorough search of the nutritional and biomedical literature on weight loss. By piecing together the scattered bits of information derived from hundreds of weight-loss studies, I found that the answer lay in the complex enzymatic and hormonal systems that control our metabolic processes. These systems or pathways determine how much food we burn for energy and how much of it we store as fat.

Some of us can eat over twice as many kilocalories as others of the same sex, age, and weight yet still not gain an ounce. Others seem to turn everything they eat into fat. Some obese people actually may have impaired or abnormal control systems and thus must eat less and exercise more to stay at an ideal body weight. To one person 3,500 kilocalories may mean weight maintenance; to another, they may mean weight gain. (I'll discuss more about our fascinating metabolic processes in Chapter 13.)

What you really need to remember is that excessive amounts of protein, fat, carbohydrate, and alcohol supply energy which the body can turn into fat. You should also remember that carbohydrate is the only *clean burning* fuel in your diet. As your body burns carbohydrate it turns it into carbon dioxide, which you exhale with each breath, along with water. Fat and

30

protein yield toxic byproducts as your body burns them. Thus, a diet overloaded with protein and fat and not enough carbohydrate (which helps hold down levels of some of the toxic by-products of protein and fat metabolism) can make you sluggish and decrease physical performance. While you are trying to lose or gain weight, the *kind* of food you eat is just as important as the *amount* you eat.

Kilocalories *do* count, but some people, because of their unique metabolic systems, burn kilocalories more efficiently than others. That's why counting kilocalories in the foods you eat can be a frustrating experience. A lot depends on how efficiently your own body handles those kilocalories.

The Hypoglycemia Myth

Under certain circumstances, exercise may lower your blood sugar so much that you may feel light headed, shaky, and tired. Athletes call this "bonking," and it happens because the concentration of sugar in your blood drops below a critical level (usually below 50 milligrams of sugar for every 3½ ounces of blood in your body). Your brain, which depends primarily on sugar for peak function, "bonks" when it is not fed properly.

Athletes who follow the Haas Peak Performance Program rarely, if ever, bonk. Bonking can be relieved immediately by eating almost any food, but your aim should not be to *relieve* a hypoglycemic attack but to *prevent* it!

Fortunately, this type of low blood sugar problem can be reversed in as little as one week—but not by eating large quantities of high-protein foods like cheese and peanut butter (this treatment for hypoglycemia has been unwisely recommended by nutritionists and dietitians for years). High-protein foods are usually high-fat foods and neither protein nor fat is really what the sugar-starved brain is hungry for.

The foods that are most effective in preventing exercise-induced hypoglycemia are the group known as complex carbohydrates: rice (brown is always preferred on the Haas Peak Performance Program), pasta, whole grains and cereals (such as whole wheat, oatmeal), breads made from unrefined flour, beans, peas, almost every known vegetable, and fresh fruits. These are some of the foods that supply the blood with sugar at a peak performance rate—neither too quickly nor too slowly.

The Care and Feeding of Your Muscles

Energy and endurance are the keys to peak performance—and this means that your muscles must work at their most efficient level.

In order to do their work, your muscles must convert fats, proteins (amino acids), and carbohydrates into energy. In simple terms, they do this by combining glycogen, the energy carbohydrate, with oxygen and fat—literally combusting glycogen (after it has been broken down into its component sugars). Glycogen is stored primarily in muscle (some is also stored in the liver) just as food is stored in the refrigerator, so that it is ready to be used when needed.

What happens when your muscles run out of glycogen? Any marathon runner can tell you: you "hit the wall." The "wall" is the term runners use to describe the painful condition of glycogen depletion. Muscles begin to burn, fatigue, and cramp causing all physical activity to stop. Marathon runners still have plenty of fat and protein left in their bodies, but when they run out of glycogen, they may as well hang up their running shoes.

Now you know why glycogen (carbohydrate) is much more important to active muscles than fat or protein. *Athletes always run out of glycogen long before they can possibly exhaust fat or protein stores.*

The type of diet you eat will actually determine how much glycogen your muscles will store. The typical high-protein, high-fat, low-carbohydrate sports diet (the same steak-and-eggs diet that caused my health problems) provides enough glycogen for about an hour of maximum physical activity. A typical "mixed diet" (the ordinary American diet) supplies enough glycogen to allow about 90 minutes of maximum activity. A high-carbohydrate diet (similar to, but not as effective as, the Haas Peak Performance Program) supplies a full two hours' worth of maximum activity because it promotes high glycogen muscle storage. The Haas Peak Performance Program goes beyond all other sports diets because it is *more than just a diet—it is a total program* that includes special food concentrates and supplements that boost stamina, energy, endurance, and sports performance.

What Kinds of Foods Fuel Your Muscles Best?

Protein? Protein plays little part in providing your muscles with energy. Extra protein cannot be stored in the body. It is converted to fat and sugar which *can* be stored, however, but is not a major source of immediate energy. Protein is essential for the growth, maintenance, repair, and protection of our bodies, but it is *not* what you eat more of to win.

Fat? The body requires a small amount of fat (about 2 to 4 grams of linoleic acid) which you can get from a large bowl of oatmeal. Peak performance in different sports and activities demands that you eat varying amounts of fats in excess of the essential 2 to 4 grams per day of linoleic acid, but excess fat, like excess protein, can hamper endurance by impairing carbohydrate metabolism (resulting in poor glycogen storage in muscles) and by limiting the amount of oxygen that blood delivers to exercising muscles.

A certain amount of fat can and should be burned during exercise because this can actually *spare* glycogen until it is really needed in the later, more physically demanding stages of a road race or tennis match. "Burning fat in the flame of carbohydrate" is the phrase biochemists use to describe the most effective and efficient way the body releases energy.

Muscles can only store a relatively small amount of fat; the rest is stored around internal organs for insulation and cushioning and under the skin (this is the fat that makes us *look* fat). When you limit your fat intake to the portions I recommend for your particular sport-specific diet (which I've outlined in Chapter 10) or the three basic levels of the Haas Peak Performance Program (explained in Chapter 5), you will provide your body with the right fuel mixture it needs to function its best.

Carbohydrates? I'm sure you guessed it. Complex carbohydrates are the best foods for peak performance because they are the only truly clean burning, readily available source of blood sugar. Complex carbohydrates such as brown rice and pasta are worth their weight in gold to professional athletes who make their living by winning; they are no less valuable to weekend athletes who want to excel at their favorite activities.

Now that we have finally slaughtered all those sacred cows of sports nutrition, you are ready to take the first step on your new peak performance program.

FOUR

Your Blood Chemistry: The Secret of Peak Performance

Every sports champion I counsel learns how to eat to win based on his or her own blood chemistry. Although my diet is based on nutritional principles that everyone follows, I make individual adjustments in the diets of champions, such as Martina Navratilova, that give them the competitive edge over their opponents. I can do the same for you.

Your Blood Chemistry

Your blood chemistry is as unique as your fingerprints. Even though I cannot personally construct your diet, I can individualize my nutritional advice for you based on your own blood chemistry, so that you can eat the same way that has helped athletes the world over achieve the winning edge.

37

There are three levels of my diet and only one is right for you with your current blood values. You can discover where to start your diet by having a simple, inexpensive laboratory test called a *blood chemistry profile.* You can get this analysis of your blood chemistry profile from your physician, public health center, local college or university, or at a hospital out-patient clinic. It will take less than ten minutes of your time and the results can be rapidly evaluated by a health-care professional.

You should not eat or drink anything (except water) for 12 hours before you have your blood chemistry profile. This is certainly not difficult to do. Just don't snack after dinner, have your blood profile first thing in the morning, and then eat breakfast. Only a fasting blood profile will yield accurate results, so skip that bedtime snack or morning beverage (only water is allowed).

After you receive the laboratory analysis of your blood (the blood chemistry profile) make sure that your physician has a copy if he or she did not do the original test.

Your blood chemistry profile can determine your risk of diet-related diseases. This evaluation is the easiest and single most powerful screening test for diet-related illness such as diabetes, gout, liver disease, kidney, and heart problems (of course, these health problems may also be unrelated to diet). It may also show if you are at risk for any of these conditions. Everyone, young and old, should have a blood chemistry profile done at least once every year.

Your Vital Values

There are dozens of blood values that make up your total blood chemistry profile, but only *five* are essential to determine which level of the Haas program is right for you. As your blood chemistry changes (which you will discover in subsequent tests), you will move from one level to the next until you approach the final and highest *peak performance level* (Level Three). The three levels cover the entire range of normal human blood chemistry so that you will easily be able to find your appropriate starting level.

These are the *five vital values*:

Total cholesterol
High-density lipoprotein (HDL) cholesterol
Glucose (blood sugar)
Triglycerides (blood fats)
Uric acid

These five vital values are the ones you are going to track as you move from level to level of the Haas program—and you will see how rapidly and how profoundly your vital values improve.

Cholesterol is present in foods of animal origin. It is also manufactured by the body from *every-*

thing we eat. A certain amount of this compound is vital: no cholesterol, no sex hormones;
but too much cholesterol in our blood can cause
grave health problems.

Since it is water based, our body must package cholesterol (which is fat soluble and therefore doesn't mix well with blood) in water-soluble
protein "containers" called *lipoproteins*. There
are four basic lipoproteins that carry cholesterol
but you need only know of one of them—HDL
or high-density lipoprotein. Most scientists now
believe that the higher your HDL value, the less
your risk of heart attack. Unlike *total* cholesterol,
carried in all four lipoprotein containers, a high
HDL is a healthy and desirable value. The more
of your total cholesterol that is carried in your
HDL protein containers, the less cholesterol is
available to clog your arteries. So keep HDL
cholesterol *high*, and total cholesterol *low* to avoid
heart attack.

Glucose (blood sugar): We've already talked
about the vital role blood sugar plays when you
are exercising vigorously (remember, low blood
sugar means "bonking"). Your blood sugar determines your energy levels, especially during
exercise and stress. For reasons that are not
completely understood, low blood sugar can even
affect your emotions, making you irritable and
easily upset.

When the concentration of blood glucose falls
below the normal fasting level (usually below

50 milligrams for every 3½ ounces of blood), hypoglycemia results. Since sugar is the brain's favorite food (and your brain cannot store sugar the way muscles can), severe hypoglycemia literally starves the brain. Poor sports performance, even unconsciousness, may result.

On the other hand, when blood sugar levels are too high, the kidneys begin to transfer some of the excess sugar to urine. This can signal the first signs of diabetes mellitus (many potential cases of this disease can be easily detected and possibly prevent by having the simple blood chemistry profile that I recommend). Again, the good news—my program can help you achieve and maintain optimal blood sugar levels.

Triglycerides (blood fats): These are fats that are to be found in ordinary foods as well as in our bodies. Triglycerides are the fats we store around our tummies, thighs, and other places that bulge when we gain nonmuscular weight. The level of *blood* triglycerides reveals many things about the foods you eat and how well your body handles those foods.

Abnormally high triglyceride values may deprive your working muscles of vital oxygen— and this means less stamina and endurance.

An elevated triglyceride reading, like elevated cholesterol, may even increase your risk of cardiovascular disease, such as heart attack and stroke. My program is constructed to *permanently* lower your serum triglycerides.

41

Uric acid: This toxic substance is actually manufactured by the body in small amounts from compounds called *purines* which are to be found in ordinary foods such as meat, seafood, and peas. Normally, our kidneys help to excrete excessive uric acid quite well. This is a vital blood value to check, however, because when uric acid blood levels increase beyond 6.5 milligrams for every 3½ ounces of blood, salts of uric acid (sodium urate) may lodge in joints and cause swelling, inflammation, pain, and damage. This condition is actually one form of arthritis called gout. Excessive uric acid may also form kidney stones, an extremely painful and health-threatening condition. A caution is in order here: whenever you attempt to lose weight through *any* type of diet and/or exercise program, you should first consult with a physician, because weight loss may temporarily elevate uric acid levels. Fortunately, this temporary rise in serum uric acid can be controlled with medications such as allopurinol and probenecid (your physician will prescribe the right medication for you), so that you will be able to safely lose weight should you desire. More good news—my program has helped to *lower* serum uric acid in many athletes who initially had high uric acid values.

Your Vital Values Determine the Level on Which You Should Enter the Diet

Most people who exercise moderately and are a bit overweight probably will have vital values that require them to begin the diet at Level One.

Those who have a regular sports or exercise program and wouldn't mind losing a few pounds in order to be really fit probably will have values consistent with Level Two.

Professional athletes in training who eat sensibly may have blood chemistry values associated with Level Three.

Your goal is level three, the peak performance level. You will be amazed to find how rapidly you can achieve it. After one month on this program, you actually will be able to measure the change in your vital values by comparing your initial blood chemistry profile with a second profile taken after four weeks.

Even if you do not choose to map your progress in this way (however, I *strongly* recommend that you do), you still will be able to measure the results on your bathroom scale and in your favorite sport or exercise.

The Haas diet program introduces a revolutionary new set of guidelines to your physician. When your personal physician receives the laboratory report of your blood chemistry profile (politely insist that your doctor give you a photocopy), he or she will consider each blood value against a normal range currently accepted by the biomedical community. *This can be a problem.*

The normal range of the five important values that determine your statistical risk of diet-related disease (as well as your entry level into the Haas program) is, according to my research, both outdated and incompatible with optimal health and sports performance.

Here's why: The normal range on most laboratory blood profile reports for serum cholesterol is between 150 and 250 (for now, let's not concern ourselves with the units such as "mg/100 ml" that follow these numbers). This "normal" range is, however, *abnormally high* in populations where there is a low rate of heart attacks—much lower than the American rate!

The normal U.S. value for HDL cholesterol (the "good" cholesterol) in women is 55 and 45 in men. Current medical thinking agrees that a higher value is better—the higher the value, the less risk of heart attack. However, there are populations with HDL cholesterol values under 30 that apparently have very low rates of heart attack. The reason: their *total* cholesterol (of which HDL is only a fractional part) is *very low—lower than the lower limit of normal (150) for people in the U.S.A.!*

The normal range of fasting blood sugar (glucose) is reported to be between 65 and 120. The problem is that this range is too broad:

athletes I counsel—amateur and professional alike—generally keep their fasting blood sugar levels below 90 in almost every case. I believe that a value above 100 is undesirable for physically active people who desire optimal health and peak performance.

The accepted normal range for triglycerides (blood fats) comes a little closer to the mark at 20 to 150. My research shows that values between 20 and 120 fall into the peak performance range.

The normal range for uric acid (a toxic metabolic waste product) is 2.0 to 6.4 in women and 2.1 to 7.8 in men. While women are much less likely to get gout than men, I recommend that everyone keep uric acid blood levels below 6 for good health and peak performance.

Caution: vigorous exercise just prior to your blood chemistry profile can normally raise the level of uric acid in your blood. Please refrain from exercise on the morning you have your blood chemistry profile taken.

The Haas diet will improve your blood chemistry in just four weeks! This is what will happen. When you eat the right foods in the right combination, your body's metabolic processes will work at their peak efficiency. Your blood will, so to speak, become *younger!*

When you were born, your HDL cholesterol was roughly equal to your LDL (low-density lipoprotein) cholesterol. When you were or are eighteen years old, your LDL cholesterol was or is roughly three to five times higher than your HDL level. By the age of forty-five, many people have a LDL cholesterol that is seven to ten times greater than their HDL fraction. That is not a healthy situation.

The growing ratio of LDL cholesterol to HDL cholesterol is associated with the aging process. I have seen my program reduce the known risk factors of cardiovascular and other diet-related diseases. Only when you achieve peak health can you reach peak performance.

Now, let's get down to the knife and fork basics of how you can eat to win!

FIVE

The Haas Peak Performance Program: Levels One, Two, and Three

The Haas Peak Performance Program differs from all other popular low-fat, high-carbohydrate regimens in two very important respects: it does not *punish* your taste buds (ample "cheating" is allowed), and is scientifically balanced according to your own blood chemistry profile to maximize your athletic performance. Each level of the Haas Peak Performance Program provides the right level of scientifically controlled "cheating" and special energy-boosting food supplements.

World-champion athletes who train four to eight hours a day, every day, place great demands on their bodies. To replace the vitamins and minerals they metabolize, these athletes would have to consume so much food in order to meet such excessive nutritional demands that they actually would get too fat to play!

What about you, the dedicated amateur athlete? I am convinced that if you follow the dietary portion of my program, the vitamin- and mineral-rich foods that I recommend will help to provide some very important nutrients that the ordinary American diet neglects: selenium, chromium, manganese, and pantothenic acid are just a few of the important ones. As you will learn, the extraordinary metabolic demands of sports and exercise may require that you *replenish* these lost nutrients through the use of special food concentrates and supplements I will describe.

A Special Note Concerning Fats and Oils Before You Start Your New Program

Most Americans are, by now, aware that our national health organizations (such as the American Heart Association) recommend that we reduce our intake of saturated fats (found mainly in animal products) and use unsaturated fats (oils from mainly vegetable sources) in place of saturated fats whenever possible. Some people take this sensible recommendation to its extreme and recommend that we use absolutely no added fats or oils (saturated or unsaturated) in our daily diets.

You may be relieved to learn that amidst our national fat phobia, there is one friendly fat that actually may reduce your risk of suffering a heart attack or stroke: it's called *eicosapentanoic*

48

acid. Since it is a hard name to remember and pronounce, let's refer to it as EPA.

Recent nutritional research has shown that EPA actually lowers serum cholesterol and serum triglycerides, both favorable reductions that can help protect you from heart attack and stroke. EPA is a highly unsaturated fatty acid, and the best dietary sources in the American diet appear to be salmon and mackerel. People who don't want to eat these fish will be happy to learn that they can find EPA capsules or oil in many health food shops throughout the country. Most scientific studies using EPA to lower serum cholesterol and serum triglyceride levels have used EPA supplements alone or with fish to achieve their beneficial effects. EPA supplements may prove useful for those people who do not eat common sources of EPA (such as salmon or mackerel) or are vegetarian.

Your new peak performance program will fall within this ideal combination of foods:

Complex carbohydrates (starches) 60–80% daily calories
Simple carbohydrates (sweets) 5–10% daily calories
Protein (animal and vegetable) 10–15% daily calories
Fats (animal and vegetable) 5–20% daily calories

As you move from Level One or Level Two, to peak performance Level Three, you will find that the percentage of simple carbohydrates (sweets), protein, and fats will *increase*, although complex carbohydrates (starches) will always provide the *greatest proportion* of your daily nutritional needs. On the Haas Peak Performance Program, starches become your *primary foods*.

Level One: The Get-In-Shape Eating Program

This is the level of the Haas Program that I designed to get you into top performance shape! In addition, as a serendipity, you also will find that you will painlessly lose those extra pounds that are slowing you down in competition.

If these are the values reported in your blood chemistry profile, start the diet at Level One:

Total cholesterol . . . . 200 or more
HDL cholesterol . . . . 30 or less
Triglycerides . . . . 150 or more
Glucose . . . . 100 or more
Uric acid, women . . . . 6 or more
  men . . . . 7 or more

If any one of your blood chemistry values matches these readings, begin the diet at Level One.

I have divided the foods that you will enjoy at all three levels into three groups: primary, secondary, and supplementary.

Primary foods are those that supply most of your daily calories. These are the complex carbo-

50

hydrates such as potatoes, breads, pasta, rice, and whole grain cereals such as oatmeal and shredded wheat, that provide the foundations of peak performance.

Secondary foods provide much of your protein requirement. You will enjoy them in sufficient quantity to achieve high-level sports performance.

Supplementary foods can be enjoyed (in the recommended quantities) as part of your meals or as snacks. As you move to higher levels in the diet, you'll find more supplementary foods and beverages.

LEVEL ONE PRIMARY FOODS

You should eat these foods or their nutritional equivalents (see 28-day home recipe plan that follows) each day:

2 large potaotes (baked, boiled, or steamed).

Topping choices for potatoes: Butter Buds butter replacer; 2 tablespoons low-fat cottage cheese; 2 tablespoons low-fat plain yogurt; 1 teaspoon bacon bits or chips (soy-bean type); 1 tablespoon chives; pepper; granulated vegetable seasonings.

Whole grains: any unrefined cereals made without sugar or salt, including shredded wheat, oatmeal, Wheateena, Quaker 100% Whole Wheat Cereal, brown rice, puffed brown wheat, puffed corn.

Spaghetti (preferably whole wheat, spinach,

or artichoke types). Top with marinara (chunk tomato) sauce, plain tomato sauce, or plain tomato sauce with any sliced vegetable such as mushroom, pepper, onions, etc. Up to 1½ cups cooked spaghetti daily with ¾ cup of sauce. Optional topping: 2 teaspoons grated Parmesan or Romano cheese.

LEVEL ONE SECONDARY FOODS

Cottage cheese (low-fat, 1%–2%): up to 1 cup.
Plain yogurt (low-fat, 1%–2%): up to 1 cup.
Legumes (cooked beans, peas, lentils): up to 1 cup.
Egg whites (no yolks): up to 4.
Chicken, turkey, fish (choose salmon or mackerel whenever possible, poached or broiled without butter), or *lobster* (steamed, boiled, or broiled): up to 1 pound *per week*.

LEVEL ONE SUPPLEMENTARY FOODS

You may eat these foods every day as you desire:
Vegetables (raw or steamed): unlimited, with four exceptions: avocado, hearts of palm, seeds and nuts, olives .
Vegetable dressings (for salads or cooked vegetables): any commercially available *no-oil* salad

dressing made without egg yolks (even though these do contain some added salt or sugar); low-fat cottage cheese or low-fat yogurt (1 tablespoon each); or my EZ salad dressing—sprinkle salad lightly with vinegar or lemon juice, 1 teaspoon of grated Parmesan or Romano cheese, and one packet Equal sugar replacer.

Fresh fruits: up to 2 per day, in addition to one fruit permitted for breakfast cereal. All known fruits are permitted.

Grated hard cheese (Parmesan or Romano): up to 3 teaspoons per dav on salads, vegetables, etc.

LEVEL ONE SNACKS

Popcorn (choose hot air popped—made without oil whenever possible): up to 3 cups (popped).

Unsalted pretzels: up to 2 ounces.

Baked brown rice crackers (baked without oil): up to 2 ounces.

Puffed brown rice (or other whole grain) cakes: up to 4.

Unsweetened applesauce: up to 1 cup.

I have chosen these basic foods to ensure that you get the proper combination of complex carbohydrates, simple carbohydrates, protein, fat, cholesterol, and sodium consistent with your metabolic and nutritional needs at Level One.

After only one month on Level One, you will see

an amazing improvement in your vital blood values and you will lose excess fat if you are overweight.

I have developed many simple recipes for delicious foods that you will enjoy at every level of the Haas Peak Performance Program. Professional and amateur athletes have tested these recipes at the training table.

Every recipe contains nutritional information that will tell you how much protein, fat, carbohydrate, cholesterol, sodium, and calories it provides per serving.

At the end of this chapter, you will find a 28-day menu for following my program while eating at home, but even if you eat more meals out than in, you can easily follow my recommendations for eating on the road in Chapter 6.

Level Two: The Stay-In-Shape Eating Program

After you have followed Level One for 28 days, you probably will be ready for Level Two (a second blood chemistry profile will determine if you are). You will have lost excess body fat; you will notice that your sports performance and endurance have improved, and you will enjoy more energy and stamina both in competition and in your daily life.

Level Two is designed to *keep you in shape* and

54

increase strength, as well as help you to continue to shed excess fat, if you desire.

LEVEL TWO BLOOD CHEMISTRY VALUES:

Total Cholesterol 170–190
HDL cholesterol . . . . 45 or more
Triglycerides 125–150
Glucose 85–95
Uric acid, women . . . . 5 or less
     men . . . . 6 or less

Level Two (as well as Level Three) adds variety and quantity to Level One. You can still enjoy every food (and Haas recipe) you ate on Level One, but you can now *add* the following foods to your Level One program.

LEVEL TWO PRIMARY FOODS

Whole grain breads (any bread made from an unrefined grain such as whole wheat, oatmeal, barley, brown rice, corn meal, etc.): up to 2 slices.

Pasta (spaghetti, macaroni, etc.): 1 cup (cooked) with Level One sauces. Level Two permits the use of red clam sauce.

LEVEL TWO SECONDARY FOODS

Beef, pork, or veal: up to ¼ pound per week.

½ cup low-fat cottage cheese.

½ cup low-fat plain yogurt (hint: add ½ sliced fresh fruit and Equal sugar replacer to taste to make a delicious yogurt dessert).

½ cup skim or nonfat dry milk (if desired).

1 cup cooked beans, peas, lentils (please rinse canned legumes with water before using—canners sometimes add salt and sugar to these products).

LEVEL TWO SUPPLEMENTARY FOODS

One fresh fruit of choice.

Low-fat frozen yogurt (any flavor): available in most supermarkets, shopping malls, and some ice cream shops; up to 4 ounces—a typical small serving. This type of yogurt does contain added sugar, but is well within the guidelines for peak performance eating.

Margarine, mayonnaise, or vegetable oil: up to 2 teaspoons *total* per day of one or more of these added fats and oils.

Alcohol: 1 3½-ounce glass of wine (white or red) or a 12-ounce can of light beer, if desired.

LEVEL TWO SNACKS

Dried fruit: up to 1 ounce of raisins, prunes, figs, etc. on cereal, in salad, or as a snack.

As you can see, your diet level determines your use of supplementary fats, oils, sweet treats, animal protein sources, and alcohol. Level One permits only those animal and vegetable fats and oils *that occur naturally in natural foods*: you may not use added fats such as butter, margarine, mayonnaise, salad dressings, or vegetable oils. Lemon juice, vinegar, or any of the no-oil salad dressings you can buy in most supermarkets can be used over salads while you're on Level One. When you follow Level Two, you may have up to 2 teaspoons of oil or oil-based dressing (this allows you to use my "low-fat stir-fry" technique for preparing foods). Peak performance Level Three allows you to enjoy up to 4 teaspoons of added oils each day.

Level Three: The Peak Performance Eating Program

When you reach Level Three of the Haas Peak Performance Program, you will be eating the breakfast, lunch, and dinner of champions. This is the diet that many world-class athletes eat to win! You probably will not lose weight when you follow Level Three—but you will maintain your ideal weight and your ideal muscle-to-body fat ratio. If you find that you *are* losing weight at Level Three, you probably are training hard and will need to increase your intake of primary foods to *maintain* your peak performance weight.

LEVEL THREE BLOOD CHEMISTRY VALUES:

Total Cholesterol . . . . 150 or less
HDL cholesterol . . . . 65 or more
Triglycerides . . . . 75 or less
Glucose . . . . 85 or less
Uric acid, women . . . . 4 or less
   men . . . . 5 or less

Level Three (as well as Level Two) adds variety and quantity to Level One. You can still enjoy every food (and Haas recipe) you ate on Levels One and Two, but you can now *add* the following foods to your Level One program.

LEVEL THREE PRIMARY FOODS

2 slices whole grain bread.
1 cup cooked pasta with Level Two sauces.
½ cup any whole grain cereal.

LEVEL THREE SECONDARY FOODS

½ cup low-fat cottage cheese.
½ cup low-fat plain yogurt.
2 egg whites.
½ cup cooked beans, peas, lentils.
¼ pound chicken, fish, turkey.

LEVEL THREE SUPPLEMENTARY FOODS

Fresh fruit: one of your choice
3 teaspoons grated Parmesan or Romano cheese (as topping for salads, pasta, or vegetables).
Alcohol: 3½-ounce glass of wine (white or red), or 12-ounce can of light beer, or 1½ ounces of hard liquor (gin, scotch, vodka, etc.)
Margarine, mayonnaise, or vegetable oil: 2 teaspoons *total* of any one or more of these fats and oils.

LEVEL THREE SNACKS

1 ounce any dried fruits.
2 cups popcorn.

Peak Performance Cooking Techniques

Never add salt to the water in which you boil anything.
Conventional cookbooks usually call for salt in

the pot. The only reason for this is that water boils faster if you add salt, but this also means unnecessary sodium in your diet.

Eat vegetables raw when possible. Cooking robs vegetables of their water-soluble vitamins and minerals such as vitamin C, B complex, calcium, and magnesium. Fat-soluble vitamins such as beta carotene (which your body converts into vitamin A) and vitamin E are more stable during cooking. The less you cook vegetables rich in water-soluble vitamins and minerals, the more of these essential nutrients you preserve.

Use a microwave oven to prepare crisp and nutritious vegetables. Microwave ovens cook vegetables without sacrificing their essential nutrients. Vegetables come out especially crisp and tender, and they retain more of their vitamins and minerals than when prepared in boiling water.

Here's My Low-Fat Stir-Fry Cooking Technique You Will Enjoy

Slice your vegetables as thin as possible. Heat a nonstick fry pan until a drop of water "dances" on it. Measure 2 teaspoons of vegetable oil (if you are Level Two or Three only) into the pan. If you are on Level One, you can stir-fry, using water only as long as you use a nonstick pan. Keep vegetables in rapid motion with a nonmetal spatula until they become bright green or translucent (1 to 2 minutes). Reduce heat to low. Add 2 tablespoons of lemon or lime juice and ¼ teaspoon soy sauce plus 1 tablespoon of water. Cover the pan with a tight-fitting lid and cook for 2 to 3 minutes. The vegetables will be crisp-tender, deliciously flavored, and will retain most of their vitamin and mineral content.

When using soy sauce as a seasoning, follow my special recipe. Dilute soy sauce with an equal part of water. For example, if you buy a 4-ounce bottle of regular soy sauce or a special soy sauce I recommend called Tamari (available in health food stores), mix it with 4 ounces of water, and then squeeze a teaspoon of lemon juice into the soy sauce—water mixture. It's a little trick I learned to enhance the flavor of the mixture, and it allows you to use much less of it, thereby reducing your salt intake.

If you can't stir-fry vegetables, bake or steam them. Some vegetables such as potatoes and the root vegetables (beets, turnips, parsnips, etc.) are not suitable for the stir-fry method. Bake them or steam them *without peeling before cooking*. A vegetable steamer is inexpensive and easy to use, but a colander placed in a small amount of unsalted boiling water and closely covered will do the trick.

Make pasta one of your primary foods. Pasta in all of its forms—spaghetti, linguini, macaroni, and all the others—is an excellent source of complex carbohydrates and very easy to cook.

For 8 ounces of pasta, boil water and slowly add the pasta so that the water never stops boiling. Cook until it is *al dente* (still firm), removing a small piece to taste for texture after it has boiled 6 minutes. Drain when done to your taste, run cold water over the pasta for a few seconds (to eliminate sticking), drain, cover with sauce, and serve.

Peak Performance Particulars

There are two special food condiments that you can enjoy on the Haas Peak Performance Program: Butter Buds and Equal.

Butter Buds is an extremely low-fat powdered butter substitute made from all natural products. A small sprinkling of Butter Buds on your baked potato or steamed vegetables will give you a delicious "buttery" taste without adding unwanted fat, cholesterol, and calories. Butter Buds also makes a delicious topping for fish and shellfish, especially when you add lemon juice and chopped parsley.

Equal sugar replacer is made from two amino acids and provides only four calories per serving packet. This sweetener, which tastes remarkably like table sugar, has no bitter aftertaste and has not caused cancer in laboratory animals.

Butter Buds and Equal are available in supermarkets and drugstores and since they both are in powdered form, you can easily carry them to restaurants where you can use them to season your food (thus, you can always order your food without salt, butter, or margarine).

CEREALS

All of us who have stood in the cereal section of the supermarket and tried to read labels detailing the ingredients know that "natural" can mean natural sugar and natural salt and a host of other undesirables! These are the most popular approved cereals for my peak performance program:

oatmeal

shredded wheat

Grape Nuts

Kellogg's Nutri-Grain cereals (wheat, corn, barley, rye) puffed brown rice, puffed whole wheat, puffed corn

Wheateena

Quaker 100% Whole Wheat

Any whole grain, all natural cereal made without added fats or oils.

A Few More Recommendations

• Chew every mouthful of food until it is liquified in your saliva.

63

• Drink soft drinks with Equal sugar replacer to keep sugar intake low.
• Drink at least 6 8-ounce glasses of water (plain or carbonated) each day.
• Use bean, pea, and lentil soups for high-nutrition, low-calorie meals.
• Avoid eating avocados, olives, and peanut butter.

Almost any diet is easy to follow if *you* do all the shopping and cooking, and eat at home seven days a week. However, my sports nutrition program is just as easy to follow on all three levels when you eat out! Let me show you in the next chapter how to do it, as I do it, and as world-champion athletes do it.

Eating In

THE HAAS 28-DAY EAT-AT-HOME
PEAK PERFORMANCE PROGRAM

Here is a 28-day, eat-at-home program I've designed for active people who enjoy quick and easy-to-prepare meals at home. These are the same delicious recipes that have helped nourish some of the world's foremost sports champions in their own kitchens.

Each daily menu includes some of the original Haas recipes you will find in the Eat to Win cookbook section of this book. All recipes are marked with a star, and each starred item is listed in alphabetical order. The recipes themselves include a breakdown of nutritional information *per serving*: calories, protein, fat, carbohydrate, sodium, and cholesterol. This is valuable information that allows *you* to control the amounts of these nutrients in your diet.

65

You may enjoy any daily menu—breakfast, lunch, and dinner—as often as you wish. All of the daily menus and the original Haas recipes conform to Level One (the strictest level) so that even if you are currently on Levels Two or Three, you can still follow my eat-at-home meal plans.

Since metabolism (the rate at which we burn kilocalories) differs from person to person, you may find that you'll lose weight when you follow my suggested recipe servings. If you wish to avoid weight loss, or if you want to gain weight, simply increase my recommended portion size. This will not change the special diet chemistry (the ratio of fats, proteins, and carbohydrates) that determines peak performance levels. Larger portions *will*, however, change the absolute amounts of sodium and cholesterol you eat. Therefore, if you are following Level One, I strongly urge you to comply with my suggested recipe portions until your blood chemistry values reach or surpass Level Two standards.

You may begin my 28-day eat-at-home program with any daily menu plan you wish—day number 25, for example, then day number 17, etc. If you find that you are especially fond of day number 2, you may enjoy this menu plan (or any other daily plan, for up to three days in a row). There is plenty of variety and each recipe is simple, easy-to-prepare, and delicious.

You may even "mix and match" by combining this eat-at-home plan with dining out several days or nights each week, as long as you follow my specific dietary guidelines for your Haas Peak Performance Program level. World-champion athletes enjoy the convenience of following my plan at home or on the road, and you will too!

Some Tasty Recommendations For Following My Eat-At-Home Plan

• Use Butter Buds butter replacer on vegetables, potatoes, fish, shellfish, and any other food that you would normally enjoy with butter or margarine.

• Use low-fat cottage cheese or low-fat yogurt as a sour cream replacement on baked potatoes. Add chives and a light sprinkling of bacon bits or chips (soybean type) for a delicious and nutritious low-calorie treat.

• Many spreads and condiments that normally contain salt or sugar are also available in a salt-free or sugar-free form. Check your supermarket for availability of these items. Some health food stores carry sugar-free and salt-free alternatives to many condiments, spreads, and dips.

• You can prepare any of the original Haas recipes in quantity (double or even triple the recipe) if you want to freeze them for quick-thaw meals at a later date. This saves you time and money, especially if you use heat-sealable clear plastic bags for frozen storage. A helpful hint: seal your meals according to portion size, so that you can conveniently reheat your meals according to the exact number of people you wish to serve.

If you are following any of the sport-specific diets I have outlined in Chapter 11, or if you are following my dietary recommendations for the special nutritional needs of women, you can still follow this eat-at-home plan because it already contains enough variety for the sport-specific diets and special feminine nutritional needs. You simply select the daily menus that conform to your individual sports diet or nutritional needs and enjoy them whenever and as often as you desire.

Day 1

BREAKFAST

Approved whole grain cereal with ½ cup skim milk
½ sliced banana, or ¼ cup raisins
Beverage

LUNCH

*½ stuffed potato
Unlimited salad with approved dressing
Beverage

*Recipe appears in Section II.

DINNER

Steamed vegetable platter
*½ stuffed potato
Unlimited salad with approved dressing
*½" slice banana bread
Beverage

APPROVED SNACKS FOR EVERY DAY (choose one)

Popcorn (preferably hot air popped—2 cups per
  day)
*Cottage fries
Salad (unlimited) with approved dressing
Raw or steamed vegetables (unlimited)
½ cup approved cereal
Baked potato
Fresh fruit (do not exceed 2 per day)

Day 2

BREAKFAST

2 slices whole wheat toast with
*Apple butter
Beverage

LUNCH

*Italian vegetable bake
Unlimited salad with approved dressing
Beverage

*Recipe appears in Section II.

DINNER
*Basic brown rice and chicken
Salad (approved dressing)
Steamed vegetable platter
*1 baked apple
Beverage

Day 3

BREAKFAST
*Oatmeal royale
Beverage

LUNCH
*Indian vegetables and rice
Salad (approved dressing)
1 fruit
Beverage

DINNER
*Coq au vin casserole
Salad (approved dressing)
*½" slice banana bread
Beverage

*Recipe appears in Section II.

Day 4

BREAKFAST
*½" slice apple bread
Beverage

LUNCH
*Cannellini-stuffed zucchini
Salad (approved dressing)
1 fruit
Beverage

DINNER
*Spaghetti with marinara sauce
Salad (approved dressing)
1 slice whole wheat bread
1 fruit
Beverage

Day 5

BREAKFAST
*3 buckwheat pancakes with
*Apple butter
Beverage

*Recipe appears in Section II.

LUNCH

*Brown rice and cottage cheese casserole
Salad (approved dressing)
1 fruit
Beverage

DINNER

*Spinach cheese pie
Salad (approved dressing)
*½" slice apple bread
Beverage

Day 6

BREAKFAST

*Haas "scrambled eggs and bacon"
1 fruit
Beverage

LUNCH

*½ "Cheddar" stuffed potato
Steamed vegetable platter
1 fruit
Beverage

*Recipe appears in Section II.

Eating In

DINNER

*Melanzane al forno (baked eggplant)
 Salad (approved dressing)
*1 slice whole wheat bread
*1 baked apple
 Beverage

Day 7

BREAKFAST

1 fruit
*½" slice whole wheat raisin bread
 Beverage

LUNCH

1 baked potato with
*Bacon, onion, chive topping
*Marinated vegetables
 Salad (approved dressing)
 1 fruit
 Beverage

DINNER

*Broccoli brown rice hollandaise
 Salad (approved dressing)
*Baked plaintains
 Beverage

*Recipe appears in Section II.

Day 8

Oatmeal with ½ sliced banana or 1 tablespoon raisins
Beverage

*1 tuna muffin
Salad (approved dressing)
1 fruit
Beverage

*Stuffed cabbage
Salad (approved dressing)
*Brown rice fruit custard
Beverage

Day 9

*1 baked apple (hot or cold)
*½" slice whole wheat toast
Beverage

*Recipe appears in Section II.

LUNCH
*2 stuffed tomatoes
Salad (approved dressing)
1 fruit
Beverage

DINNER
*Tini Linguini
Salad (approved dressing)
*Noodle pudding
Beverage

Day 10

BREAKFAST
*1 blueberry bran muffin
1 fruit
Beverage

LUNCH
*1 cup chili bean soup
*Cucumber salad
*1 baked apple
Beverage

*Recipe appears in Section II.

DINNER

*Tuna casserole supreme
 Steamed vegetable platter
*1 apple muffin
 Beverage

Day 11

BREAKFAST

*1 slice whole wheat toast with
*Haas peanut butter (1 tablespoon)
 Beverage

LUNCH

*Chik 'n' chili (1 cup)
*Broccoli and onion salad
 1 fruit
 Beverage

DINNER

*Italian stuffed peppers (1 pepper)
 Salad (approved dressing)
*Banana noodle custard
 Beverage

*Recipe appears in Section II.

Day 12

*1 orange muffin
1 fruit
Beverage

*Potato soup (1 cup)
*Caesar salad
*1 corn muffin
Beverage

*Fish and mushroom marinade
*Baked potato with mushroom topping
Steamed vegetables
1 fruit
Beverage

Day 13

*½" slice earth bread with
*Apple butter
Beverage

*Recipe appears in Section II.

*Ranchero chili
*Broccoli and onion salad
*1 slice earth bread
 1 fruit
 Beverage

DINNER
*Macaroni and cheese Lombardo
 Salad (approved dressing)
 1 fruit
 Beverage

Day 14

BREAKFAST
*½" slice apple bread with
 Beverage

LUNCH
*1" slice tomato salmon loaf
 Steamed vegetables
*Hot German potato salad (½ cup)
 1 fruit
 Beverage

*Recipe appears in Section II.

DINNER

*Spinach noodle casserole
Salad (approved dressing)
*½" slice apple bread
Beverage

Day 15

BREAKFAST

Repeat breakfast menu of first 14 days

LUNCH

*Black-eyed pea soup (1 cup)
Salad (approved dressing)
1 fruit
Beverage

DINNER

*Veal scallopini
Salad (approved dressing)
1 fruit
Beverage

*Recipe appears in Section II.

Day 16

LUNCH
*Italian vegetable bake
*Bean and vegetable salad (½ cup)
1 fruit
Beverage

DINNER
*Sweet and sour chicken
*Cucumber salad (½ cup)
1 fruit
Beverage

Day 17

LUNCH
*Italian macaroni and beans (1 cup)
*Broccoli and onion salad (½ cup)
*½" slice holiday cake
Beverage

DINNER
*Chicken curry
1 fruit
Beverage

*Recipe appears in Section II.

Day 18

LUNCH
*Kidney bean soup (1 cup)
*½" slice whole wheat bread
Salad (approved dressing)
Beverage

DINNER
*Crabmeat au gratin
Salad (approved dressing)
1 fruit
Beverage

Day 19

LUNCH
Baked potato with
*Barbecue chicken topping
Steamed vegetables
*½" slice banana bread
Beverage

DINNER
*Corn and chicken frittata
Steamed vegetables
Salad (approved dressing)
1 fruit
Beverage

*Recipe appears in Section II.

Day 20

LUNCH
*Potato casserole (1 cup)
Salad (approved dressing)
*1 baked apple
Beverage

DINNER
*Eggplant moussaka
*Bean and vegetable salad (½ cup)
*Cranberry relish (½ cup)
Beverage

Day 21

LUNCH
*Waldorf salad deluxe (1 cup)
*½" slice whole wheat bread
Beverage

DINNER
Broiled white fish with
*Dill sauce deluxe
Baked potato with
*Snappy Cheddar topping
Salad (approved dressing)
Beverage

*Recipe appears in Section II.

Day 22

LUNCH

*Tuna Haas on whole wheat pita bread
Salad with approved dressing
1 fruit
Beverage

DINNER

*Glazed ratatouille
Salad with approved dressing
2″ slice crustless pumpkin pie
Beverage

Day 23

LUNCH

*Sweet potato soup (1 cup)
*½″ slice whole wheat bread
1 fruit
Beverage

DINNER

*Corn and chicken frittata
*Cucumber salad (½ cup)
*½″ slice whole wheat raisin bread
Beverage

*Recipe appears in Section II.

Day 24

LUNCH
*Potato casserole (1 cup)
Steamed vegetable platter
1 fruit
Beverage

DINNER
*Imam Bayeldi (stuffed eggplant)
Salad with approved dressing
Steamed vegetables
*½" slice apple bread
Beverage

Day 25

LUNCH
Baked potato with
*Chicken in wine sauce topping
Steamed vegetables
*Oatmeal fruit bar
Beverage

DINNER
*Pasta with garlic sauce
Salad with approved dressing
1 fruit
Beverage

*Recipe appears in Section II.

Day 26

LUNCH

*Chicken salad on whole wheat pita bread
Sliced tomatoes
1 fruit
Beverage

DINNER

*Chicken casserole (1 cup)
Salad with aproved dressing
*½" slice apple bread
Beverage

Day 27

LUNCH

Baked potato with
*Horseradish topping
Steamed vegetables
1 fruit
Beverage

DINNER

*Chili pie (2" slice)
Salad with approved dressing
*2" square oatmeal fruit bar
Beverage

*Recipe appears in Section II.

Day 28

LUNCH

*Howard's onion soup (1 cup)
*½" slice earth bread
1 fruit
Beverage

DINNER

*Italian white beans and pasta
Salad with approved dressing
*French apple bake (½ cup)
Beverage

*Recipe appears in Section II.

SEVEN

Eating Out

Most of us eat out quite often, whether it means grabbing a quick sandwich during the workday or enjoying a leisurely meal at a good restaurant. "How can I follow the Haas Peak Performance Program on the road?" Nancy Lieberman asked me when I became her nutritional coach. "Whether I'm having a pizza or dining at the Four Seasons, I can't control what they serve me."

But that's just what you *can* do, and I'm going to show you how easy the program is to follow—and it pays off in competition.

Look for Restaurants That Serve Your Favorite Primary Foods as Staples

Italian restaurants are, of course, always going to have plenty of pasta on hand. Indian restaurants specialize in serving rice, barbecued chicken, delicious vegetable dishes, and marvelous low-fat flat breads. Chinese and Japanese cuisines offer their traditional rice dishes, noodles, vegetables, and are light on animal protein, such as meat, chicken, or fish. Mexican restaurants offer tortillas (made from corn, lime, flour, and water), beans and rice—all delicious and all peak performance foods. Almost without exception, restaurants that feature the cuisine of other lands offer plenty of complex carbohydrates, vegetables, breads, and fruits. One exception to this rule is the traditional French gourmet restaurant. Calorie-rich sauces or entrees made with egg yolks, heavy cream, butter, cheese, and other high-fat foods are unacceptable for your new peak performance program.

Fortunately, nouvelle cuisine (the newer, lighter French way of cooking) is featured at many French restaurants and this is good news for Haas dieters. Nouvelle cuisine restaurants go lightly on rich cream sauces, emphasizing instead fresh vegetables, fish, poultry, and fresh fruits to create delicious food that conforms more closely with my dietary recommendations.

During 1982, I traveled to Stuttgart, Germany, with Martina Navratilova to supervise her diet when she played in the Porsche Grand Prix Tournament. Her performance in that event was awesome. When she beat Tracy Austin in the finals, the German press proclaimed Martina a "legend in her own time."

That evening, Porsche gave Martina a victory dinner and we arrived a little late. When we came to the enormous buffet table bedecked with platters of sausages, cheeses, rich cakes oozing with custard and whipped cream, vegetables smothered in heavy cream and cheese sauces—chicken and fish were nowhere to be found—Martina looked to me for advice. "Help!" she whispered.

We circled the table twice, finally spotting the only peak performance food on the entire table and, from a basket of breads, I took two rolls—one for each of us.

We returned to our table, each carrying a huge plate containing only one roll, to the astonishment of our host, Ed Peter, a Porsche executive, and everyone else in the room.

What the other guests didn't know was that I had checked the menu beforehand and taken care to order plenty of baked potatoes, chicken, steamed vegetables, salad, and fresh fruits, which Martina and I enjoyed before we arrived at her victory party!

Helpful Advice for Eating Out

Restaurants that serve American-style foods may not offer pasta, rice, or tortillas, but they usually will have baked potatoes, vegetables, chicken, fish, and fresh fruits. That great American invention, the salad bar, allows you to create a peak performance dish very easily. Load your plate with lettuce, green peppers, garbanzo beans, tomatoes, and any other fresh vegetables offered, except avocado. But do *not* use the house dressings (although you can sprinkle your salad with bacon bits if they are the "substitute" type made from soybeans; avoid real crumbled bacon). Use lemon juice or vinegar and sprinkle grated Parmesan cheese on top, toss and enjoy your salad the peak performance way!

Here is my advice for eating outside the home: *Double up on complex carbohydrates and cut your protein in half*. Order half of the usual restaurant portion of animal protein (or share half with a companion or take the uneaten portion home in a doggy bag). Order a baked potato (or even two, if you desire), and a large salad (remember, do not use commercial dressings). Top your baked potato with a sprinkling of Butter Buds you have brought in your pocket, or ask for yogurt or cottage-cheese topping (low-fat if possible).

Order fresh fruits for dessert. Most American-style restaurants serve melon, grapefruit, and fresh berries in season.

Don't be self-conscious about ordering this way. None of these requests is terribly unusual or hard to fill, and I've personally found that if you explain about how you are eating to win, you'll probably get a lot of interest and super service!

Create your own Haas Peak Performance dishes at your favorite restaurants. Be a creative orderer. You'll be surprised how glad the restaurant proprietor or chef will be to please discerning customers, especially if they are regulars.

Gene Mayer, the well-known tennis pro, enjoys spaghetti marinara with chunks of lobster. He never has a problem when he asks the chef to add a plain broiled lobster to the sauce.

Some athletes tell me they don't have time to read the instructions on a pay telephone, let alone a long diet list, so here are some simple guidelines for eating out.

BREAKFAST CHOICES

Choose one:

Whole grain cereal (shredded wheat, oatmeal, Grape Nuts, or any other low-fat, sugar-free [less than 2 grams of fat per 4-ounce serving]) whole grain cereal with ½ cup skim milk and 1 fresh fruit

or

2 pancakes, preferably buckwheat (¼" thick, 4" in diameter, approximately) without butter. Use Equal sugar substitute or applesauce with cinnamon instead of syrup or follow Martina's example and sprinkle the pancakes with cinnamon, and Equal, and ladle on the liquid Butter Buds.

LUNCH CHOICES

Choose one:

Spaghetti marinara (with up to 2 teaspoons of grated Parmesan cheese).

Shrimp, lobster, or crabmeat cocktail (4 ounces) with lemon, lime, or red cocktail sauce (no mayonnaise).

Chicken or turkey sandwich: 2 thin slices of poultry with plenty of lettuce, tomatoes, mushrooms, sprouts, etc. on whole grain bread (no butter or mayonnaise; mustard, if desired).

Baked potato with low-fat yogurt or cottage cheese topping.

Bean burrito or bean tostado without cheese with tomato, lettuce, onion, peppers, mushrooms, etc.

Soup (12-ounce bowl): split pea, bean, lentil, vegetarian vegetable, Manhattan clam chowder, chicken and chicken with rice.

Fresh fruit salad (2 or 3 sliced fresh fruits except avocado) topped with low-fat cottage cheese.

All of the above entrées may include as much salad or steamed vegetables as you care to eat.

DINNER CHOICES

Choose one of these entrées. You may eat the same main course as many times a week as you care to.

Lobster tail (steamed, boiled, or broiled without butter): 4 ounces after shell is removed, with lemon or lime juice and/or red cocktail sauce.

Crab legs or claws (steamed, boiled, or broiled without butter): 4 ounces after shell is removed; same condiments as above.

Scallops (steamed, boiled, or broiled without butter): same condiments as above.

Turkey or chicken (broiled, baked, boiled, or barbecued): always remove the fatty skin before eating poultry.

Fish (baked, broiled, poached, or barbecued): 4 ounces, preferably salmon or mackerel because these fish are rich in EPA, the "friendly" fat that helps protect you against cardiovascular disease.

Spaghetti or linguini marinara with up to 2 teaspoons of grated Parmesan or Romano cheese.

Spaghetti or linguini with red clam sauce with up to 2 teaspoons of grated Parmesan or Romano cheese.

12-ounce bowl of bean, pea, or lentil soup

With your entrée, choose *one* of these side dishes:

Baked potato with Butter Buds or low-fat yogurt or low-fat cottage cheese and/or spiced with chives, ketchup, mustard, pepper, steak sauce, barbecue sauce, or bacon bits (soybean type).

Vegetables (steamed in unlimited quantity) with Butter Buds and/or lemon or lime juice.

Raw vegetable salads (avoid avocado, olives, and hearts of palm): unlimited quantity. Dress with vinegar, lemon juice, up to 2 teaspoons grated Parmesan or Romano cheese (if you have not used these cheeses with your entree) or "Russian" dressing made with cottage cheese and a dollop of ketchup; bacon bits or chips (soybean type) and Butter Buds may also be added to salads.

Rice, preferably brown (steamed or boiled): Butter Buds or grated Parmesan or Romano cheese (up to 2 teaspoons) may be used to top your rice.

If you desire dessert, choose one of these:
Fresh fruit or fresh fruit cup (8 ounces).
Frozen soft-serve low-fat yogurt (4 ounces): any flavor.
Fruit sherbet (4 ounces): any flavor.
Fruit pie (apple, blueberry, key lime, or lemon meringue): one small slice no more than twice each week (because they contain larger amounts of sugar and fat than do the fresh fruits from which they were made).

These beverages are approved and can be ordered in virtually all restaurants:
Coffee (with Equal sugar replacer and/or skim milk): up to 2 cups per day (or as your physician prescribes). I personally recommend the water-processed decaffeinated brands. Check the product label to determine if your favorite brand is this type.
Tea (I recommend decaffeinated tea available

in most supermarkets): up to 8 ounces per day.

Alcohol beer: 12 ounces of light beer. Wine: (red or white): 1 3 ½-ounce glass. Hard liquor (vodka, for example): 1½ ounces.

Water (tap, bottled, or carbonated): *always* the best beverage.

These food choices are the ones I advise for professional athletes who are on Level Three of the Haas Peak Performance Program. If you are still on Level One or Level Two, avoid foods and drinks that are not yet permitted on your diet level.

Fast Foods for Athletes

Every day, trusting athletes (along with millions of nonathletic Americans) devour bushels of burgers and sip scores of shakes without the slightest idea of the nutritional value of these fast foods.

There's no need to wonder just how nutritious these foods are—I've already done the research for you. If you are a true fast-food fanatic, here are my recommendations.

• Consider eating south of the border. Mexican fast foods are among some of the best in the business for peak performance eating. According to the latest research published by independent testing laboratories, Mexican fast foods such as bean burritos (without the cheese topping) and bean tostados offer a less fattening, higher

95

fiber alternative than most other fast-food meals. Laboratory analysis reveals that compared to America's most famous fast-food hamburger, a typical Mexican fast-food bean burrito without cheese (but topped with lettuce and tomato) has 40% less calories, one-third the fat, cholesterol, and salt, twice as much fiber, about six times as much vitamin A, and slightly more thiamine (vitamin B-1) and vitamin C.

• In my opinion, Wendy's offers Haas Peak Performance dieters more of what they need than most other fast foods chains: plenty of complete carbohydrates from their chili and unlimited salad bar. These foods provide plenty of protein, iron, calcium, vitamins A, B-complex, C, E, magnesium, zinc, selenium, and fiber without providing excessive calories. There are two things you should remember when enjoying these peak performance fast-foods:

(1) Wendy's puts a full quarter pound of beef in their bean chili, and that amount limits this dish to those people on Level Two and Level Three (no more than twice a week) and, (2) avoid using prepared dressings on your salads. Instead, use my on-the-spot dressing recipe of vinegar, Equal, and grated Parmesan cheese.

• You can easily transform any ordinary fast-food pizza into a *peak performance pizza* by (1) ordering a 12" plain cheese pizza; (2) sliding the cheese topping off (the tomato sauce will remain on the cheese-soaked crust); and (3) sprinkling a small amount of grated Parmesan cheese over the pizza slice.

Of course, as you move from Level One to Levels Two and Three, you don't have to remove the original cheese topping (unless you prefer to); Level One and Level Two dieters may enjoy two slices of pizza per meal; those who have reached peak performance Level Three may have an additional slice per meal.

What To Do When You Dine In "Hostile" Territory

You probably will find yourself sooner or later, in a no-win eating situation: a business luncheon or dinner, a wedding reception, a birthday celebration, a five-star gourmet restaurant that specializes in veal cordon bleu, chocolate mousse, and other high-fat delights. What can you do when faced with a preplanned or fixed menu that contains almost no peak performance dishes?

You have three options: (1) be unsociable and refuse to eat; (2) eat very little and wait until you get home; (3) enjoy whatever is served and resume your diet immediately thereafter. From a nutritional standpoint, you can choose option 3 without risk of blowing your peak performance program *as long as you limit this kind of dietary deviation to once in a blue moon* (of course, you should avoid option 3 the night before or the day of an important athletic competition).

On the night Martina defeated Chris Evert Lloyd in the finals of the Daihatsu Challenge Cup in Brighton, England, I decided to surprise Martina with one of her favorite dinners—Peking Duck with all the trimmings—even though at that time it was not permitted on her peak performance diet. Since she did not have to play another tournament for two weeks, I decided that this diet deviation would be quite acceptable. I located a restaurant in London (about an hour and a half down the road from Brighton) and off we went. It wasn't until the waiter brought the main course that Martina realized what I had planned.

Her appetite was as big as her smile—before I could dig in, half the duck was gone! A well-deserved treat for a deserving champion.

Martina and I don't worry about an occasional cheat on our peak performance programs and neither should you. Enjoying a variety of foods (even an occasional cheat) is one of the luxuries of eating to win, as long as you stick to my peak performance program in the long run.

EIGHT

The Drink of Champions

Jimmy Connors knows it. So do John McEnroe, Martina Navratilova, Harold Solomon, and Gene and Sandy Mayer. I have told all of these world-class tennis players about the single most important nutrient they need to enhance their athletic performance and endurance.

The scientific use of this seemingly magical substance has helped to improve the energy, stamina, performance, and cramping tolerance of these stars—and it will do the same for you!

What is it? *Water*. Every chemical reaction in your body, including energy production, takes place in a watery environment. If your blood, muscles, and other organs do not receive optimal amounts of water, they will not function at peak performance levels.

Carefully controlled scientific studies have shown that when you lose *as little as 2 pounds of water during exercise, your ability to perform hard*

99

work can drop 15%! A 7-pound water loss, which is not extraordinary for a professional tennis player in humid and hot weather, can decrease work ability by a very damaging 30%. *Athletes lose more contests through dehydration than any other nutritional deficit.*

During my career as sports nutrition consultant, I have watched many improperly nourished athletes win. I've seen overly tired, and even seriously ill players win—but I have never seen a dehydrated athlete win. I have watched some of the best athletes of this century lose key competitions because of avoidable dehydration.

I saw Muhammad Ali defeated in his last fight—not just by the fists of his opponent, nor just by his age, but also by diet, medication, and dehydration.

Ali was taking thyroid medication in order to promote weight loss before the fight, and this helped weaken him. He ate the traditional high-protein training diet that does very little to help the body store water in the muscles, and this set the stage for decreased endurance. He became severely dehydrated as the fight progressed, and dehydration helped defeat the greatest boxer in the history of the sport. I wonder whether Ali, with his unrivaled boxing skills, could possibly have won that fight (even though he was fighting past his prime) had he followed the advice I'm going to give you.

Take a Lesson from Jimmy Connors

Jimmy Connors has proved that water is his victory drink. I had followed Jimmy's tennis career casually for years, but it was not until his wife, Patty, consulted me that I became personally involved in his victories and defeats. As Patty regained her ideal weight and robust health under my guidance (after recovering from surgery and the normal weight gain that accompanies postsurgical inactivity), Jimmy and I talked about his sports diet, and about the vital importance of water before, during, and after competition.

"I'm a ham-and-gravy man," Jimmy told me, "and what I drink is sodas—a dozen a day."

I had watched Connors fight his way to three Wimbledon finals only to lose from what appeared to be fatigue in the later stages of each match. Admittedly, he faced Bjorn Borg in two of these finals, and Arthur Ashe in the third, so he was fighting the toughest competition in the world at that time. Yet I believe that Jimmy could have won at least two of these matches if only he had had more energy and stamina.

We talked some more about diet and the value of water.

In 1982, Jimmy Connors won the Wimbledon championship and the U.S. Open title. I believe that the most significant dietary changes he made as a result of our discussions were these: (1) he modified his precompetition meal of steak to a high complex carbohydrate dish of spaghetti; (2) he learned to drink water, water, and more water *before, during, and after* each match.

While I was discussing my peak performance principles with Jimmy, I got to know one of his fiercest rivals, John McEnroe. John also embraced my optimum hydration program, and now I suspect that these two champions will compete at the water cooler as well as on the court!

Thirst does not prevent dehydration. The human body contains many wonderful built-in safety signals that warn us about a problem before it occurs, but thirst is not one of them. Many athletes can tolerate a water loss of up to 5% of their body weight before their thirst makes them drink. Unfortunately, by then the debilitating effects of dehydration already have occurred. *Thirst does not keep up with water loss*, and this time lag prevents active people from drinking enough water at the precise time their bodies most need it.

All athletes should make sure that they are properly hydrated before exercise. The body can absorb only a relatively small amount of water (about 1 to 2 pints an hour) from the stomach during exercise, so you should drink at least 1 pint of water before you actually begin exercise or competition.

What About Mineral Loss During Exercise?

When we sweat, we do lose a small amount of vital minerals and salts, and we must make sure that the body has ample stores of these essential nutrients. Competition also depletes blood sugar and glycogen (the storage form of carbohydrate energy), both of which are necessary for energy and stamina. Why not drink "sports drinks" to replace these nutrients?

As observed, commercially touted sports drinks give your body *much more* sodium and potassium and sugar than it needs. Sugar and salt both act to draw vital body water *into* the stomach and *away* from the parts of the body that most need water during exercise: the muscles.

These drinks stay in the stomach too long to benefit your athletic performance. *Pure water* leaves the stomach and enters the bloodstream much faster. During exercise, particularly competitive exercise, digestion virtually ceases, which means that the energy that the sugar in these drinks is meant to provide is not immediately available to the muscles and brain.

When large amounts of salt (and sugar) finally do leave the stomach and enter the blood, more water is drawn from the working muscles in order to dilute the high salt concentration in the blood. This deprives the hot, over-worked muscle cells of what they need most—more water.

103

We do indeed have to make sure that the proper electrolyte (salt and mineral) and fluid balance of the body is maintained, but not by drinking lots of salt and sugar. Researchers working with the American College of Sports Medicine have determined that the maximum concentration of sugar, salt, and potassium in any sports fluid replacement beverage should be, for every 8 ounces of fluid, 5.9 grams of sugar, 55 milligrams of sodium, and 46 milligrams of potassium. This is a great deal less than what is to be found in sports drinks. Yet no more than this concentration of nutrients can be absorbed efficiently from your stomach and delivered efficiently to the areas of your body that require them.

Here is my formula for a simple, scientifically sound fluid replacement beverage that meets the ACSM guidelines—and the needs of the athlete's body—precisely.

QUICKFIX

Mix and chill:
1 cup water
2 tablespoons fresh orange juice
1 pinch (⅓ teaspoon) table salt

Mix a jug of Quickfix the day you are going to exercise or compete and keep it well chilled.

Drink 2 cups of Quickfix about 15 minutes before exercise or competition. Active athletes, who
are competing in a hot, humid environment, or
those who sweat profusely even in moderate
temperatures, should drink 1 to 2 pints of
Quickfix during each hour of strenuous activity,
plus two cups of Quickfix beyond thirst requirements *after* the event.

Hidden Water—Your Secret Sports Weapon

High-protein, high-fat, low-carbohydrate diets
actually dehydrate the unfortunate athlete who
eats this traditional way. This is what happens:

Protein requires much more water for its digestion than does complex carbohydrate. That
is why water is drawn into the stomach and
away from other parts of the body, including
the muscles.

Less water—as much as one third less—can
be stored in muscles. During heavy exercise, this
water deficit can mean the difference between
victory or defeat.

High-protein, low-carbohydrate diets are also
high-fat diets. The human body responds to
this unnatural nutritional balance by going into
ketosis. This is a condition in which incompletely
burned fat forms toxic compounds called ketones,
which act to further dehydrate working muscles.

Athletes who follow my peak performance program (which is a *maximum* hydration program), store much more water in their muscles than do those who follow the old-fashioned steak-and-eggs regimen.

This is because the complex carbohydrates (which constitute the majority of daily peak performance nourishment) are the body's prime source of glycogen. Glycogen, as you will remember, is what your muscles burn (along with fat), and glycogen can be stored in the muscles (and liver). Moreover, each molecule of glycogen holds on to 3 molecules of water, and this water can be released to the muscles when you need it most—during exercise.

Athletes who eat peak performance foods carry a concealed weapon into sports combat—extra water stored in their muscles!

Primary foods on every level of the Haas Peak Performance Program carry their special bonus of hidden water. Foods with a high moisture content such as fruit and vegetables (90% or more water) and potatoes (75% water) augment your daily liquid intake of Quickfix or pure water to ensure that *you never will be beaten by dehydration.*

A Little More Watery Wisdom

Use water to cool your skin during competition. Marathon runners cool their overheated bodies by splashing water on the head and other exposed body surfaces—and so should you, no matter what your sport. This is especially important for athletes who are tall or broad (or fat) because the more body, the more surface that is exposed to the endurance-draining effects of heat, humidity, and direct sunlight.

Make sure beforehand that water will be available wherever you compete or exercise. Race officials, racquet club managers, and health club instructors will tell you about the location and availability of water supplies during your event. If you don't believe that there will be enough water available for you, don't take chances—*bring your own.*

Haas Peak Performance Program Guidelines For Fluid Intake

• *Drink* at least 6 to 8 cups of water or Quickfix each day.
• *Drink* 2 cups of water or Quickfix about 15 minutes prior to exercise or competition.
• *Drink* at least 1 cup of water or Quickfix every 15 to 30 minutes during exercise or competition.
• *Drink* at least 2 cups of water or Quickfix beyond your thirst requirements after exercise or competition.
• *Drink* chilled rather than warm liquids for faster absorption from the stomach into the blood.

Chilled drinks also help to decrease elevated body temperature.

• *Drink* 1 additional cup of water or Quickfix if you have had caffeinated drinks (colas, tea, coffee) within 12 hours of exercise or competition.

NINE

The Special Nutritional Needs of Active Women

One of the most exciting developments in the sports world during the last decade has been the enormous talent, skill, and endurance displayed by the new breed of female athletes.

Women have broken through social, psychological, legal, and even physical barriers to improve their performance beyond what most sports professionals thought was possible.

In the past few years, women have been shaving minutes off their previous records in running, while men are only taking seconds off theirs.

In 1981, Allison Roe ran the New York City Marathon in a record-breaking time of 2 hours, 25 minutes and 9 seconds. Her time was good enough to have won the men's Gold Medal for the marathon in the 1952 Olympics!

In 1967, Katherine Switzer ran in the Boston Marathon illegally, because women at that time were barred from competing in that event. In

1984, for the first time, the Olympic Games will include women in the 26-mile, 385-yard race!

How many husbands remember the money they lost to their wives when they bet that Bobby Riggs would beat Billie Jean King?

Although the performance of female super-star athletes is thrilling, I personally find the ever-increasing number of women who have become dedicated amateur athletes even more exciting because, as a sports nutritionist, I know the enormous health benefits conferred by regular physical activity and sports.

Even our national ideal of beauty has changed. We no longer admire the fleshy female screen stars of the fifties; our new godesses are slim, taut, and fit (and all the most fashionable clothes are designed for Farah Fawcett or Cheryl Tiegs, not Venus).

You've come a long way baby, and my peak performance program will take you the rest of the way—so let's start by learning about your uniquely feminine nutritional needs. You can easily follow these guidelines whether you're following level one, two, or three of the Haas Peak Performance Program or any of the sport-specific diets I've outlined in Chapter 11.

How Many Calories per Day?

The National Academy of Sciences Council on Food and Nutrition recommends that the average American woman eat 2,200 kilo-calories each day from the foods that comprise the ordinary American diet. My research has convinced me that this recommendation is excessive; professional female athletes I counsel often do not need to eat this many kilo-calories a day. (Of course, a female athlete in serious training needs more calories to *maintain* her body weight than the average active woman.)

I have found that most women who exercise or enjoy sports about three times a week generally have about 18 to 22% of their total body weight in fat tissue. These moderately active women usually require no more than 1,800 kilocalories to maintain their ideal weight. Not infrequently I counsel weekend female athletes who actually gain weight at this level of caloric intake.

Does it frustrate you to watch as men eat rich, high-calorie foods without pangs of guilt or apparent weight gain? If it does, take heart in the fact that you, as a woman, are special, and the reason men can eat more than women and get away with it (even men of comparable size and weight) is that they've got muscles where you've got curves!

Fat (adipose) tissue burns far fewer kilocalories than muscle, and if you don't exercise, you literally have to starve yourself to lose weight. Muscle tissue, on the other hand, is metabolically active tissue and burns plenty of pesky calories. The more muscle and the less fat you have (called your muscle-to-fat ratio) the more kilocalories you burn while watching the six o'clock news or running in the Boston Marathon!

Since men have higher muscle-to-fat ratios than women they generally look more muscular and enjoy greater strength than the opposite sex—differences that both sexes, I presume, fully appreciate. On the average, men weigh more than women, which means that they burn more kilocalories even if they're overweight and out of shape. It is bigger bodies and more muscle that allows men to seemingly pig-out without penalty.

The bad news then is that as a female, athletic or not, you must eat less to stay in good shape; the goods news is that compared to the ordinary American diet that you probably are now eating, on the Haas Peak Performance Program you will get to eat *more* because my peak performance foods and recipes are less fattening!

Ironing Out Your Iron Needs

Women have a higher iron requirement than men (especially due to blood loss during menstrual periods and to increased fetal nutritional needs during pregnancy). The National Academy of Sciences Council on Food and Nutrition recommends 18 milligrams (mg.) of iron each day (more for pregnant and lactating women).

If you eat the ordinary American diet, you would have to consume 2,800 to 3,000 kilocalories a day to get enough iron-rich foods to satisfy this requirement.

Eighteen hundred kilocalories for perfect weight maintenance—2,800 to 3,000 to get enough iron. Is this womanhood's Catch 22?

PEAK PERFORMANCE FOODS ARE THE ANSWER

Peak performance foods rich in iron include:
Legumes: peas, beans, lentils (including soups)
Fresh fruits
Whole grain cereals and breads
Broccoli and Brussels sprouts
Popeye's peak performance food, spinach, is famously rich in iron, but it also contains a substance called oxalic acid, which tends to bind iron, making it hard for your body to absorb it. Iron-rich whole wheat flour also contains phytic acid. I am not advising women to avoid such nutritious foods; rather, I am emphasizing that they should not rely solely on these foods as their primary sources of iron.

Your body absorbs iron more efficiently from animal foods than from vegetable foods because the iron in animal foods is carried in a slightly different form which more easily gets into your blood. The iron from vegetable foods, however, can be transformed into its more efficiently absorbed form if you eat *vitamin-C-rich foods at the same time*. Fresh fruits, and vegetables such as broccoli and tomatoes provide plenty of vitamin C along with iron. There is one vegetable source of iron that I strongly recommend for its exceptional iron content as well as its ample supply of protein, other vital vitamins and minerals, and fiber. *I recommend that active women eat at least 3 to 7 cups of beans, peas, or lentils (including soups) every week on every level of my program.*

In my opinion, all athletes should avoid taking iron supplements unless absolutely necessary (prescribed by a physician for the treatment of a health problem). The human body does not readily or easily excrete iron; if too much iron is stored by the body, especially in the liver, serious damage and disease may result. Iron constipates many athletes who supplement their diet with it, and it can also create damaging free-radicals (which can prematurely age you and damage virtually any part of your body—more about these molecular villains in Chapter 10) if you don't also take in enough vitamin E and other antioxidants.

An example of the danger of high iron intake can be found in the Bantu people of Africa, who brew their beer in large iron pots. Minute amounts of iron are leached into the beer. When the unsuspecting Bantu natives enjoy their favorite brew, their livers store the excess iron, resulting in a severe blood disease called Bantu siderosis.

This is an extreme example of the danger of excessive and inadvertent iron intake. The Bantus were not aware that iron pots brewed a dangerous health problem into their beer, but we know that excess iron can be dangerous.

Special Sports-Related Iron Deficiency

If a female athlete enjoys contact sports, such as basketball or martial arts, she may need to eat even more iron-rich foods, such as broccoli, beans, and peas, as well as supplement her diet with vitamin C, vitamin E, and antioxidant minerals such as selenium and zinc because she may suffer trauma or "occult" blood loss: small blood vessels in the body can rupture with sports contact—an event that may go unnoticed in the heat of competition.

I consider jogging to be a contact sport because every time your feet hit the ground, slight trauma occurs in your feet. Women who participate in contact sports should be sure that they eat my recommended dietary sources of iron and try to consume at least 6 to 7 cups of legumes per week, in addition to 2 fresh fruits each day. A contact sport such as football, jogging, karate, wrestling, soccer, or basketball increases the body's need for vitamin C, vitamin

E, selenium, zinc, vitamin B-6, and iron beyond that required for noncontact sports such as swimming, cycling, and golf.

To sum up: *active women do not need to take iron supplements (unless they have a particular health problem that demand such supplementation on the advice of a physician.)* After reviewing hundreds of blood chemistry profiles on female athletes and studying volumes of scientific research, I am convinced that peak performance foods contain, calorie-for-calorie, enough iron for the athletic woman.

Extra Riboflavin and Calcium

Skim and low-fat milk and milk products such as cottage cheese, yogurt, and hard and soft cheeses contain two vital nutrients that are particularly important to all active women: *riboflavin (vitamin B-2) and calcium.*

Riboflavin plays an important role in your body's metabolism of protein, fat, and carbohydrate. Because women in sports are concerned with maintaining strong muscle tissue (and in some cases, as with female weight lifters, in *building* muscle tissue) and want to burn unwanted body fat, they need extra riboflavin to maximize this metabolic process.

Supplemental riboflavin and other B vitamins are necessary for peak performance. The skim and low-

116

fat dairy products that I recommend provide a good supply of riboflavin for sedentary, nonactive women; women engaged in strenuous exercise, however, may get only *half* the riboflavin they require for peak performance. Recent sports nutritional research has determined that female athletes do not eat enough riboflavin to replace the extraordinary losses of this "sports" vitamin, and so supplementation with this and the other B vitamins is necessary to restore body stores to optimal levels. Although research in this area still remains inconclusive, several female world champions I advise supplement their diet with 5 to 40 milligrams of riboflavin per day.

What about calcium? Women in general, and athletic women in particular, need to supplement their diets with calcium (calcium supplements must also contain magnesium for proper absorption by the body). Most women lose calcium and other important minerals such as magnesium from their bones *every day of their lives*! This loss contributes to the disease called osteoporosis, which is currently epidemic among older women in the United States. By the time many women reach fifty or sixty years of age, they have lost over one-third of their bone mass! Under such circumstances, bones become hollow, brittle, and can actually fracture at the slightest touch!

Excess dietary protein, from animal *and* vegetable sources contributes to daily calcium losses in the urine—the more protein you eat, the more calcium you lose. That's why the Haas Peak Performance diet recommends no more than 15% of your daily calories come from protein. This recommendation provides an extra margin of protein safety, so that even the most active of athletes will get all the protein they need for peak performance and peak health.

Astronauts, bedridden hospital patients, and inactive women share a common attribute—all lose more calcium each day than they replace! Weightlessness and inactivity cause abnormal calcium losses; high-protein diets increase those losses further. My advice: follow the Haas Peak performance protein recommendations, eat peak performance foods rich in vitamins and minerals, and supplement your diet with the sports vitamins and minerals that you'll learn more about in Chapter 12. Don't get caught short: some of our astronauts, who were in peak physical condition before their space flights, still have not been able to replace all the calcium they lost in space.

Calcium balance studies reveal that women who eat high-protein diets (about 150 grams of protein per day or more—a typical protein intake for most Americans) cannot prevent dangerous calcium losses in their urine even when they take one gram of supplemental calcium each day! African women, on the other hand, eat less protein than Americans (about 40 to 50 grams per day) and less calcium (about 350 to 500 milligrams per day), yet they do not lose calcium in their urine—they store it in their bones. African women bear two to three times more children than their American counterparts, yet these natives have stronger, denser bones, and don't suffer from osteoporosis as they age.

Even though your new peak performance program will not cause you to lose calcium in your urine, I recommend that all active women supplement their diet with a calcium-magnesium formulation (the ratio of calcium to magnesium should be 2-to-1 for proper balance and absorption) to protect against calcium losses that occur in sweat and urine. Vigorous physical activity, especially under hot and humid conditions, requires that you drink large amounts of fluids. Since calcium and magnesium are water-soluble minerals, active women run the risk of losing these and other minerals in their sweat and urine. Every female athlete I counsel supplements her diet with 500 to 1000 milligrams (½ to 1 gram, respectively) of calcium and half as much magnesium. Most calcium-magnesium supplements that you can purchase at health food stores, drug stores, and supermarkets contain calcium and magnesium in the proper 2 to 1 ratio.

Active Women Should Not Eat Three Meals A Day

Am I recommending starvation? Of course not. I counsel athletic women to eat *up to six meals each day*.

Women usually have more body fat than men, as I have explained, and tend to deposit more calories as fat rather than as lean, muscular tissue—Mother Nature's way of providing an extra storehouse of energy for the fetus in the event of pregnancy. Many small meals a day deposit less fat than one or two large meals, even if you eat the same food and the same amount of food.

When you eat many small meals, your body has a chance to metabolize those kilocalories efficiently, burning them for energy and storing them as glycogen instead of as fat. That's why smaller, more frequent meals result in better weight loss *and* weight maintenance as long as you remain physically active. *Physical activity and sports promote lean, taut bodies that burn food for fuel and store excess calories as glycogen rather than as fat on the Haas Peak Performance Program.*

Some years ago, nutritionists studied the eating patterns of Balinese women, who were much less obese than comparable populations (including our own), and found that they normally ate as many as eight small meals a day. These observations have also been confirmed in the laboratory, both in human beings and in animals.

Active women who follow the Haas Peak Perform-ance "mini-meal" program get a special bonus—more energy. When you eat this way, you will maintain your blood sugar at its ideal level, avoiding the huge swings in blood sugar that rob many people of their energy and stamina throughout the day. No more midafternoon slumps for you—you will enjoy a vital flow of energy all day long. Time formerly spent resting, napping, or trudging along through your day's work is now time gained—profitable and energy-rich.

It's easy to follow these dietary recommendations regardless of whether you're on Level One, Two, or Three, even if you're eating on the road, without kitchen facilities.

SAMPLE MENU

BREAKFAST

½ cup whole grain cereal (hot or cold)
Sliced fresh fruit topping of choice
Equal sugar replacer (if desired)
½ cup skim milk (low-fat if skim isn't available)

MIDMORNING

1 fresh fruit

LUNCH

Large mixed garden salad
Oil-free dressing
1 cup low-fat cottage cheese
or
1 bean burrito (at a Mexican fast-food restaurant)
or
1 cup bean, pea, or lentil soup

MIDAFTERNOON

1 fresh fruit

DINNER

Chicken chow mein with rice, or
12-ounce bowl of bean, pea, or lentil soup, or
Barbecued chicken breast, or
4-ounce broiled (without butter) fish fillet
Above served with baked potato (Butter Buds topping, if desired), large fresh garden salad (oil-free dressing)

MIDEVENING

1 fresh fruit, or
4 ounces frozen yogurt (any flavor)

This is a *sample pattern* to show how easy it is whether you are home, on the job, or on the road. This menu pattern is compatible with Level One. You can add more variety as you move to Levels Two and Three. Therefore, *you can eat up to six meals during each day, every day, regardless of the level of your Peak Performance Program.*

A Special Case for Unequal Rights for Women: Drugs

Women do not require the same drug dosages as men because, as a general rule, they metabolize them more slowly. Every mother knows that infants require baby aspirin rather than regular aspirin because it provides one quarter the strength of a tablet meant for adults. The reason: babies have less body mass to metabolize drugs than do adults.

Although medical researchers have known for years that drug dosage should be prescribed according to body weight (there are, of course, exceptions to this pharmacological principle), the over-the-counter drugs that we find on every drugstore and supermarket shelf may provide label directions indicating lower dosages for children than adults, but *they do not provide different dosages for men and women.*

What about drugs in the everyday foods we consume, such as coffee, tea, chocolate, and cocoa? All of these drugs are chemically related to "speed" (amphetamine), yet men, women, and children may all ingest identical amounts of these foods, despite enormous differences in body weight. I assure you that one hundred milligrams of caffeine (the approximate amount of caffeine in one cup of freshly brewed coffee) provides a much stronger and longer lasting stimulant effect to a 100-pound woman or child than it does to a 250-pound male. I urge all women, active and nonactive (and especially when pregnant), to discuss this matter with their physician whenever they take prescription or nonprescription drugs.

Remember: the amount of caffeine and other stimulants in ordinary foods and beverages varies according to amount and method of preparation, but the drug effect *increases* as body weight *decreases*. The mathematics are as sobering as the coffee we drink: 4 cups of our nation's favorite breakfast beverage will give a 100-pound woman approximately the same caffeine-stimulant effect as 8 cups will provide a 200-pound man!

Amenorrhea and Active Women

The scientific and lay press recently has called attention to amenorrhea (irregular or missed menstrual periods) in female athletes who decrease their body fat below 15%. Does the amenorrhea associated with sports activity and lean bodies adversely affect health or sports performance?

While all the answers are not yet in, the preliminary findings of studies that examine sports amenorrhea indicate that it occurs in athletes in all sports and particularly in endurance sports (such as long-distance running, cross-country skiing, and ballet dancing). Sports amenorrhea does not appear to pose a health risk to active women, nor does it prevent the ability to become pregnant after regular menstruation resumes. This simply may be the body's way of preventing a woman from conceiving *during the time that she has inadequate stores of body fat (energy) to ensure that the fetus will be well provided for*.

What Oral Contraceptives Do

Women who take oral contraceptives should know that these drug-hormones increase their body's daily requirements for vital nutrients such as the B-vitamins, choline, and most likely, other nutrients that future scientific studies will reveal. Active women, especially those who regularly enjoy strenuous sports or exercise, should take special care to replenish these and other nutrients I have already mentioned, *especially if they take oral contraceptives*.

One unfortunate side effect that some oral contraceptives may cause is depression. This type of depression is not due to psychological factors but rather to the fact that oral contraceptives can deplete the body of choline, a naturally occurring substance found in many foods and manufactured by the body. The brain uses choline and other nutrients to manufacture a special chemical "messenger" (called acetylcholine) that helps the brain cells and other nerve cells throughout the body transmit signals and messages essential to normal function and life itself.

Some women who use oral contraceptives and become depressed for no apparent reason may actually require more choline and other nutrients that the body needs to manufacture acetylcholine. I have seen several depressed female athletes who completely eliminated their unexplained depression by taking supplemental choline and following my peak performance program. While there are many and multiple causes of depression that are not due to choline deficiency, choline supplementation deserves further research, for it may help women avoid unnecessary and potentially harmful prescription medications that are currently prescribed to manage depression. I urge you to discuss the possibility of choline supplementation with your physician if you take oral contraceptives and suffer from unexplained depression.

You can easily follow my recommendations for the special nutritional needs of active women on any level of the Haas Peak Performance Program, whether you follow Level One, Two, or Three or any of the sport-specific diets I will explain in Chapter 10. As you have just discovered, if you are an active woman, you have some *very special needs* that most sports-care professionals *and* female athletes have neglected far too long. I've already told you how to replenish those vital nutrients you lose through physical activity, stress, poor diet, and drug use. Now I'm going to show you *how to stay young longer* and, if you sustain a sports injury, *how to heal faster and stronger.*

T E N

Heal Faster—Stay Younger: The Antioxidant Story

I first talked to world-famous marathon champion Bill Rodgers in 1980, when he was thirty-two. Most runners consider the thirties as the time when aging begins to take its toll, by decreasing a runner's maximum aerobic capacity (the amount of oxygen the body can extract from the blood and use effectively) by about ½ to 1% every year. By age forty-two, a runner can lose 10%—and a drop of even 4 or 5% literally can put you out of the running.

"I guess the thirties are all downhill," Bill said sadly. But he was wrong. With the right nutritional program, the expected effects of aging that eventually end all athletic careers don't have to happen anymore.

Bill is also famous for his junk-food diet, but as he told me, it is sometimes exaggerated by the press. When we both addressed an eager audience of runners at the Bill Rodgers Running Clinic, Bill stated that he agreed with my high-carbohydrate nutritional program. Bill, who sometimes gets up in the middle of the night to snack on milk and cookies (hardly ideal, but still carbohydrate), does eat more junk food than I would recommend. However, Bill is 5' 8" and weighs all of 128 pounds. When he runs 20 miles each day, his body requires an extra supply of calories. Three years after our first conversation, Bill is still competing in world-class events, although not as frequently as he once did. He is a fantastic athlete, but I am convinced that if he had followed my peak performance program and included age-retarding antioxidant supplements in his diet he would be even better than he is today. I am going out on a limb to predict that Martina Navratilova, who conscientiously follows my nutritional advice and relies on my antioxidant formulas, will still be at the top of her sport ten years from today!

Sadly, most professional athletes believe that their careers will begin to deteriorate the day they blow out thirty candles. Why should the normal consequences of aging have to lead to defeat at the very time when hard-won skill and experience give athletes the greatest competitive edge?

Ask this question of Fred Stolle, famous tennis champion and world-renowned coach of top players such as Vitas Gerulaitis. Fred has faithfully followed my peak performance program for more than two years and has racked up some impressive victories (and prize money). Ask Stan Smith, now over ten years older than the average world-champion tennis player.

After adopting the peak performance program, Stan recently scored two major wins by boosting his stamina, energy, and endurance—demonstrating that the traditional decline in sports performance with age is not inevitable. *You literally can tie the hands of time with my high antioxidant peak performance program.*

My own father (okay, in this case, I'm slightly prejudiced), who formerly took six medications to control heart disease, high blood pressure, and rheumatoid arthritis, recently won a 10-kilometer road race in his age group by using my antioxidant formulas. No more chest pain, no more high blood pressure, no more arthritic pain, *and no more drugs!* Oh, by the way, he is sixty-seven years old.

Professional athletes and weekend athletes alike who embrace my antioxidant, peak performance program, are living proof that aging can be retarded and in some cases, *reversed.*

How to Help Mother Nature Cheat Father Time with a Little Help From Your Friends

Your new-found friends are substances called antioxidants. You may not know them by this

130

term, but you eat them every day (although probably not nearly enough) in common foods. Beta carotene, ascorbic acid, and dl-alpha tocopherol are among the most common and most powerful antioxidants—a chemical class that also includes some food additives, preservatives, amino acids, and a number of prescription drugs used to treat health problems.

I have studied antioxidant activity for the last ten years, and more researchers are now investigating and documenting the beneficial role of these agents.

Antioxidants not only can help stave off the effects of premature aging, but they also can help to heal sports injuries faster and stronger. Actually, aging and sports injury have a lot in common. In a biochemical sense, *aging can injure and injury can age*.

The mechanisms of aging and injury damage, as well as the pain and stiffness of arthritic disease, all share a common factor: cellular damage due to the activity of *free-radicals*. These sinister-sounding substances are highly reactive and toxic chemical fragments within our bodies, very unstable and very unhealthy.

Free-radicals destroy healthy tissue, including the primary genetic material in our cells, DNA, by electrocution. Free-radicals will always be with us; in fact, some free-radicals are essential to life. Health problems (and premature aging) occur when there are too many free-radicals and not enough antioxidants to "insulate" our cells from electrocution. Free-radicals enter the body through food, tobacco smoke, even from the air we breathe and the water we drink. Actually, the free-radicals are often created *after* these substances enter our bodies and therefore can be quenched by antioxidants if the antioxidants are present in sufficient quantities.

There are two ways in which research scientists are currently attacking the problem of free-radical damage. One is the search for a free-radical scavenger drug that will gobble up these little subversives before they can attack and destroy healthy cells. These "Pac-Man" drugs are still in the experimental stage, but there is another way of controlling the damage that free-radicals do to us.

This method, which I recommend, is called antioxidant therapy. Ironically, oxygen is one reason we live *and* die. Oxygen carried in our blood plays a major role in the formation of free-radicals, and antioxidants inhibit the transformation of these elements or atoms (which, in their normal state, are simply called radicals) to the potentially damaging free-radical state.

We have seen how free-radicals contribute to the aging process by damaging cells. Antioxidants cut down on the number of free-radicals so that fewer cells are destroyed and therefore *youth lasts longer*.

The role of free-radicals in tissue injury and rheumatoid arthritis is a bit more complex. These two conditions are similar because the inflammatory process causes pain, soreness, and swelling, both in simple sports injury such as a sprained ankle and in an attack of rheumatoid arthritis.

Let's examine what happens when you sprain your ankle. What you have done is to tear the ligaments (which can be thought of as leather straps) connecting your muscles. This triggers the inflammatory response, which is the body's prime defense against injury and infection.

In a nutshell, here is what is happening inside, when outside you see a discolored and swelling ankle and feel a great deal of pain.

1. Chemical substances called inflammatory mediators are released into the extracellular fluid (the fluid that bathes your body's cells) around the injured site.

2. Chemicals, such as histamine (that's the stuff that causes itching, burning, and runny noses with allergies) and bradykinin, cause the small blood vessels around the damaged tissue to enlarge. More blood flows into the area and makes your ankle look red and feel hot.

3. At the same time, the walls of the small blood vessels change, in a protective response, so that the body's "warrior" cells, such as

antibodies, neutrophils, and macrophages, can pass to the site of injury.

4. More fluid passes into the tissues and your ankle swells (this is called edema).

5. White blood cells, called neutrophils, contain substances named lysozomes, which produce powerful protein-dissolving enzymes. These enzymes actually may destroy already damaged tissue (which means premature aging).

6. The inflammatory mediators, histamine and bradykinin, also stimulate nerve endings in the injured area, and this causes pain. These substances are released by the body in response to injury and help prevent further injury by making physical activity too painful to continue.

7. When macrophages and other "warrior" cells are damaged or destroyed in this process, they release fat-related compounds called prostaglandins. Prostaglandins add to the pain-producing potential of the inflammatory mediators, and this is when your ankle *really* hurts. (Recent research has shown that ordinary aspirin inhibits the synthesis of prostaglandins.)

How Do Antioxidants Soothe the Inflammatory Process?

Free-radicals are produced at many stages of the inflammatory process. They are autocatalytic, which means that they can, themselves, create

134

more free-radicals. Eventually this chain-reaction stops, but not before it attacks healthy cells. This can retard healing; it can also weaken the previously injured tissue, making it more susceptible to reinjury.

During the period when you were host to the inflammatory process, you probably consulted a health-care professional. And the recommendation was most likely what sports-care experts call RICE: Rest, Ice, Compression, and Elevation of the injured area (usually *above the heart,* if possible). Some professionals also recommend drugs to help reduce inflammation and soft tissue swelling. You might have been advised to take simple aspirin or been given a prescription for stronger medications (which may have harmful side effects) such as phenylbutazone ("bute," as it's commonly called by the athletes who take it) and indomethacin.

What *should* be recommended along with RICE is:

1. A fat-restricted diet
2. Antioxidant therapy

We have seen that antioxidants inhibit the excessive production of the free-radical particles that can injure, age, and even kill healthy cells. But what is the role of *fat*? Why restrict fat in the diet of an injured athlete?

A high-fat diet means a high free-radical potential in your body. The more fat you eat—especially the unsaturated type—the more free-radicals your body makes, and the longer an injury takes to heal. *High-fat diets aggravate sports injuries and needlessly increase healing time.*

What About Arthritis?

Oddly enough, the same inflammatory process that causes pain, swelling, and damage in common sports injuries is also the same process that occurs when joints become inflamed—a condition known as arthritis. Since there are over a hundred forms of arthritis caused by many factors, some of which remain unknown, we have no cure for this painful and crippling disease.

Free-radicals also contribute to the pain, swelling, and joint injury of arthritis. Here is what I believe happens: Serum iron accumulates in the membranes and fluids surrounding affected joints and interacts with oxygen to form free-radicals, called superoxide anion radicals. These, in turn, damage red blood cells, causing them to leak their contents into the inflamed area, which then produces the most damaging of all the free-radicals known—hydroxyl radicals—that destroy DNA and break down the protective fluid that normally lubricates joints. The less fluid, the more stiffness and pain. The free-radicals also interact with unsaturated fats in the body, producing even more free-radicals and more injury. During this process, lysozomes (little sacs that contain powerful protein-dissolving enzymes) are destroyed, leaking their enzymes into the damaged area, which further increases the damage to joint membranes.

Most physicians who specialize in the study and treatment of arthritis and related diseases will tell you that diet has little do do with causing arthritis or relieving its pain and stiffness. I strongly disagree.

As athletes age, so do their joints. High-fat, high-cholesterol diets that are low in natural antioxidants such as vitamin E, beta carotene, vitamin C, and antioxidant metals such as selenium and zinc contribute to the damage done by oxygen and other unavoidable free-radical stimulants.

Any athlete who follows my peak performance program, relies on antioxidants to prevent excessive production of harmful free-radicals. Antioxidants can reduce the damage from most traumatic sports injuries and minimize free-radical destruction of joint tissues.

I, personally, have seen athletes who were sidelined with joint pain, inflammation, and swelling who rapidly returned to peak function when they used the right combination of *diet and antioxidant supplements*.

Nancy Lieberman, the number-one women's pro basketball player, sustained a serious injury that required surgery. As Nancy's sports nutrition advisor, I am happy to report that her recovery was amazingly fast. She regained almost full range of motion in a matter of weeks, and the swelling, a normal consequence of surgery, was minimal. The low-fat nutrition program I created especially for Nancy and the antioxidant formulas I gave her minimized the free-radical damage from surgical anesthesia (due to the toxic chemicals that surgeons must use to prevent pain during surgery), kept edema and inflammation to a minimum, and strengthened the collagen that rebuilds strong tissue after surgery.

Let's Get Down To Specifics

We have two sources of antioxidants: the foods we eat and the supplements we can buy in most pharmacies, supermarkets, and health food stores. (You also may obtain antioxidants by prescription from your physician.)

Naturally occurring antioxidants in our foods help to prevent free-radical damage. The selection of foods rich in these vital substances is the first step in achieving optimal protection on my peak performance program.

Your own kitchen can be a storehouse of some of the most effective and important antioxidants:

Vitamin E
Vitamin C

Beta carotene (pro-vitamin A)
B-complex vitamins:
   Thiamine (B-1)
   Pyridoxine (B-6)
   Pantothenic acid (B-5)
   PABA (para-aminobenzoic acid)
   Selenium
   Zinc
Sulfur-containing amino acids
BHT (butylated hydroxytoluene)

These are just a few of the common antioxidants you'll find in your refrigerator and kitchen cabinet. Let's examine more closely some of the foods rich in these widely available anti-oxidants that can *help you heal faster and age more slowly.*

VITAMIN E (DL ALPHA TOCOPHEROL ACETATE)

Vitamin E is the primary deterrent of free-radical formation in your body when you eat unsaturated fats. Vitamin E is depleted by high-unsaturated-fat diets. (remember, a low-fat diet aids injury healing); so the more fats you eat (the unsaturated ones are usually liquid at room temperature, and are therefore technically called oils), the more vitamin E you need.

Vitamin E is fat soluble, which means that it can be stored in the body. Since vitamin E can be destroyed by freezing, you should use fresh food sources, if these will be your primary supply of this important antioxidant.

VITAMIN-E-RICH FOODS

Wheat germ
Whole grains (brown rice, whole wheat, oatmeal, cornmeal)
Asparagus
Spinach
Sweet potato
Beet greens
Turnip greens
Brussels sprouts
Broccoli

The amount of vitamin E in these common foods varies tremendously according to storage time, method of preparation, where they were grown, and what chemicals they were exposed to from the time they were harvested until they reach your table. When you enjoy commonly served portions of these vitamin-E-rich foods (such as you are served in restaurants) you will consume about 10 to 15 I.U.'s (International Units) of vitamin E in its various forms. And since the Haas peak performance program is a low-fat diet, your need for vitamin E is not increased as it would be if you ate large amounts of unsaturated fats.

VITAMIN C

Vitamin C is a water-soluble antioxidant vitamin, which means that you must regularly replenish your body's supply. Some nutritionists have mistakenly assumed that since you can avoid scurvy—the famous vitamin C "deficiency" disease—on as little as 9 milligrams a day (a small baked potato provides 45 milligrams), then your need for vitamin C is very small.

This potent antioxidant is unstable in the presence of both heat and oxygen, so it is best to eat vitamin-C-rich foods raw, if possible. The fresher, the better. If you cook vegetables, use as little water as possible. (Try steaming to retain this vitamin.)

Vitamin C also helps your body heal from sports injury and surgery better and faster, and helps protect it against the damage from anesthesia (due to free-radical formation). I believe that vitamin C supplementation, beyond the amount you can reasonably expected to receive from any foods, is extremely important before and after surgery.

Vitamin C blocks the formation of many carcinogens (cancer-causing substances) found naturally in foods and in the body. It functions equally well as a preservative in foods to which carcinogenic compounds have intentionally been added, such as in the case of nitrates and nitrites. These chemicals prevent contamina-

141

tion of foods by dangerous micororganisms and therefore they play an important role in keeping us healthy. It is wise to supplement our diets with additional vitamin C if we eat foods adulterated with other potentially harmful chemicals, but our national nitrate phobia actually is ill-founded: we produce more naturally occurring nitrates in our own bodies than most of us get from our diet. (Your saliva, on any given day, contains a much greater concentration of nitrates than food manufacturers add to foods to protect against botulism and other dangerous diseases.)

VITAMIN-C-RICH FOODS

Citrus fruit (oranges, grapefruit, lemon, lime)	Spinach (raw)
	Turnip greens
Tomatoes	Collard greens
Strawberries	Watercress
Brussels sprouts	Black currants
Peppers (raw)	Papaya
Potatoes	

Since vitamin E and vitamin C work synergistically (the combined effects of these two antioxidants is multiplicative rather than additive), foods that provide each vitamin should be included in your diet if you do not take antioxidant supplements. The Haas Peak Performance Program provides about 300 milligrams of vitamin C on all three levels. Athletes and people who enjoy regular, strenuous physical activity should supplement their diets with additional vitamin C.

BETA CAROTENE

Beta carotene is called pro-vitamin A because it is tranformed by the body into active vitamin A at a safe rate when it is needed. Beta carotene is relatively nontoxic in amounts far greater than you would be able to survive if you ingested an equivalent amount of active vitamin A. Vitamin A poisoning can result in serious nerve and liver damage, and even death when ingested in amounts exceeding 50,000 International Units per day for several months or more.

Beta carotene comes from the vegetable kingdom; active vitamin A is found only in animal foods. Recent studies have shown that beta carotene, a potent antioxidant, helps protect against the damaging effects of air pollution and even reduces the risk of getting lung cancer.

You can identify many vegetables rich in beta carotene by their color—usually orange, dark green, or yellow. The Haas Peak Performance Diet is rich in beta carotene. Since this antioxidant is fat soluble, your body can store an ample supply. Beta carotene is not susceptible to destruction by cooking, like vitamin C and other water-soluble vitamins. And if you spend a great deal of time in the sun, as many active people do, you'll be pleased to know that recent research indicates that beta carotene can protect against potentially damaging (and aging) effects of solar ultraviolet-B radiation. Beta carotene is a potent inhibitor of a type of free-radical called singlet oxygen.

BETA-CAROTENE-RICH FOODS

Pumpkin	Endive
Carrots	Kale
Sweet potatoes	Romaine lettuce
Winter squash	Turnips and turnip greens
Summer squash	Spinach
Broccoli	Fresh tropical fruits
Tomatoes	papaya, canteloupe,
Chard	mangos, etc.)
Escarole	

B VITAMINS

Thiamin (vitamin B-1) is vital to the energy-release system in the body. It is essential to several enzyme systems that regulate the metabolism of protein, fat, carbohydrate, and alcohol. Moreover, thiamin is part of the complex system that helps transmit nerve impulses throughout the body.

144

Athletes who drink alcoholic beverages need much more thiamin than they get from my peak performance foods. Fred Stolle, still a great tennis talent and a great coach as well (Vitas Gerulaitis owes much to Fred), is an Australian, and the Aussies love their beer. One famous sports writer and television commentator has written that beer is like "mother's milk" to an Aussie. The first day Fred came to me for counseling, he said, "I'm willing to give up steak, but you can't take away my bloody beer!"

I didn't. What I did do for Fred was to construct a peak performance program *around* his drinking habits—which included a "six-pack" in the evening after he'd put in a hard day on the courts. Fred simply traded some high-calorie foods (thereby reducing total daily calories, sugar, and fat intake) for the beer he loved. This trade-off helped keep Fred's serum triglycerides (blood fats) at an acceptable level, helped reduced his beer belly (even though he still got to enjoy his favorite brew), and added antioxidant-rich foods and supplements to protect against the toxic effects of alcohol.

Fred's peak performance program provided him with foods and food supplements that research has shown will protect against the harmful effects of alcohol on the body. For example, beer, wine, and hard liquor form toxic substances called aldehydes (as well as free-radicals) that can destroy liver, kidney, and brain cells.

Aldehydes (most of us who took high school biology probably dissected a frog that was preserved in formaldehyde) serve a useful function in preserving or "pickling" dead animal tissue, but they serve no beneficial purpose in live animals—especially humans!

The program I constructed for Fred provided him with a number of antioxidants to partially offset this "pickling" process by stopping the aldehydes and free-radicals from doing damage to vital organs. Today, Fred relies on his antioxidant "cocktail" every day so that he can enjoy his postmatch six-pack and still play to win the next day. Fred relies on a special formula (which I constructed according to his personal blood chemistry) including the antioxidants beta carotene, dl-alpha tocopheryl acetate, B-complex vitamins, ascobyl palmitate, zinc, selenium, and an amino acid mixture including cysteine ("Maxi-Life," made by Twin Laboratories) to play at his peak performance level.

Fred's diet, also rich in antioxidants and other protective nutrients, includes a tuna fish sandwich (a Haas recipe) on whole wheat bread (which Fred eats every day), a limited amount of fresh fruit (depending upon his current blood chemistry profile), a special vegetable mixture on whole wheat toast called Vegemite (which Fred has flown in from his native Australia), and shellfish (again, according to his blood chemistry profile), which are rich in specific trace minerals that give Fred his competitive edge.

My peak performance program has worked very well for Fred, lowering his serum cholesterol to 150, as well as controlling any possible rise in blood fats commonly associated with alcohol consumption. However, Fred is a trained athlete and a hard-working tennis coach—in top shape. The program I designed for him is based on his unique nutritional needs and level of physical activity. I do not recommend the use of alcoholic beverages, even by world-class athletes like Fred, unless I personally can monitor the blood chemistry changes that occur with my antioxidant protection and peak performance programs.

THIAMIN (VITAMIN B-1)-RICH FOODS

Beans (any type)
Baked beans (vegetarian style in tomato sauce
   —the small amount of sugar in the sauce
   will not hamper your peak performance because the sauce is fat-free; if you're active
   you easily burn up the added sugar)

Bread (whole grain)	Spinach
Oatmeal	Broccoli
Brown rice (there's no	Peas
thiamin in "polished"	Oranges
white rice	Cucumbers

Wheat germ
Artichoke
Asparagus

Caution; don't boil away your thiamin. Thiamin is a water-soluble vitamin and is attacked by oxygen and destroyed by heat. Eat thiamin-rich foods, raw or steamed; vegetables should be cooked until just done (*al dente*). Thiamin is available in supplemental form in almost every B vitamin formulation on the market.

PYRIDOXINE (VITAMIN B-6)

Pyridoxine is involved in a multitude of metabolic processes, including protein transport. Pyridoxine plays a most important role for athletes in the conversion of stored muscle glycogen to energy-producing glucose (blood sugar).

Pyridoxine is also water soluble and is destroyed by light and heat, so be sure to take the same cooking and storing precautions as you do with other water-soluble vitamins such as vitamin C and thiamin.

Some scientific evidence shows that pyridoxine protects against artery damage resulting from high-protein diets and a disease called homocystinemia. This protective effect is due to the antioxidant properties of pyridoxine and is also the reason that this vitamin antioxidant protects cells from other damaging chemicals that we eat and breathe.

PYRIDOXINE (VITIMIN B-6)-RICH FOODS

Leafy vegetables (loose leaf lettuce, spinach, cabbage, etc.)
Whole grains and cereals
Beans

Peas
Lentils
Tuna fish (water-packed)
Bananas

Pyridoxine is a potent antioxidant that plays an important role in protein metabolism. It actually transports amino acids, the building blocks of proteins, to the sites of important metabolic reactions that determine your level of peak performance. This vitamin antioxidant is so important that all athletes I counsel take additional pyridoxine.

PABA (PARA-AMINOBENZOIC ACID)

PABA is a B-complex vitamin and antioxidant that protects cell membranes, including red blood cell membranes, from free-radical destruction. PABA works with pyridoxine (B-6) in preventing certain types of anemia that rob athletes of vital oxygen during physical activity. PABA is also a popular antioxidant that, when applied to the skin, helps protect it from premature aging and skin cancer.

PABA-RICH FOODS

Whole grains and cereals
Leafy vegetables
Beans
Peas
Lentils
Potatoes

PABA, like beta carotene, protects against ozone damage caused by air pollution and ultraviolet solar radiation. *PABA is a must for all who compete or exercise in polluted cities.* PABA antioxidant protection is important for our Olympic athletes who will compete in the 1984 Olympic games in Los Angeles. Like all active people exposed to free-radical initiators (chemicals in smog and other forms of air pollution), Olympic athletes should supplement their peak performance program with PABA supplements. Even if you attend the Los Angeles 1984 Olympic games as a spectator, you would do well to include PABA supplements in your antioxidant arsenal.

PANTOTHENIC ACID

Pantothenic acid gets its name from the Greek word for "everywhere," because this B-vitamin antioxidant is present in every living cell. Pantothenic acid plays a key role in energy production and is an important antistress vitamin. Scientific studies have conclusively demonstrated that this antioxidant extends the life expectancy of laboratory animals.

Pantothenic acid is a key antioxidant for athletes who compete in extreme conditions, especially cold weather. Two long-distance swimmers who broke the currently existing record for the butterfly stroke (the most demanding and difficult stroke in swimming) by more than 10 miles accomplished this historical feat by following the Haas Peak Performance Program. As part of their personalized program, I gave James and Jonathan DiDonato (identical twins, who set their new world record side by side, every stroke of the way), a special antioxidant formula containing large amounts of pantothenic acid to help them battle the cold water and winds that could lead to the life-threatening condition called hypothermia (this is when internal body temperature drops low enough to kill). Today, thanks to my peak performance program and plenty of pantothenic acid, the DiDonato Twins are immortalized in the *Guinness Book of World Records*. Athletes who use pantothenic acid in supplemental form should ask for calcium pantothenate, the calcium salt of pantothenic acid.

SELENIUM

Selenium is a trace mineral (which means that the body requires very small amounts—too small to be seen by the human eye). This antioxidant forms part of several enzyme complexes that protect fats (oils) from creating free-radicals. It also plays an important role in helping vitamin E function as an antioxidant. Finally, selenium helps our body's cells kill potentially dangerous bacteria.

The ordinary American diet does not supply much selenium because selenium is usually milled or processed out of foods such as white rice, white bread, and other commonly processed or manufactured foods that Americans enjoy.

SELENIUM-RICH FOODS

Whole grains and cereals
Wheat germ
Brewers yeast
Fresh fruits
Fresh vegetables
Garlic

Onions

The selenium content of foods depends on the selenium content of the soil in which these foods were grown. Some parts of the United States are selenium poor, and so it's difficult for consumers to determine just how much selenium their cup of brown rice provides. The soils with the highest selenium content are found in the great plains between the Mississippi River and the eastern Rockies. The soils lowest in selenium content are in the Northeast, Florida, and the Pacific Northwest.

Athletes who take selenium supplements must know that large doses of selenium can be toxic. Even though the body requires selenium in microscopic amounts, most athletes still do not get enough of this antioxidant from their highly refined diets. Selenium supplements contain dosages well within safe limits. However, some athletes think that if a little is good, a lot is better.

AMINO ACIDS

Amino acids, the molecules that make up every protein in our foods and bodies, can also function as antioxidants. The human body can manufacture almost all the amino acids essential to life; there are less than a dozen that we absolutely must get from our foods, and these are called essential amino acids. But just because many amino acids are not essential doesn't mean that they are not important. They definitely are!

Research on the antioxidant role of amino acids demonstrates that cysteine, commonly found in chicken and fish, may provide valuable protection from free-radical damage. You can purchase pure, supplemental cysteine from health food stores, both individually and in multiple vitamin/mineral formulas. *If you take cysteine supplements, you must also take pyridoxine (vitamin B-6) as well, to balance the increase in cysteine intake.* Remember, pryidoxine helps to transport amino acids and protects arteries and other tissues from high-protein diets. Supplemental amino acids increase protein intakes and pyridoxine requirements.

SYNTHETIC ANTIOXIDANTS

Despite what the advocates of all-natural, additive- and preservative-free foods claim, food additives are not *all* bad. While most of us probably are concerned with eliminating harmful chemicals in our foods, most additives do not contribute to disease; in fact, they help prevent it!

Food preservatives, such as TBHQ (tertiary butylated-hydroxyquinone), BHA (butylatedhydroxyanisole), and BHT (butylatehydroxytoluene) provide antioxidant protection in foods and food packing. Research scientists have demonstrated that the *known benefits* that we derive from anti-oxidant additives far outweigh any supposed or alleged risks.

Athletes who use cooking oils (commercial brands have very little antioxidants to protect the oil from rancidity and free-radical formation) can purchase BHT and add it to these oils to increase their shelf-life.

ANTIOXIDANT MEDICATIONS

Your own physician can prescribe very power-ful antioxidants which, by law, are used only to treat specific diseases. L-DOPA, a medication for Parkinson's disease, retinoic acid (a vitamin A-related compound), a new and successful treat-ment for serious acne, and ergoloid mesylates, which physicians prescribe to combat senility, all provide antioxidant protection. There are many other available prescription medications with potent antioxidant power that physicians prescribe for health problems. You should con-sult with your physician and ask him to evaluate prescription antioxidants for *your own antiaging or injury healing use.*

When Should You Increase Your Antioxidants?

Take this quiz to find out:

	YES	NO
I have a serum cholesterol count above 180.	___	___
I smoke (anything).	___	___
I live with a smoker.	___	___
I work with smokers in the same room.	___	___
I live in an area with heavy air pollution.	___	___
I drink more than 1½ ounces of hard liquor a day.	___	___
I take one or more prescription drugs daily.	___	___
I use recreational drugs.	___	___
I work under fluorescent lights each day.	___	___
I work close to electric fields.	___	___
I am exposed to ionizing radiation (air travel, X-ray technicians, etc.).	___	___
I currently have a sports injury.	___	___
I exercise strenuously four or more days a week.	___	___
I want to avoid cardiovascular disease, cancer, cataracts, arthritis, and other "aging" diseases.	___	___
I want to achieve peak performance in my active life.	___	___

If you have answered yes to any of these questions, then you may want to supplement your peak performance program with antioxidants. The more yeses, the more your body demands these protective substances for optimal health and peak performance.

My recommendation: choose foods within the guidelines of the Haas Peak Performance Program which I have recommended for their antioxidant-rich content. And by all means, eliminate all the risk factors that increase your antioxidant requirements: smoking, drinking, recreational drugs.

ELEVEN

The Sport-Specific Diets

Different sports make different demands on your body. Jogging, skiing, swimming, and aerobic dancing are endurance sports that require *aerobic* metabolism. Running, swimming, cycling, and martial arts call for *high-energy anaerobic* activity; many sports demand both types of metabolism.

I have counseled and studied champion athletes in almost every field of competition, and I have learned that each type of sport (depending upon whether it demands aerobic metabolism, anaerobic metabolism, or *both*) requires a different diet chemistry. To my knowledge, no other sports nutritionist has developed the detailed instructions that will enable you to *eat to win* in your favorite sport or activity.

Only when you have completed Level One—the *get-in-shape level* of my program—when your blood chemistry values meet or surpass the standards I have established for entering Level Two, the *stay-in-shape level*, should you follow the *sport-specific* eating plans that follow.

Your blood chemistry values must meet or surpass these levels before you adapt my sport-specific diet recommendations:

Cholesterol	180 or less
HDL cholesterol	45 or more
Triglycerides	150 or less
Glucose	6 or less
Uric acid, men	6 or less
women	5.5 or less

I am going to give you detailed, sport-specific diets for these popular sports and activities:

1. Jogging, Skiing, Aerobic Dancing, Cycling, and Swimming

2. Soccer, Football, Basketball, Boxing, Wrestling, Karate (and other Martial Arts), and Ice Hockey

3. Weight Lifting and Weight Resistance (machine) Training

4. Tennis and other Racquet Sports

5. Golf

But first I want to give you my recommendations for your vital *pregame meal* and tell you *what* and *how* to eat after competition in order to replenish everything you lost during physical activity.

Recommendations for Competitors in All Sports

YOUR PRECOMPETITION MEAL

Locker room lore abounds with fact and fiction surrounding the best foods to eat just prior to competition. Collegiate and professional football coaches and trainers provide plenty of steak and eggs to fuel the fires of ferociousness in their players; U.S. Olympic athletes receive little if any dietary advice as a class and are therefore left to their own devices. Boxers wolf down lots of red meat, while triathlon competitors load up on carbohydrates. Tennis players? Each player has his or her own special pregame meal based more on superstition ("I won my last match eating bacon and eggs, so I'll eat the same way") than on scientific principle.

Bacon and eggs (one of the *worst* precompetition meals you can eat) notwithstanding, there is no *single* precompetition meal that is best or right for every athlete in every sport. But there are some very helpful and very scientific principles I can give you to help you select the best precompetition meal to suit your chosen sport and your personal tastes, as well.

1. Don't eat a large meal before competition or exercise. Your body cannot perform at its best if your stomach is overloaded with fats, protein, and carbohydrates. Since physical activ-

ity severely retards digestion, you should go into battle with that lean and hungry look. Keep food intake to a minimum to satisfy hunger (no more than 250 kilocalories, if possible). This is equivalent to about 4 slices of whole grain bread or ¼ cup of whole grain cereal with ½ cup of skimmed milk and 1 fresh fruit. Wait at least two hours *after eating* before beginning your favorite sport or exercise.

2. Your precompetition or preexercise meal should consist primarily of complex carbohydrates (about 60 to 80% of the kilocalories in your pregame meal should come from whole grains, cereals, fruits, breads, pasta, and vegetables). This will keep fats and oils to a minimum, thereby allowing your body to adequately assimilate the energy from these peak performance foods at an optimal rate (about 2 kilocalories per minute prior to competition). Of all the nutrients you eat, fats and oils leave the stomach last. They also slow down the stomach-emptying time of other vital nutrients that you need for energy and endurance.

3. Drink water *beyond what your thirst requires*. This is the single most important recommendation I can make—because lack of water is the single most frequent fatal flaw in the diet of almost every athlete I've studied or advised. Drink at least 1 cup of water for every 50 pounds of body weight *before* you begin physical activity.

Then drink at least 1 cup of water (8 ounces) for every 15 minutes of physical activity.

4. Take ergogenic acids (see Chapter 12) at least two hours prior to competition. As long as you take these peak performance aids at least two hours before exercise or sports participation, you will allow enough time for them to enter your blood and do their work. Remember: the presence of food in the stomach, especially fatty foods, slows gastric emptying time; take ergogenic aids with small meals or single foods which do not provide more than 250 kilocalories, but not on a totally empty stomach.

YOUR POSTCOMPETITION MEAL

This meal must do two things for you: (1) give you the nutritional building blocks to restore the glycogen your muscles have burned during exercise, and (2) replace the fluid, vitamins, minerals, and protein your body needs every day.

Athletes in all sports need to replenish their competition-weary muscle with the same basic nutrients. Although each athlete's nutritional needs vary from sport to sport, day to day, I have created an ideal postcompetition meal to meet the metabolic requirements of the most demanding sports and physical activities.

No matter what level of the Haas Peak Perform-

ance Program you follow, you can enjoy this ideal postcompetition meal after your match.

1. Four ounces of fish or poultry (strict vegetarians should eat 2 cups of beans, peas, or lentils; lacto-vegetarians should eat 1 cup of low-fat cottage cheese and 1 cup of beans; lacto-ovo vegetarians should eat 2 egg whites [no fatty, cholesterol-laden yolks, please], ½ cup of low-fat cottage cheese or yogurt, and ½ cup of beans).

2. Two baked or boiled potatoes or 1 cup of cooked pasta with plain tomato or marinara sauce.

3. One cup of green, yellow, or orange steamed or raw vegetables such as broccoli, hard yellow squash, or carrots.

4. Two fresh tropical or citrus fruits (about ¾ cup of cut fruit) including banana, papaya, pineapple, orange, grapefruit, etc.

5. Water according to thirst, *plus* at least 1 additional pint.

People who enjoy noncompetitive physical activities such as aerobic dancing, weight or machine training, or calisthenics, require the same special pre- and postperformance nutrition immediately before and after exercise. Many of these popular "solo" or noncompetitive activities still require that you *compete against yourself.* My pre- and postcompetition guidelines will give you the vital peak performance nutrition you need to be your personal best during competition or individual workouts.

When you have achieved the blood chemistry values I recommend for entering Level Two of my peak performance program, you can follow the sport-specific diets outlined in this chapter, but first it is vitally important that your blood chemistry values meet or exceed the levels I recommend for Level Two. If you participate in more than one sport, choose the sport-specific diet that provides the highest level of kilocalories from complex carbohydrates. This will ensure that you achieve peak performance levels in the most physically demanding sport you enjoy.

SOME IMPORTANT SECRETS OF THE CHAMPIONS THAT WILL HELP YOU EAT TO WIN

1. Maintain your present body weight. Do not lose more than 2 pounds of body weight in one week if you intend to compete at your peak performance level. This extremely valuable secret has become one of the most important rules of sports nutrition—my way. Unfortunate is the athlete who violates my rule and follows a crash weight-loss diet in order to qualify for competing in a specific weight category, such as heavyweight or lightweight. Boxers, wrestlers, and martial arts competitors who attempt drastic weight loss shortly before competing generally lose not only the weight but the match as well!

Drastic weight loss just prior to any type of athletic competition (more than 2 pounds in 1 week) will decrease your maximum aerobic capacity (the amount of oxygen your blood can carry and deliver to your muscles during strenuous physical activity) and severely diminish your athletic endurance. The agony of defeat can be caused by what you *don't* eat! Always maintain your body weight just before and during competition—even if that competition (such as a tennis tournament) lasts two weeks.

2. Don't drink alcohol after competition if you have to compete the next day. Alcohol dehydrates (robs) your body of its precious water supply, and along with the water go vital nutrients such as B vitamins, calcium, magnesium, and potassium—the very peak performance nutrients you need to win. You'll enjoy your favorite drink all the more if it's your victory toast!

3. How soon should you eat after competition? *Listen to your body*. Mother Nature in her infinite wisdom has decreed that strenuous physical activity should delay hunger, and for good reason: you need to replace the most vital nutrient lost through athletic competition—water. Your first duty is to replenish your body's water supply before you do anything else. Drink, drink, drink. Then, and only then, can you eat, eat, eat.

To sum up:

1. Follow my pre- and postcompetition guidelines for meals that you eat immediately before and after athletic competition or workouts.

2. Return to your regular program level (based on your blood chemistry values) in between competition or workouts.

3. When your blood chemistry values meet or exceed Level Two standards, you may follow the sport-specific diet programs outlined in the next section.

4. If you enjoy more than one sport, always choose the diet that provides the most kilocalories from complex carbohydrates.

The Haas Sport-Specific Diets

I have created the following sport-specific diets to fulfill the unique nutritional needs of professional and amateur athletes in fourteen of the most popular sports. If you enjoy more than one of these sports, *always choose the sport-specific diet that provides the greatest amount of daily kilocalories from complex carbohydrates.*

These are five sport-specific diet programs that cover all fourteen sports:

CATEGORY ONE
Jogging

Skiing
Aerobic dancing
Cycling
Swimming

CATEGORY TWO
Tennis and other racquet sports

CATEGORY THREE
Weight lifting
Weight resistance (machine) training

CATEGORY FOUR
Soccer
Football
Basketball
Baseball
Boxing
Karate (and other martial arts)

CATEGORY FIVE
Golf

All of these sports require that you use the largest muscles in your body—leg muscles. The amount of muscle glycogen you store and the enzymes you manufacture to burn that glycogen efficiently will determine your level of endurance and performance in these sports.

Each sport can demand a wide range of energy expenditure (in general, according to the duration of the event) from a few hundred kilocalories to a few thousand! Cross-country skiing and marathon running may require 2,000 or more kilocalories in one event.

James and Jonathan DiDonato, the identical twin world-champion long-distance swimmers, follow my sport-specific swimming diet even though one eats meat and the other is a lacto-vegetarian (a person who eats vegetables and milk products only). James is actually a "Haas lacto-vegetarian": he eats only skimmed and low-fat milk products). James simply supplements beans, peas, or lentils (which are excellent vegetable sources of protein) and skimmed or low-fat milk products for animal protein sources and such as chicken, turkey, and fish.

A special note for triathlon athletes: the triathlon is one of the most demanding and potentially dangerous competitive events yet devised. The current record of 9 hours and 8 minutes for the 2½-mile open ocean swim, 112-mile bicycle race, and 26-mile 385-yard marathon run sounds impressive, yet I predict that a well-trained triathlon athlete could break this record by a *wide margin* (just as the DiDonato twins demolished the existing record for the long-distance butterfly swim by more than 10 miles) if he or she followed my regimen for ultra-athletic competition. I have not included this diet here because it is necessary for me to work directly and intensively with triathlon athletes, using computers and highly sophisticated biochemical technology, to achieve proper individualized results.

PORTION SIZE

Weekend athletes usually are unaware of the enormous physical demands that world-class competition places on competitors; nor are they generally aware of the enormous appetites of these competitors—Gene and Sandy Mayer, world-champion tennis professionals, each ate at one sitting Big Macs and several orders of French fries (large), and washed it all down with a couple of milk shakes—of course, that was before they adopted this program!

Rather than restrict yourself to a specific portion size (although I have listed suggested portions ranges below) let appetite rule the portions you eat. Most athletes I've advised discover that this is sound and prudent advice, and I believe that you will too. You will also be surprised to find that shortly after you begin the program your appetite will automatically readjust itself. The appetite center in your the brain is like the thermostat in your house: once you set it, it stays there until you reset it. The chemical composition of your diet, as well as the intensity and duration of your exercise or sport, will set your "appestat" (your appetite thermostat lo-

cated in the hypothalamus) to its peak performance level. You will find that your desire for
food precisely matches your body's need for
energy. Athletes who begin my program report
that for the first time they are in touch with
their body's needs and requirements. A high-
complex-carbohydrate diet based on foods with
a naturally low-fat content rich in vitamins and
minerals provides the body's sensitive appetstat
with the right chemical balance to eliminate over-
and undereating. The Haas peak performance
foods supply the perfect diet chemistry (based
on your own blood chemistry) for appetite
control. If your body requires more food, you'll
feel hungry; once you meet your body's nutritional needs, you'll feel full and satisfied. My
clinical experience has taught me that when
overweight people discard the ordinary American diet (about 45% fat, 15% protein, and 40%
carbohydrate) and adopt my program (5 to 20%
fat, 10 to 15% protein, 60 to 80% carbohydrate),
they reach their ideal weight safely and gradually without the health risks associated with
rapid weight loss or crash dieting. If you want
to gain muscular weight, simply eat larger portions of the foods I recommend and follow an
exercise program (such as weight training) designed to help you increase muscle mass. Extra
daily calories from complex carbohydrates—not
from protein—is the secret of building muscle
tissue during weight training.

THE BASIC EATING PLAN

The American life-style has conditioned most of us to regard specific foods as appropriate for breakfast, lunch, or dinner. The Hass peak performance program does not restrict any food or food group to specific meals or time of day. You may enjoy your favorite breakfast cereal for lunch, or your favorite pasta recipe for breakfast (as many marathon runners do). These peak performance meals are just as effective whether you eat them morning, noon, or evening.

The original Haas recipes you will find in the second section of this book provide you with fail-safe eating regardless of your diet level or the sport-specific diet of your choice. I have created each recipe to conform to my strictest standards for peak performance so that you can enjoy them, as the world champions do, any time you desire (when you dine at home, you can easily follow the 28-day menu plan outlined in Chapter 6, which uses my recipes exclusively).

My basic eating plan—the foundation for all the sport-specific diets—divides all the foods you will enjoy into three categories in order of importance: carbohydrate sources; protein sources; and fats and oils. There is also a special section on condiments and beverages.

For your convenience, I have listed *suggested portion sizes* for an ideal reference athlete. You can judge your own nutritional needs against those of this reference athlete. This imaginary reference athlete weighs 150 pounds and burns 600 kilocalories in exercise or sports every day (equivalent to 1½ hours of singles tennis or 1 hour of slow jogging or regular aerobic dancing). If you weigh more than 150 pounds or expend more than 600 kilocalories per day, you may increase my suggested portions accordingly; if you weight less than 150 pounds or burn less than 600 kilocalories per day, you'll need to proportionally decrease these suggested portions. Female athletes should also follow my advice to meet their uniquely feminine needs, as I've explained in Chapter 9.

FOOD CATEGORIES

There are three food categories (carbohydrates, proteins, and fats) and two supplemental categories (beverages and condiments) that supply peak performance nutrition for each sport-specific eating plan. Under Category One (carbohydrates), you'll find the maximum *daily* limits listed next to each specific carbohydrate food source—your individual sport-specific diet will tell you the maximum amount of these carbohydrate sources you can choose each day. You may eat less than the maximum amounts I've listed, but to achieve peak performance in your chosen sport or activity, do not exceed these limits. The same advice applies for Category Two (protein) and Category Three (fats and oils). You may use the recommended condiments as desired within reasonable limits. I've listed the maximum allowable amounts for each approved beverage. Only water—the drink of champions—is permitted in unlimited quantities.

CATEGORY TWO: PROTEINS (10 TO 15% DAILY DAILY KILOCALORIES)

Cereals
Fresh fruits
Dried fruits
Fruit juices
Potatoes
Brown rice
Pasta
Vegetables (raw or steamed)
Whole grain breads
Whole grain pancakes
Desserts: original Haas recipes only

CATEGORY TWO: PROTEINS (10 TO 15% DAILY KILOCALORIES)

Skim milk
Nonfat dry milk, prepared
Low-fat, part skim cheeses

Grated Parmesan or Romano cheese
Low-fat cottage cheese, ½ to 2% fat
Low-fat yogurt, 1 to 2% fat
Meats:
    Poultry
    Fish
    Shellfish
    Veal
    Beef, lean cuts only
    Duck
    Pork
    Lamb
    Venison
Legumes: beans, peas, and lentils, any type
Nuts and seeds
Protein supplements: Specific amino acids used only as ergogenic acids

CATEGORY THREE: FATS AND OILS (5 TO 15% DAILY KILOCALORIES)

Only 1 portion (up to 1 tablespoon, total fats and oils) is permitted per day from the following list:
Olive oil
Any other vegetable oil (safflower, corn, sesame)
Margarine, reduced-calorie type (Weight Watcher's)
Margarine, regular type

Mayonnaise, reduced-calorie type (Weight Watcher's)

Mayonnaise, regular type

Avoid: peanut oil (it strongly promotes atherosclerosis), butter, and lard

Special Condiments

The following condiments may be used in reasonable amounts to taste:

Butter Buds butter replacer

Equal sugar replacer

Any oil-free salad dressing (Herb Magic, Tillie Lewis, Medford Farms, Italian flavor only, Bonaparte)

Vinegar (any type)

Mustard (regular or spicy)

Ketchup (Low-sodium, low-sugar varieties are available in the diet section of supermarkets and in most health food stores.)

Steak sauce (A-1; Worcestershire; most steak sauces are high in sodium so use sparingly. If you follow a sodium-restricted diet, check with your physican before using).

Barbecue sauce (most brands or those served in restaurants; usually high in sodium and sugar —use sparingly. If you follow a low-sodium, low-sugar diet, check with your physician before using.)

Lemon or lime juice

Bacon bits or chips, soybean type (These usually contain sugar and salt. If you are following a low-sodium or low-sugar diet, check with your physician before using).

Any other salt-free or sugar-free herb or spice such as cinnamon, nutmeg, paprika, fresh garlic or garlic powder, basil, thyme, pepper.

Beverages

Water (tap, bottled, carbonated, salt-free carbonated beverages are available in most supermarkets if you follow a sodium-restricted diet).

Coffee and tea (use water-processed decaffeinated coffee; decaffeinated teas are available in most supermarkets and health food stores).

Vegetable juices (carrot, tomato, V-8, up to 8 ounces per day. These juices contain sodium. If you follow a sodium-restricted diet, check with your physician before using.)

Alcoholic Beverages:
  Light Beer
  Regular beer
  Wine, white or red
  Champagne
  Hard liquor (vodka, scotch, rum)

Hot chocolate, reduced calorie (Swiss Miss Lite or Carnation brand, for example)

Diet soda, non-caffeinated (These beverages contain sodium. If you follow a sodium-restricted diet, check with your physician before using.)

APPROVED CEREAL LIST

The cereals listed below will vary from sport-specific diet to diet—some cereals are too high in fat or sugar or both for peak performance in certain sports. In general, the more calorically demanding a sport, the more liberal will be the approved cereal list for that sport.

Shredded Wheat	Alpen
Grape Nuts	Muesli
All Bran	Bran Chex
Quaker 100% Whole Wheat	Kellogg's Nutri-Grain
Wheatena	Raisin Bran
Oatmeal	Puffed brown rice or wheat

Cereal toppings: use skimmed or nonfat dry milk and fresh fruit of choice. Use Equal sugar replacer for sweetening cereal.

SKIM AND LOW-FAT DAIRY PRODUCTS

Do not use milk as a beverage. Milk is a *food* in liquid form. It contains substantial amounts of protein and sugar (lactose) which can decrease endurance if consumed in excessive quantities. As you've already learned, too much protein can dehydrate you and excess sugar can cause "bonking" (hypoglycemia). Use milk as a "topping" or "condiment" such as on cereals.

Low-fat cottage cheese and yogurt also contain protein and lactose in concentrated form, so you should limit your intake of these dairy products to prudent levels—approximately 2 cups per day.

FRESH FRUITS

Fresh fruits are a good source of simple and complex carbohydrates. You should eat about *five times* more complex than simple carbohydrates. If you limit your fresh fruit intake to the amounts I recommend daily for each sport-specific eating plan, you'll comply with this important performance carbohydrate rule.

FRUIT JUICES

Fruit juices are a *concentrated* source of sugar—not *complex carbohydrates*—and you should avoid them whenever possible or at least, drink no more than a cupful. You can dilute your favorite fruit juice with an equal portion of water (which is more consistent with the chemical composition of your own blood) if you want to enjoy your favorite fruit juice.

VEGETABLES

Eat as many steamed or raw vegetables as desired. Pick a variety of colors to get a variety of nutrients—red, orange, yellow, and green. Athletes remember which vegetables to choose by thinking of Roy Green—R: red; O: orange; Y: yellow; GREEN: Legumes (beans, peas, or lentils). Legumes are excellent sources of protein, iron, calcium, and fiber and you should try to include them in your diet at least three days each week if you enjoy them.

ANIMAL PROTEIN

Try to avoid the fatty meats such as lamb, duck, pork, ham, and other luncheon meats. Choose lean protein sources such as fish (you may eat two fish that are relatively high in fat, salmon and mackerel, because they are rich sources of EPA, the "friendly" fat), chicken (white meat), turkey (white meat), and shellfish: lobster (always your first choice), crab, oyster, clams, scallops, and shrimp (always your last choice). Shellfish is a source of cholesterol, as is chicken and fish, but on a high-carbohydrate, high-fiber, low-fat diet, you can enjoy these foods without raising your serum cholesterol. Use prudence and moderation. My research shows that when you limit your animal protein intake to between 10 to 15% of your daily calories, you get more than enough protein without running the risk of dehydration (and the vitamins and minerals that you lose with water). This translates into about 4 ounces of animal protein (not including dairy products) per day, on the average, or about 1½ pounds of animal protein per week.

FATS AND OILS

World-class endurance athletes require much more fat and oil than do weekend warriors. The recommendations above are my "middle-of-the-road" fat and oil recommendations for the average sports participant. As you've already learned, you are unique, with a unique blood chemistry and a unique set of nutritional needs. These recommendations are within the guidelines for healthy eating established by our national health organizations such as the American Heart Association. In general, a good rule of thumb to follow concerning the use of fats and oils is to include sparingly good sources of essential fats and oils that naturally occur in foods: the "friendly" fat, EPA, found in salmon and mackerel; the "essential" fat (linoleic) that occurs in foods such as oatmeal, corn, and brown rice. And if you do add other fats and oils to your foods, use them in the amounts I've suggested for optimal health and peak performance.

WHY I ALLOW THOSE CONDIMENTS ON MY DIET PROGRAM

The occasional use of condiments that contain salt and/or sugar such as ketchup, pickle relish, mustard, steak sauce, barbecue sauce, etc. is permitted because of their low to negligible fat content. If you don't abuse the use of these condiments, they won't abuse you! As always, if you follow a sugar- and/or sodium-restricted diet, check with your physician before using any foods, food products, or condiments that contain these substances.

CATEGORY ONE: JOGGING, SKIING, AEROBIC DANCING, CYCLING, SWIMMING

Research scientists who study people (individuals as well as the populations of whole countries) report that men and women who participate in daily aerobic exercise (exercise that raises your heart rate above 120 beats per minute) generally are slimmer, fitter, and healthier than their more sedentary friends and relatives. Moreover, when these active people eat a low-fat, low-cholesterol, high-complex-carbohydrate diet, they don't suffer from the diet-related degenerative diseases—heart disease, diabetes, hypertension, obesity, stroke, for example—with the epidemic frequency that sedentary people who eat high-fat, high-cholesterol diets do.

Jogging, skiing (and especially cross-country skiing), aerobic dancing, cycling and swimming are some of the best aerobic physical activities. However, no amount of exercise alone is enough to afford you maximum protection against diet-related disease. Proper nutrition is essential for optimal health, longevity, and peak performance.

Viki Fleckenstein, top U.S. Ski Team racer and U.S. Olympic Team competitor, uses the sport-specific Category One plan to eat to win. Viki's event, the slalom, demands great strength and endurance and peak effort. Viki visited my sports nutrition clinic in Florida last year in order to boost her already excellent stamina to peak performance levels. I believe that Viki, one of the first skiers to follow my program, will stay at the top for a long time to come.

If your favorite sport requires long sustained effort, eat to win the way Viki does:

Approved Cereal List
Shredded wheat
Grape Nuts
All Brain
Wheatena
Oatmeal
Nutri-Grain

Quaker 100% Whole Wheat
Puffed brown rice or whole wheat

Eat up to 1 cup per day for each continuous hour of sport or exercise. Top with ½ cup skim or nonfat dry milk and 1 fresh fruit of choice. Use Equal sugar replacer if you desire additional sweetner.

Additional fresh fruit: up to 3 fresh fruits of your choice per day.

Dried fruits: up to 1 ounce per day.

Fruit juices: up to 6 ounces per day.

Potatoes: up to 4 per day.

Brown rice: up to 2 cups (cooked) per day.

Pasta: up to 2 cups (cooked) per day.

Vegetables: raw or steamed; as desired; avoid avocado, hearts of palm, and olives.

Whole grain breads: up to 2 slices per day.

Whole grain pancakes (made without egg yolks): up to 2 6-inch pancakes per day with approved topping.

Desserts: up to one serving, original Haas recipe.

Skim and nonfat dry milk, prepared: up to 1 cup per day.

Low-fat, part skim cheeses: up to ½ ounce per day.

Grated Parmesan or Romano cheese: up to 2 teaspoons per day.

Low-fat cottage cheese and yogurt: up to ½ cup per day.

Meats: up to 4 ounces any type per day.

Legumes: up to 1 cup per day,

Nuts and seeds: up to 1 ounce per day, any type.

Fats and oils: up to 1 teaspoon, any type.

Ergogenic acids: as required (see Chapter 12).

See the basic sport-specific eating plan for approved beverages and condiments.

CATEGORY TWO: SOCCER, FOOTBALL, BASKETBALL, BASEBALL, BOXING, KARATE

In contrast to sports such as jogging, cycling, and swimming where movement is virtually continuous, these sports often require athletes to expend bursts of *discontinuous*, explosive energy, with intermittent periods of reduced physical demand or rest. Football players, basketball players, soccer players, and ice hockey players have time outs and rest periods at half-time; boxers, wrestlers, and martial arts competitors rest between rounds.

These sports demand endurance, but not exactly the type required for marathon running, cycling, long-distance swimming, or cross-country skiing.

The caloric costs of these sports can be tremendous: a 15-round boxing match or typical basketball game requires more kilocalories than jogging or dancing for 30 minutes—so this sport-specific diet provides more kilocalories than Category One does.

Athletes who enjoy Category Two sports are usually concerned with body-building, and my recommendations include the right mixture of protein, fat, and carbohydrate to build, maintain, and replenish injured or torn down muscle tissue. When you follow this specific eating plan (and eat the right foods in the right combinations) you train your muscles to utilize blood sugar and fat efficiently to give you the explosive power you need.

Approved Cereal Lists
Shredded wheat
Grape Nuts
All Bran
Quaker 100% Whole Wheat
Wheatena
Alpen
Muesli
Bran Chex
Nutri-Grain
Puffed brown rice and whole wheat
Eat up to 1 cup per day for each continuous hour of sport or exercise. Top with ½ cup skimmed or nonfat dry milk and 1 fresh fruit of choice. Use Equal sugar replacer if you desire additional sweetener.

Additional fresh fruit: up to 6 fresh fruits of your choice per day.

Dried fruits: upto 2 ounces per day.

Fruit juices: up to 8 ounces per day.

Potatoes: up to 4 per day.

Brown rice: up to 3 cups (cooked) per day.

Pasta: up to 4 cups (cooked) per day.

Vegetables: raw or steamed as desired; avoid avocado, hearts of palm, and olives.

Whole grain breads: up to 6 slices per day.

Whole grain pancakes (made without egg yolks): up to 3 6-inch pancakes per day with approved topping.

Desserts: up to 2 servings, original Haas recipe.

Skim and nonfat dry milk, prepared: up to 2 cups per day.

Low-fat, part skim cheeses: up to 1 ounce per day.

Grated Parmesan or Romano cheese: up to 3 teaspoons per day.

Low-fat cottage cheese and yogurt: up to 1 cup per day.

Meats: up to 4 ounces any type, per day.

Legumes: up to 2 cups per day.

Nuts and Seeds: up to 2 ounces per day, any type.

Fats and oils: up to 2 teaspoons, any type.

Ergogenic aids: as required (see Chapter 12).

See the basic sport-specific eating plan for specific condiments and beverages.

CATEGORY THREE: TENNIS AND OTHER RACQUET SPORTS

Tennis and other racquet sports require both aerobic and anaerobic activity. I've developed this sport-specific eating plan to give you the competitive edge to outlast and wear down your opponents through extraordinary stamina and extra power for explosive bursts of energy.

Many people don't consider tennis a true endurance sport (usually the people who play an occasional game of social mixed-doubles); but many players, from amateur weekend addicts to Wimbledon champions, may spend over six hours in match play. Tennis champions (and those amateur enthusiasts who play until it's too dark to see the ball) may require the endurance of a marathon runner and no less explosive speed than a soccer player. This sport-specific plan will provide you with both.

The caloric cost of racquet sports varies, of course, according to whether you are playing singles or doubles, as well as according to your level of skill. A good game of singles (tennis, squash, or racquetball) can burn as many kilocalories as a jogger would expend in an equal amount of time.

Approved Cereal List
Shredded wheat
Grape Nuts
All Bran
Wheatena
Oatmeal
Nutri-Grain
Puffed brown rice and whole wheat
Eat up to 1 cup per day for each continuous

hour of sport or exercise. Top with ½ cup skim or nonfat dry milk and 1 fresh fruit of choice. Use Equal sugar replacer if you desire additional sweetener.

Additional fresh fruit: up to 2 fresh fruits of your choice per day.

Dried fruits: up to 1 ounce per day.

Fruit juices: upto 6 ounces per day.

Potatoes: up to 2 per day.

Brown rice: up to 1½ cups (cooked) per day.

Pasta: up to 1½ cups (cooked) per day.

Vegetables: raw or steamed; as desired; avoid avocado, hearts of palm, and olives.

Whole grain breads: up to 2 slices per day.

Whole Grain pancakes (made without egg yolks): up to 2 6-inch pancakes per day with approved topping.

Desserts: up to 1 serving, original Haas recipe.

Skim and nonfat dry milk, prepared: up to 1 cup per day.

Low-fat, part skim cheeses: up to ½ ounce per day.

Grated Parmesan or Romano cheese: up to 2 teaspoons per day.

Low-fat cottage cheese and yogurt: up to ½ cup per day.

Meats: up to 4 ounces, any type, per day.

Legumes: up to 1 cup per day.

Nuts and seeds: up to 1 ounce per day, any type.

Fats and oils: up to 1 teaspoon, any type.

Ergogenic aids: as required (see Chapter 12).

See the basic sport-specific eating plan for specific condiments and beverages.

CATEGORY FOUR: WEIGHT LIFTING AND WEIGHT RESISTANCE (MACHINE) TRAINING

Weight training demands explosive, anaerobic activity that places unique demands on your muscles. Weight training can also be aerobic, if you use the circuit-training technique: highly repetitive lifting and moving to the next weight station or routine as quickly as possible without giving your heart rate a chance to slow down. Research has demonstrated that you must engage in *continuous* lifting for at least 20 minutes for it to become aerobic.

Large amounts of muscle tissue may be torn down during exhaustive weight training, so your sport-specific eating plan provides the necessary nutrients for building and rebuilding muscle tissue. Weight lifters do not need the large amounts of muscle glycogen that marathon runners rely on to go the distance. However, weight lifters have made a serious sports nutrition error in the past by mistakenly increasing their protein intake when, in fact, they should have increased their consumption of complex carbohydrates. My sport-specific eating plan for weight lifters reverses this error.

Approved Cereal List
Shredded wheat
Grape Nuts
All Bran
Wheatena
Oatmeal
Nutri-Grain
Quaker 100% Whole Wheat
Puffed brown rice and whole wheat

Eat up to 1 cup per day for each continuous hour of sport or exercise. Top with ½ cup skim or nonfat dry milk and 1 fresh fruit of choice. Use Equal sugar replacer if you desire additional sweetener.

Additional fresh fruit: up to 4 fresh fruits of your choice per day.

Dried fruits: up to 1 ounce per day.

Fruit juices: up to 6 ounces per day.

Potatoes: up to 6 per day.

Brown rice: up to 3 cups (cooked) per day.

Pasta: up to 4 cups (cooked) per day.

Vegetables: raw or steamed; as desired; avoid avocado, hearts of palm, and olives.

Whole grain breads: up to 6 slices per day.

Whole grain pancakes (made without egg yolks): up to 3 6-inch pancakes per day with approved topping.

Desserts: up to 2 servings, original Haas recipe.

Skim and nonfat dry milk, prepared: up to 2 cups per day.

Low-fat, part skim cheeses: up to ½ ounce per day.

Grated Parmesan or Romano cheese: up to 3 teaspoons per day.

Low-fat cottage cheese and yogurt: up to 1 cup per day.

Meats: up to 4 ounces, any type, per day.

Legumes: up to 2 cups per day.

Nuts and seeds: up to 1 ounce per day, any type.

Fats and oils: up to 1 teaspoon, any type.

Ergogenic aids: as required (see Chapter 12).

See the basic sport-specific eating plan for approved beverages and condiments.

CATEGORY FIVE: GOLF

Golf—really good golf—demands exquisite and elegant neuromuscular coordination, and the pros win or lose based upon the amount of it they can muster. Mental concentration is no less important. The best golfers possess the mental abilities of concentration and focus enjoyed by chess masters and brain surgeons.

Under the stress of competition (or a heavy wager), a golfer's blood sugar can plummet to hypoglycemic levels—along with any chance of winning. Special brain chemicals which improve concentration and brain-to-muscle communication must be present in optimal quantities for championship play. Golf demands a constant optimal concentration of these neurochemicals as well as finely tuned muscular movements.

My sport-specific eating plan for golfers provides a fail-safe nutritional plan for maintaining blood sugar at peak performance levels, even under the stress of competition. Golfers who use the ergogenic aids I've described in Chapter 12 should focus on optimal concentrations of vital nutrients such as phenylalanine, tyrosine, choline, B vitamins, and other compounds that the brain needs to manufacture its vital peak performance chemicals.

The caloric cost of golfing is, of course, directly dependent upon whether you walk (and how far) the five or six miles of the course or whether you ride in a golf cart, where all the energy is burned by the motor, not your body. Sadly, for most golfers, the majority of golf courses today require that players use golf carts (in order to speed up play). I urge you, if at all possible, to try to do as the pros do, and play at least some of your matches on a course where you can walk. You'll derive many more physical benefits from your game.

I advise all golfers to carry a source of readily available carbohydrate during match play in order to help stabilize blood sugar levels and to keep concentration at peak levels. Apples, bananas, and whole wheat bagels are all excellent portable sources of complex carbohydrates. Always snack on these foods when you feel fatigued or sense that your concentration is slipping away.

Golfers who play in the hot sun or in humid weather are going to lose fluid and minerals through sweat. Follow my hydration guidelines for fluid replacement (Chapter 4) conscientiously. They're definitely par for the course I recommend. So, duffer (temporarily, I hope) or club champion, follow this sport-specific eating plan to make your game the very best it can be.

Approved Cereal List
Shredded Wheat
Grape Nuts
All Bran
Wheatena
Oatmeal
Nutri-Grain
Quaker 100% Whole Wheat
Puffed brown rice or wheat

Eat up to 1 cup per day for each continuous hour of sport or exercise. Top with ½ cup skim or nonfat dry milk and 1 fresh fruit of choice. Use Equal sugar replacer if you desire additional sweetener.

Additional fresh fruit: up to 2 fresh fruits of your choice per day.

Dried fruits: up to 1 ounce per day.

Fruit juices: up to 6 ounces per day.

Potatoes: up to 2 per day.

Brown rice: up to 1 cup (cooked) per day.

Pasta: up to 1 cup (cooked) per day.

Vegetables: raw or steamed; as desired; avoid avocado, hearts of palm, and olives.

Whole grain breads: up to 2 slices per day.

Whole grain pancakes (made without egg yolks): up to 2 6-inch pancakes per day with approved topping.

Desserts: up to 1 serving, original Haas recipe.

Skim and nonfat dry milk, prepared: up to 1 cup per day.

Low-fat, part skim cheeses: up to ½ ounce per day.

Grated Parmesan or Romano cheese: up to 2 teaspoons per day.

Low-fat cottage cheese and yogurt: up to ½ cup per day.

Meats: up to 4 ounes, any type, per day.

Legumes: up to 1 cup per day,

Nuts and seeds: up to 1 ounce per day, any type.

Fats and oils: up to 1 teaspoon, any type.

Ergogenic aids: as required (see Chapter 12).

See the basic sport-specific eating plan for approved beverages and condiments.

TWELVE

The Athlete's Chemistry Set

At the age of eight, chemical equations and formulas fascinated me more than the Saturday afternoon John Wayne double feature at the local movie. Well, things haven't changed much in 26 years. My laboratory is much larger and more sophisticated (as is my chemistry knowledge), but, come Saturday, you can still find me in the lab—developing new formulas to help top professional athletes *win through chemistry*.

Most of the professional athletes I've met believe that chemicals, natural or synthetic, can boost their performance to new heights. They are also convinced that research scientists very often withhold this vital information; and I must confess, *they are absolutely right!* Scientists often wait years to test, retest, and validate their original findings before releasing useful and beneficial information to the general public. While this slow procedure helps to protect the lay public against prematurely using scientific findings that aren't fully tested, it can also needlessly delay the introduction of new and important information and products that the public wants and needs.

As a research scientist, I am ethically and professionally obligated to give my unbiased appraisal of ergogenic (energy-enhancing) chemicals. It is perfectly true that these natural and artificial substances can and do boost athletic endurance and performance. It is also perfectly true that many of these ergogenic acids have the potential to harm the well-intentioned but ill-informed athlete who uses them without proper supervision.

I do not approve of the use of such dangerous drugs as *amphetamines, cocaine,,* and *anabolic steroids*. Athletes in *all* sports use these drugs from time to time. Other less powerful but just as undesirable substances on my *don't take list* include *ephedrine, isoproterenol* (prescribed for asthma and nasal congestion—one Olympic swimmer had to relinquish his gold medal for the innocent use of asthma medication before competition), and *phenylpropanolamine* (a closely related compound of aphetamine, and the active ingredient in most over-the-counter appetite suppressants and cold medications).

You should never use any of these drugs or related compounds to boost your athletic endurance or sports performance. They make losers out of winners.

Why do athletes insist on using substances such as amphetamines despite the health risks involved? As a professional sports nutrition consultant, I have talked to dozens of users, and most of them truly do not believe that these drugs can damage or even kill.

They can and they do. And if they don't get you one way they can get you another. Mercury Morris, Miami Dolphin three-time Super Bowl champ turned cocaine dealer, today is playing ball not with the pros but with fellow inmates in a Florida prison.

I'm going to show you how to win with chemistry the right way—the *only* way as far as I'm concerned—with chemistry, *my way*.

The Chemicals That Boost Performance

These are the natural, nonprescription substances that give the athletes I counsel the competitive advantage over their opponents, the same ones you can use at work or play to achieve your highest level of performance—*peak performance*.

CAFFEINE

Most of the pros I counsel are surprised to learn that this ordinary food substance (you'll find it in plentiful supply in coffee, tea, cocoa,

pirin compounds and other over-the-
medications, soft drinks, etc.) actually
ves their minds as much as it does their
sports performance.

Caffeine is a potent stimulant of the cerebral
cortex, the intellectual part of the brain. Its main
action is to produce a clearer, more efficient
flow of thoughts, and better ability to associate
ideas. Caffeine improves (reduces) reaction times
to sensory stimuli and increases motor activity—
your ability to perform skillful movement *faster
and more efficiently*. Research has shown that
typists, for example, type faster and with fewer
mistakes after drinking two cups of coffee (about
200 to 250 milligrams of caffeine).

Caffeine also has multiple and opposite effects in other parts of your body. For example,
it can dilate the coronary arteries that supply
your heart muscle with blood, markedly increasing blood flow while, at the same time, con-
stricting the small arteries (aterioles) that serve
the brain. Caffeine and related compounds
(especially those used in asthma medications)
relax the smooth muscles of the bronchi in the
lungs, improving breathing. Caffeine and caf-
feinelike drugs therefore can be of considerable
therapeutic value to asthmatics.

Because of its effect on the arteries in the
brain, migraine headache sufferers have used
caffeine for years as a quick and easy way to
control pain. Athletes, especially marathon

runners, use caffeine for a different reason: it allows them to run faster without "hitting the wall"—running out of muscle and liver glycogen. Caffeine actually tells the body to burn more fat and less carbohydrate (glycogen) during endurance exercise. Thus, drinking *two* cups of coffee just before a long race gives runners an advantage over competitors of the same running ability who eschew their morning java. As you've already learned, it is glycogen that keeps runners from running out of steam, especially in the later stages of a long race.

My recommendation: caffeine provides endurance athletes with an unquestionable scientifically demonstrable advantage over opponents of roughly equal athletic ability. You should not expect to benefit from caffeine's ergogenic effects unless you compete in an *endurance* sport, such as long-distance running or cross-country skiing. *Caution:* if you do not regularly use caffeine (either in foods, medications, or caffeine supplements), if you are pregnant or lactating, or if you have a medical condition that may be worsened by caffeine (such as cardiovascular disease, high blood pressure, diabetes, etc.), you should consult with your physician before attempting to use this naturally occurring ergogenic substance.

How much caffeine do you need? None. Caffeine is a nonessential chemical for human life. It is not a vitamin, mineral, fat, carbohydrate, or protein. It is a naturally occurring alkaloid, closely related to theophylline (found in tea) and theobromine (found in cocoa). These compounds, the methyl xanthines, are structurally related to *uric acid*, one of the five "vital values" that you'll find in your blood and on your blood chemistry profile analysis. Since you'll want to keep your serum uric acid within my recommended peak performance range, limit your use of caffeine (if you use it at all) to athletic competition only.

The average cup of brewed coffee contains approximately 100 to 150 milligrams of caffeine; instant coffee contains less: about 80 to 90 milligrams. A cup of tea (brewed and instant) provides about three times less caffeine than coffee. Instant cocoa contains much less caffeine (about 10 to 15 milligrams), while some cola soft drinks supply a generous 40 to 60 milligrams of caffeine.

Experimental evidence on marathon runners indicates that 250 to 350 milligrams of caffeine is an effective, ergogenic dose. Several studies used twice this amount, given to participants in two equal doses, one dose about an hour before competition, the second about halfway through the race. This dosage is well within the limits of normal human consumption of caffeine, but as with any other drug, one must consider the differences in human metabolism, body weight, and drug interactions (caffeine may interact with other substances you take at the same time), and individual blood chemistry before the proper dose of caffeine can be determined. There is no one single dose that's right for everyone. Consult an experienced sports nutritionist or other sports-care professional before you use caffeine to achieve peak performance.

CALCIUM LACTATE

Anyone who has ever done any form of physical activity too long is familiar with that burning feeling in the muscles that prevents further activity. Lactic acid is one cause of that burning sensation.

When you start to exercise, your muscle cells begin to burn sugar (glucose) at a faster rate. If the exercise is not too vigorous or intensive, glucose combines with oxygen and fat to produce among other things *energy*, in the form of ATP. ATP is a high-energy compound that stores and releases the kind of energy that fuels every cell in the body.

At some point, the physical activity may become too intensive or strenuous for your cells to provide enough oxygen to efficiently burn glucose. When this happens, glucose cannot be burned and converted to ATP; instead, glucose forms a substance called lactic acid. Lactic acid can be used for energy (indirectly and slowly) but lactic acid build-up in the blood and muscles eventually shuts down muscular contraction. Your muscles burn, even cramp, and you are forced to stop physical activity.

Paradoxically, you can use lactic acid (I recommend the nonacidic salt of this compound called *calcium lactate*) to boost your endurance!

Research scientists have long known that people who exercise harder and longer keep their blood lactate levels lower. This is due to a demonstrable biochemical adaptation in muscle metabolism (because increased synthesis of muscle enzymes helps keep lactate levels low). The ability of your body to dispose of lactate generated by exercise is one limit of physical fitness. The scientific research on lactate to date has revealed three important conclusions that you should know about:

1. You can augment the rate of removal of lactic acid (lactate) from your blood by physical training. In general, the harder you train, the faster your body removes excess lactate from the blood.

2. Your level of physical fitness depends on the rate of lactate clearance from the your blood. You can improve your fitness *and* rate of lactate clearance through the Haas Peak Performance Program because it induces the synthesis of enzymes necessary for lactate clearance. *The Haas Peak Performance Program "teaches" your muscles and liver how to clear lactate from your blood* and convert it back to sugar through a biochemical process called gluconeogensis (gluco = sugar; neo = new; genesis = creation—the creation of newly formed sugar from lactate).

3. You can augment the rate of clearance of lactate from your blood *by taking L-(+)-lactate supplements*! Paradoixcally, if you take calcium lactate supplements—the very substance that cripples athletic endurance—you actually will be able to increase your maximum work time. Here's why. By increasing the lactate load delivered to your blood, your muscles and your liver undergo an *adaptation response* producing more enzymes to process the excess lactate. Whether you exercise or take lactate supplements this adaptation response is the same. The result is that whenever your blood is presented with a large lactate load, as is the case with strenuous exercise, that lactate load will be lowered rapidly and efficiently. About three-fourths of the lactate will be converted to carbon dioxide (which you exhale with each breath); the rest will be converted to potential energy in the form of sugar which can then be *reused* by exercising muscles. When you follow my program of diet and use the recommended supplements (including calcium lactate), you boost your endurance potential far more than with lactate supplements alone.

How much lactate do you need? Research scientists have used up to 20 grams of calcium lactate (some researchers use sodium lactate, but calcium lactate provides additional calcium while avoiding unnecessary sodium) in human trials with success and no apparent adverse effects. Food manufacturers use lactic acid and lactate in many food products. The Food and Drug Administration regards calcium lactate as a safe food additive.

As with any ergogenic acid, I strongly urge you to take calcium lactate supplements under the direction of an experienced sports-care professional. Five grams of calcium lactate taken four times a day may be relatively harmless in well-trained, healthy athletes, but *you* may require much less when you begin a lactate supplementation program.

OCTACOSANOL

Octacosanol is a 28-carbon, straight-chain molecule in the chemical class of compounds chemists call alcohols. It occurs naturally in the vegetable kingdom in such foods as whole wheat and other whole grains. Scientists often have mistakenly attributed the effects of octacosanol to vitamin E, an error that has caused many people to supplement their diet with the wrong compound.

The reason is simple: most vitamin E studies that used wheat germ oil as the sole source of vitamin E (and there are many in the biomedical literature) actually measured the effects of octacosanol. Wheat germ oil is one of the most potent sources of this substance. The beneficial effects of octacosanol in these studies (mistakenly attributed to vitamin E) then encouraged further testing of "vitamin E"—testing which involved synthetic vitamin E or vitamin E derived from octacosanol-free sources. Since octacosanol was not present in these vitamin E preparations, many vitamin E studies could not duplicate the original studies that demonstrated positive results—*benefits that came from octacosanol, not vitamin E.* That's one major reason why some studies show that vitamin E improves athletic endurance and others demonstrate no effect.

Clinical studies have tested octacosanol on a variety of medical problems ranging from multiple sclerosis, amyotrophic lateral sclerosis, cerebral palsy, and arthritis. Scientists have also tested the related compounds, triacontanol and dotriacontanol on similar neuromuscular disorders.

My interest in octacosanol lies not in the treatment of disease, but in the improvement of athletic endurance and performance. Based on my own research with octacosanol, I believe that this naturally occurring substance can improve your own endurance and performance, at work or play.

Dr. Helmut F. Prahl, formerly associated with

the Standard Oil Company, Monsanto Chemical Company, Bjorksten Research Foundation, and now executive director of Dynatron Research Foundation, has developed a process to isolate octacosanol in pure cyrstalline form. Only one vitamin and mineral company in the U.S. currently markets this pure crystalline form of octacosanol, Twin Laboratories, in Deer Park, New York.

My own research has shown that athletes who take octacosanol as part of my program do, indeed, report improved endurance, stamina, alertness, and speed. Octacosanol does not appear to have any side effects, and I have observed no adverse changes in the blood chemistry profiles of these athletes. While these preliminary results are encouraging, I must continue to test octacosanol before I can give you a more definitive answer.

How much octacosanol do you need? Athletes use between 1,000 to 5,000 micrograms (mcg.) of 95% pure crystalline octacosanol to boost their endurance. But just as with any ergogenic aid, your dosage depends on your body weight, sex, age, health, other drugs you may be taking, and a host of other variables. And once again, I urge you to consult an experienced sports-care professional before supplementing your peak performance diet with this or any other ergogenic aid.

GINSENG

Ginseng is the general name for a class of naturally occurring steroidlike compounds that contain a steroid nucleus bonded to a sugar molecule and an alochol (or phenol) group. The Chinese, for thousands of years, have taken ginseng in one form or another as a rejuvenating tonic. Since the change in United States foreign policy has generated a cultural and scientific exchange with the Chinese, ginseng and the mystique that surrounds it has stimulated great interest among athletes in search of ergogenic aids.

There are few scientifically sound studies on the effects of ginseng. This makes it difficult, if not impossible, for athletes to evaluate the many claims made for this almost magical substance. Even more confusing, there are many varieties of ginseng (the root of the ginseng plant contains the "active" ingredients) marketed in the United States.

Ginseng is available in liquid and powder form and is approved (as a water extract) by the Food and Drug Administration for use in beverages such as tea. Most health food stores carry a variety of ginseng extracts and ginseng-containing products.

Ginseng is also an antioxidant that can quench free-radicals, thereby preventing premature aging and destruction of healthy cells and

207

tissues. Just as with all other antioxidants we've discussed so far, more is not necessarily better.

A recent two-year study conducted at the University of Southern California's Los Angeles Department of Bio-behavioral Sciences demonstrated that prolonged and excessive use of Korean red panax ginseng led to high blood pressure, insomnia, skin rash, and diarrhea. The study also noted that participants were taking other stimulants at the time such as tea (theophylline and caffeine) and coffee (caffeine). The results of this study may indicate that those persons who use one or more natural stimulants, such as caffeine, should not take ginseng as well.

How much ginseng should you take? Our present knowledge of ginseng is limited to very few valid and reliable studies. Athletes who use ginseng generally take anywhere from 1 to 5 grams in capsule form, although ginseng tea is becoming popular as an ergogenic beverage. The use of ginseng as an ergogenic aid requires the direct supervision of a sports-care professional. If you presently have high blood pressure or take any medications (including nonprescribed over-the-counter medications such as appetite suppressants, cough medicines, or asthma drugs), I urge you to consult with your physician before supplementing your diet with ginseng. Ginseng may offer athletes a competitive edge when properly used. If abused, as with almost any other substance, it can lead to serious health problems.

PHENYLALANINE

Phenylalanine is a commonly occurring amino acid found in almost everything we eat. I believe that phenylalanine can help athletes in all sports (as well as active people at work or play) because it is a primary precursor to two excitatory neurotransmittters (stimulatory chemicals that carry messages from nerve cell to nerve cell in the brain and other parts of the body: norepinephrine and dopamine). These neurotransmitters help keep you awake, alert, and depression-free.

Athletes also use phenylalanine to lose weight. Phenylalanine stimulants the production of norepinephrine, which can act as an appetite suppressant. Phenylalanine also causes the release of CCK, a hormone made in the brain and other parts of the body that naturally depresses your appetite. The more phenylalanine you eat, the less you crave food—at least, that's the theory.

Phenylalanine is chemically related to amphetamine and phenylethylamine, the mood-elevating stimulant found in cocoa and chocolate. Fortunately, phenylalanine and phenylethylamine are much safer than amphetamine, but as with all ergogenic aids, caution should temper your use of this natural substance.

How much phenylalanine should you take? L-phenylalanine (the D-form is not an ergogenic aid) requires other vitamins, such as vitamin C and vitamin B-6 for conversion to norepinephrine and other neurotransmitters. Another closely related amino acid, tyrosine, provides the same effects as phenylalanine and is, in fact, one step closer in the synthesis pathway to norepinephrine; thus both the phenylalanine *and tyrosine* content of your diet should be calculated before you decide how much phenylalanine to take. A good food composition book, such as the thirteenth edition of *Food Values of Portions Commonly Used*, by Jean Pennington and Helen Church (Harper and Row, New York, 1980), will tell you how much phenylalanine and tyrosine (the totals of both of these amino acids are given under the single entry of phenylalanine) you eat each day. The Haas Peak Performance Program provides a generous portion of phenylalanine and tyrosine (about 2.5 grams per day). A 4-ounce chicken breast, for example, contains a full gram of tyrosine and phenylalanine.

Athletes supplement their diets with phenylalanine by starting with doses of 50 to 250 milligrams, and gradually take as much as 2 grams, always on an empty stomach, because other amino acids in foods compete with phenylalanine for entry into the brain. By taking phenylalanine on an empty stomach, athletes ensure prompt delivery of phenylalanine to the brain and shorten the time it takes the brain to convert it into norepinephrine. You can purchase phenylalanine (an essential amino acid) in any health food store.

Since phenylalanine is chemically related to amphetamine and phenylpropanolamine (the active ingredient in most over-the-counter appetite suppressants), people with high blood pressure should use caution when supplementing their diet with this amino acid.

I am currently experimenting with phenylalanine and related compounds in boosting athletic performance and endurance in both professional and amateur athletes. While all of the results are not yet in, I predict that you will be reading more about this ergogenic aid and similar compounds (L-DOPA, a compound that helps those afflicted with Parkinson's disease, for example) in the near future.

CALCIUM PANTOTHENATE

Calcium pantothenate is the calcium salt of pantothenic acid, also known as vitamin B-5. The body requires this vitamin in the energy metabolism of proteins, fats, carbohydrates, and alcohol. It has been labled the "antistress" vitamin because laboratory research has demonstrated improved survival rates and increased stamina in animals subjected to physical and mental stress but given calcium pantothenate. Pantothenate is required for the synthesis of acetylcholine, a neurotransmitter that is used by the brain and other parts of the nervous system to communicate between nerves themselves and between nerves and muscles.

When James and Jonathan DiDonato broke the world distance record for the butterfly stroke, they did it using the Haas Peak Performance Program, which included calcium pantothenate. I included this vitamin as part of their program because it provides improved endurance and it reduces the chances of *hypothermia*, as noted earlier, a life-threatening condition in which body temperature drops precipitously, often resulting in death if the condition is not reversed within a short period of time. Before the DiDonato twins came to me for counsel, they attempted to swim the English Channel (20.5 miles) without the benefit of the added protection of calcium pantothenate. They were pulled from the water suffering from severe hypothermia just in time. The water temperature was 58 degrees, but the wind chill factor that day reduced their body temperature to dangerously low levels.

How much calcium pantothenate should you take? The Haas Peak Performance Program provides approximately 10 to 20 milligrams of pantothenate per day—more than enough to meet normal nutritional needs. For peak performance, athletes may require many times more than even my diet normally can give them.

Professional athletes who require the endurance and added protection of supplemental calcium pantothenate usually take between ½ a gram (500 milligrams) to 3 grams of this vitamin. By using the *calcium salt of pantothenic acid*, they avoid the unnecessary and unwanted acidity that pantothenic acid would cause and they boost their intake of calcium at the same time.

Calcium pantothenate is a water-soluble vitamin with very low toxicity. It does not appear to aggravate high blood pressure as some ergogenic aids do, but always check with a sports-care professional or physician before using it.

The information I've provided you with in this chapter—your new "chemistry set"—can give *you* the competitive edge over any opponent. Used wisely and with the proper precautions, your new chemistry set will help you achieve your *personal best*.

THIRTEEN

The Diet Chemistry of Peak Fat Loss

One secret of peak performance that leads to winning is achieving your ideal muscle-to-fat ratio. For most people, even a few world champions I've counseled, this means losing excess body fat while building strong muscle tissue.

As you have seen, Level One of my peak performance program helps you attain maximum fat loss while you improve your vital blood chemistry values. As a scientist, I always want to know *why*, so I would like to show you just why my peak performance program favorably changes your muscle-to-fat ratio.

Modern men and women can control their environment at the touch of a thermostat, dive to the bottom of the oceans, soar through outer space, call up entire libraries by pushing the proper buttons or keys, capture fleeting images and sounds to reexperience at will—but we are all still living in the body of a cave dweller. And that, in a sentence, is why so many of us are overweight.

Our Primitive Metabolic Machinery Turns Most Modern Foods Into Fat

Almost every cell in the human body contains a mechanism for converting food into energy—the same mechanism that was essential to the life of primitive men and women. This process is called the Kreb's Cycle (pedantic professors refer to it as the "tricarboxylic acid cycle") and the more you know about it, the easier it will be to understand how you can burn fat and stay ideally slender for a lifetime.

The Kreb's Cycle is a central part of the biochemical mechanism the body uses to burn calories, turning food into energy (such as ATP). The Kreb's Cycle is the great melting pot of metabolism, for it is in this cycle that everything a person eats and drinks—protein, fat, carbohydrate, and alcohol—comes together to be burned, recycled, stored, or modified according to the body's needs.

The Kreb's Cycle can, for example, help turn sugar, protein, and alcohol into fat, carbon dioxide, water, and ATP. It can help change sugar into protein, and protein into sugar. About the only biochemical trick it can't perform is to change fat into sugar (there is a rare exception

215

to this rule, but it is not important for most of us).

What does the Kreb's Cycle have to do with *your* excess poundage? Just about everything! We have seen that the Kreb's Cycle can and does make fat *from everything we eat and drink*, with only a few exceptions, such as salt and water. Obviously, if there were some way for you to control the fat production capability of the Kreb's Cycle, you could slow the production of unwanted fat.

One way to do this is to "encourage" the Kreb's Cycle to turn more food into substances such as carbon dioxide and water (which we exhale and excrete). *The more water and carbon dioxide your Kreb's Cycle produces, the less fat it will produce.*

How can you encourage your own Kreb's Cycle to do this? Let me give you a helpful phrase to remember: *fat burns in the flame of carbohydrate*. This principle of biochemistry is so important that you should commit it to memory, because it's the key to choosing peak performance foods that will keep you slender for life.

This principle really says that the Kreb's Cycle can burn fat (from your diet or around your stomach) most efficiently and cleanly during physical activity *only when there is enough carbohydrate present in the cycle at the same time.*

If you do not eat enough carbohydrate (the

216

best kind of carbohydrate comes from unrefined cereals and grains, such as potatoes, brown
rice, and oatmeal), the Kreb's Cycle will not do
its best work—it will burn fat inefficiently and
produce toxic by-products called ketone bodies,
the enemies of peak performance! Fat burns best
with plenty of exercise and plenty of complex
carbohydrates.

Carbohydrate Spares Protein During Fat Loss

This is another important principle of biochemistry that you should also memorize. In simple
terms, when you reduce your food intake (in
order to consume less kilocalories to lose weight),
your body will begin to "eat itself" in order to
provide the Kreb's Cycle with the fuel it needs
to produce ATP (the energy-rich molecule that
you just can't live without). *You can control*
whether your body will "eat" fat (which is what
you want), or muscle (which is definitely what
you don't want) if you eat enough carbohydrate.
I designed my programs to do just that. When
you follow my recommendations for each level
of the program, you will be able to lose excess
body weight without sacrificing vital muscle
tissue; you can even *build new muscle tissue* during your peak weight-loss program if you desire
to do so. Carbohydrates, *not protein*, are the key
to achieving peak performance weight-loss.

You now know that fat burns in the flame of carbohydrate, and that carbohydrate spares protein during weight loss, but there is one more principle you need to learn before class is over: there are *two* kinds of carbohydrate—*simple* and *complex.* Simple carbs usually taste sweet: table sugar, honey, and syrups. There are exceptions, such as the simple carbs in beer, milk, and milk products. Complex carbs are commonly called starches, and this category includes foods such as pasta, potatoes, breads, cereals, grains, and vegetables. Some foods, as fresh fruits, contain simple and complex carbs.

The carbohydrates you should eat for peak performance weight loss are the complex carbohydrates. They provide the most nutrition for the least calories.

Consider the much maligned potato, mistakenly shunned by weight-conscious people as a fattening food. A medium-size potato provides only *85 kilocalories*—30% fewer than you'll get from a good size apple! This wonderfully balanced vegetable contains plenty of vitamin C, B vitamins, trace minerals, and fiber—but absolutely no cholesterol and almost no fat. It certainly isn't the potato that promotes fat storage; it's the toppings most people put on them that do the damage.

Pasta is another complex carbohydrate that most people consider fattening. Again, its the high-fat sauces that they ladle on top that pile on the pounds.

Brown rice—the very mention of this food used to make many of my nutrition professors livid—is one of the best complex carbohydrates you can eat for peak performance. Brown rice has a bad reputation among many nutritionists and hospital dietitians, because about ten years ago the medical literature reported the death of someone who followed the macrobiotic diet. This person ate a diet composed almost exclusively of brown rice for an extended period of time ("Diet Number Seven" is the infamous all-brown-rice diet recommended by the founder of the macrobiotic diet, George Osahwa). Diet Number Seven notwithstanding, brown rice, as part of a *total* nutritional regimen or program, is a nutritious complex carbohydrate that will help to keep you fit, trim, and healthy.

Here are a few of the reasons why I recommend that you eat *six to eight* times more complex than simple carbohydrates:

1. Simple carbohydrates stimulate the pancreas to produce a high level of insulin. This means that you will feel hungry more often if you favor them over complex carbohydrates. High insulin production also stimulates fat production; insulin actually tells the body to *make and store fat*.

2. Simple carbohydrates increase the amount

of triglycerides (fat) in the blood, which reduces athletic endurance and promotes cardiovascular disease.

3. Simple carbohydrates increase the amount of cholesterol in the blood.

4. Simple carbohydrates increase the amount of uric acid in the blood, which can cause gout (a form of arthritis) in susceptible people.

To sum up: simple carbohydrates provide poor nutrition; they're less filling than complex carbs; they "tell" your body to make more fat, cholesterol, and uric acid; they promote dental caries (cavities); they stimulate your appetite so you wind up eating more, even though you are already well nourished.

There is nothing wrong with enjoying some simple carbohydrates every day, and you can, as long as you follow the program I've outlined. It ensures that you will eat the proper ratio of complex-to-simple carbohydrates to promote fat loss, muscle retention (or muscle gain, if you so desire), and optimal health.

A Few Words About Fat

Why eat large amounts of the very substance—fat—you are trying to burn? That's exactly what you'll do if you follow traditional high-protein (high fat) "sports" diets or weight-loss schemes. It is about time you learned the truth: to lose weight, spare muscle, and achieve blood chemistry values in the peak performance range *concentrate on complex carbohydrates.* Our prehistoric ancestors thrived on them—and so will you!

FOURTEEN

Peak Sexual Performance

"My personal experience has convinced me that peak peformance in middle- and long-distance races is possible within hours of sexual activity."
—Dr. George Sheehan

"I am well aware of a world-class sprinter who, one half hour after masturbating, went out and set a world's record."
—Dr. William Masters

"It isn't sex that wrecks these guys, it's staying up all night looking for it."
—Casey Stengel

More Sex in Your Life and More Life in Your Sex

Highly conditioned marathon runners and week-end sports enthusiasts alike have told me that my peak performance recommendations have greatly improved their sex lives!

The physical requirements of peak sexual performance can rival those of any endurance activity or sport: high aerobic capacity, abundant energy, stamina, strength, mobility, concentration, neuromuscular coordination, proper hydration, and optimal health. A recent readership poll by *Runner's World* revealed that physically active people felt that their level of fitness increased their sexual pleasure, satisfaction, and fulfillment.

The athletes who follow my program report profound improvement in both the frequency and enjoyment of their sexual activity. There are many chemical and biochemical reasons for this.

Sexual peak response can be partially or even totally determined by *diet chemistry* and *level of fitness*.

The latest scientific studies bear this out. For example, researchers have recently discovered that *beta-endorphins*, which are chemicals similar to opium (they're manufactured in the brain and throughout the body), play a role in sexual pleasure. The type of diet you eat, the right amounts of vitamins and minerals, and other environmental stimuli can affect beta-endorphin levels, and, by extension, the sensations of sexual pleasure.

Sex hormones are manufactured by the body, and these powerful chemicals help to stimulate sexual desire and drive. The proper foods, vitamins, and minerals, and amount of body fat are among the factors that play a large role in determining the relative amounts of these hormones in the blood.

Large amounts of serum cholesterol and triglycerides can obstruct the body's cardiovascular system, and this may cause chest pain during sex, or even impotence. Proper nutrition and exercise can lower the amount of serum cholesterol and triglycerides, and in some cases, even reverse arterial obstruction that causes these undesirable symptoms of cardiovascular disease.

Stimulation of the *neuroendocrine system* in laboratory animals makes them act "younger." Neuroendocrine hormones may be modified by many factors, including diet and supplementary vitamins and minerals, to provide this "fountain of youth" effect.

Fat and Sex Don't Mix

Excess body fat often can turn sexual desire into indifference because it upsets sex hormone balance by transforming androgens (male hormones) into estrogens (female hormones). Although our bodies make both kinds of hormones every day (female sex hormones are made from male sex hormones), a change in the *ratio* of androgens to estrogens can play biochemical havoc with sexual desire as well as sexual performance and fulfillment. Too much of one hormone and not enough of the other (we each need *both* for normal sexual function) actually can turn lust into lethargy for the overly fat person. An imbalance in the ratio of male to female sex hormones can decrease the level of LHRF (leutinizing hormone releasing factor) in the brain. LHRF can act as a natural aphrodisiac when present in sufficient quantities; a low LHRF level can mean a low sex drive for an obese man or woman.

I was in the men's number-one locker room at the All England Lawn Tennis Club (Wimbledon) in July 1982 with, among others, John McEnroe, Jimmy Connors, and Bill Norris, the trainer for the U.S. Davis Cup team and the Association of Tennis Professionals, when I was asked (the questioner must remain anonymous), "Does sex affect athletic performance, or does athletic performance affect sex?" All other conversation stopped. You could hear the proverbial pin drop.

"Yes," I answered.

A few puzzled looks later, I explained what I meant by my singular reply.

Sex Is an Athletic Event

Your heart is racing at over 160 beats per minute, your respiration rate is ten times more than normal, your lungs feel "heavy," and you're sweating profusely. Are you running the Boston Marathon, playing tennis with Bjorn Borg, or going 15 rounds with Muhammad Ali? No, you're just having vigorous sexual intercourse!

You can achieve peak sexual performance, just as you can in any other form of exercise, through proper "training." Peak sexual performance, like peak sports performance, requires a *scientific* approach. Please don't misunderstand— I'm just as romantic as the next person—but optimal health and fitness through nutrition and exercise can also *enhance romance!* My professional experience has convinced me that many people, even world champions, could better enjoy time spent in the bedroom by adopting my scientific approach in the dining room!

Vigorous, extended sexual activity actually can enhance sports performance, just as sports participation can enhance sexual performance. Sex and sport evoke similar body responses, which means that both activities can improve your physical fitness. More stamina on the court (through proper sports nutrition and hard training) can mean more energy in bed and vice versa.

One Problem with Achieving Peak Sexual Performance

I cannot divulge the personal stories that the sports champions and amateur athletes whom I counsel have confided to me, but I *can* tell you that many of them report a dramatic improvement in the frequency, intensity, and duration of their sexual performance. Peak sexual performance, however, is not without its drawbacks.

Occasionally, an athlete's spouse or lover (who is not following my program) will call me, complaining that he or she cannot keep pace with the partner's newly found sexual stamina or desire. My reply: *begin the Haas Peak Performance Program yourself!*

Poor diet can prevent peak sexual performance. Diet-related health problems, such as cardiovascular disease, diabetes, obesity, and high blood pressure (and the effects of some of the drugs prescribed to control these problems) can promote impotence and decrease sexual desire:

Poor diet can mean sluggishness, lethargy, and excess body fat, which can be sexually unattractive to a sexual partner.

High blood pressure is often treated with drugs that may induce impotence, due to their effects on the central nervous system or the hormonal system that controls sexual arousal and desire.

Diabetes can also cause impotence due to impaired circulation that can reduce the blood supply to the penis which is necessary to achieve erection.

Atherosclerosis (narrowing or complete obstruction of parts of the cardiovascular system) can lead to impotence due to impaired circulation and/or avoidance of sexual activity because it may bring on severe chest pain (angina pectoris).

Elevated serum cholesterol and triglycerides may be treated with drugs that can induce impotence or depress the libido.

My peak performance program has already eliminated many of the symptoms of cardiovascular disease (and helped reduce and even eliminate prescribed medications that can lead to sexual problems) in many people who follow it. This is one important reason that I strongly recommend that you work with your physician when you change your diet and begin to exercise. It is possible and quite likely that my program can improve certain diet-related health problems. Many people who enjoy the Haas Peak Performance Program are able to reduce their drug dependence and, in some cases, even eliminate the need to take such medications; but I must stress that *you should never attempt to modify or discontinue any physician-prescribed medication without your physician's recommendation to do so.*

Sex at ninety can be as fulfilling as sex at twenty—and maybe even more! The Haas Peak Performance Program can restore youthful vitality and improve sexual performance at any age because the better health, ideal body weight, and high energy levels it produces all contribute to sexual longevity.

The twenty-year-old athlete may ask, "How

can I sustain my present sexual vigor as I grow older?" while the sixty-year-old may wonder, "How can I regain the sexual vigor of my youth?" My answer to both is: follow the scientific principles of the Haas Peak Performance Program!

SECTION II

THE
EAT TO WIN
RECIPE BOOK

Foreword

My *Eat to Win* recipes have nourished some of the world's best athletes and will provide you with a delicious way to achieve your own peak performance levels at work or play. These recipes, created with the help of Hilarie Porter, M.S., have been successfully tested during the most grueling training schedule of amateur and professional athletes. They have provided champions such as Jimmy Connors, Gene Mayer, Viki Fleckenstein, Nancy Lieberman, and Martina Navratilova with the peak performance food chemistry they need to eat to win.

Each recipe provides the essential information you'll need to reach your own peak performance levels. This vital nutritional information is listed according to serving size so that you'll know exactly how many calories and how much protein, fat, carbohydrate, cholesterol, and sodium each portion supplies. These are the six

233

most important values you'll need to know, regardless of the nutritional program you may now follow.

Great care has been taken to make each recipe as simple and easy to follow as possible. You don't have to be a skilled cook or chef to enjoy these delicious peak performance recipes. Since the recipe ingredients are composed of ordinary supermarket foods, you'll be able to prepare them as soon as you go shopping.

Each recipe will vary somewhat in its nutritional content, but you may select *any* of the following recipes, regardless of your program level—One, Two, or Three. If you are following a low-sodium diet, or a regimen that restricts fat and cholesterol, you can easily determine which recipes are best for you by adding the daily totals of the nutrients that are listed with each one. If your daily sodium limit is 2 grams, or if you must eat less than 100 milligrams of cholesterol per day, the *Eat to Win* recipes will help to keep you within your daily limits. If you have a health problem or follow a medically supervised diet, your physician can help you decide which recipes are best for you.

Preparing the *Eat to Win* recipes requires no special equipment. Some kitchen appliances, however, can make meal preparation easier: microwave ovens, blenders, food processors, electric mixers all are handy to have, but are not essential to the preparation of these recipes.

You can make almost every *Eat to Win* recipe in extra quantity, to be frozen and stored until needed. Volume recipe preparation not only saves you time but money as well. We have tested the frozen shelf-life of most of these recipes for up to three months without significant loss of flavor. Heat-sealable clear plastic bags are a wonderful way to store single or multiple servings of each recipe; you can do all your cooking at one time, and then simply defrost and reheat (this is where microwave ovens make life easier) whenever you desire.

The *Eat to Win* recipes do not require you to use significant amounts of fats or oils to prepare dishes that normally would require their use. Frying foods in nonstick cookware, broiling, steaming, poaching, baking, and sauteeing in water are all methods that help you reduce the amount of fat calories in your diet. When some fat or oil is essential to the preparation of a recipe, you may use a nonstick pan lightly sprayed with lecithin (Pam spray, for example).

Many active people who don't have the time to spend preparing complicated or lengthy recipes will find the eat-to-win recipes a refreshing change from conventional, time-consuming recipes that may have discouraged them from creative cooking in the past. There is plenty of room for creative cooking with these recipes as long as you don't exceed the recommendations for your current peak performance level. You may use salt-free and sugar-free condiments as you wish. If you find that any recipe contains a particular condiment that does not appeal to you, you may simply omit it. It's not the condiments that make these recipes special; it's the basic food chemistry that really makes the difference. You actually can change the taste of any recipe with the right condiments without changing the essential peak performance chemistry.

Once you hve mastered the art of low-fat cookery (it's really much easier than cooking *with* fats and oils), you will probably find, as most of the athletes I counsel do, that greasy, fat-laden dishes no longer appeal to you. You can easily modify your formerly favorite high-fat recipes by adapting them to my low-fat cooking methods, and by substituing low-fat ingredients for high-fat ones. Here is just a sample of the changes you can make in your favorite high-fat recipes to creat new, low-fat dishes à-la Haas:

• Replace butter or margarine with Butter Buds butter replacer; when you absolutely must use butter or margraine, choose a low-fat margarine such as Weight Watcher's brand (it has half the fat and half the calories of regular butter and margarine and contains no cholesterol).

• Replace mayonnaise with my recipe for Haas mayonnaise. Haas mayonnaise may be used in any recipe that calls for conventional mayonnaise. There are also several brands of low-fat, cho-

lesterol-free mayonnaise available in most supermarkets that you can use if you must use
mayonnaise.

• Replace peanut butter (or other nut butters)
with the Haas peanut butter recipe. Conventional peanut butter contains fats and oils that
promote atherosclerosis (in laboratory animals)
and despite its mistaken reputation of being a
high-protein food, over 75% of the calories in
peanut butter come from fat (only 18% of the
calories come from protein).

• Replace whole eggs with egg *whites*. Recipes (including omelettes) that call for whole
eggs or egg yolks can be made just as easily and
successfully with egg whites alone. Egg yolks
supply over 250 milligrams of cholesterol per
yolk, and nearly 80% of the calories in a yolk
comes from fat! Egg whites, on the other hand,
contain no fat or cholesterol, yet supply quality
protein.

• Replace sour cream with low-fat yogurt or
blended low-fat cottage cheese. There are also
low-fat, low-cholesterol sour cream replacement
products available in many supermarkets that
can help cut unnecessary fat calories.

• Replace whole milk products with skim and
low-fat milk products. Low-fat cottage cheese
(available in most supermarkets in an uncreamed,
½% fat form), low-fat yogurt (1 to 2% fat), and
skim milk or nonfat dry milk (zero fat) are excellent foods that will help you to reduce the

amount of saturated fat and cholesterol in your diets.

• Replace your favorite cheese with a small amount of grated Parmesan or Romano cheese. Parmesan and Romano cheeses have such a strong flavor that you can often use much smaller quantities of these cheeses to flavor recipes that call for larger amounts of mozzarella, Swiss, and Cheddar. One level tablespoon of grated Parmesan cheese contains just 1.5 grams of fat, only 4 milligrams of cholesterol, and a mere 23 calories. One ounce of Cheddar, on the other hand, provides 9 grams of fat, 30 milligrams of cholesterol, and 112 calories!

Recipe Index

BREADS AND MUFFINS

APPLE BREAD
APPLE MUFFINS
BANANA BREAD
BLUEBERRY BRAN MUFFINS
CORN MUFFINS
EARTH BREAD
ORANGE MUFFINS
WHOLE WHEAT BREAD
WHOLE WHEAT RAISIN BREAD

DESSERTS

BAKED APPLES
BAKED PLANTAINS
BANANA NOODLE CUSTARD
BROWN RICE FRUIT
CUSTARD
CRANBERRY RELISH
CRUSTLESS PUMPKIN PIE
FRENCH APPLE BAKE
HOLIDAY CAKE
NOODLE PUDDING
OATMEAL FRUIT BARS

BREAKFAST

BUCKWHEAT PANCAKES
HAAS "SCRAMBLED EGGS
AND BACON"
OATMEAL ROYALE

ENTRÉES

BASIC BROWN RICE AND
CHICKEN
BROCCOLI BROWN RICE

HOLLANDAISE
BROWN RICE AND COTTAGE
CHEESE
CANNELLINI-STUFFED
ZUCCHINI
CHICKEN CASSEROLE
CHICKEN CURRY
CHICK 'N' CHILI
CHILI PIE
COQ AU VIN CASSEROLE
CORN AND CHICKEN
FRITTATA
CRABMEAT AU GRATIN
EGGPLANT MOUSSAKA
FISH AND MUSHROOM
MARINADE
GLAZED RATATOUILLE
IMAM BAYELDI
INDIAN VEGETABLE AND
RICE CASSEROLE
ITALIAN MACARONI AND
BEANS
ITALIAN STUFFED PEPPERS
ITALIAN VEGETABLE BAKE
ITALIAN WHITE BEANS
MACARONI AND CHEESE
LOMBARDO
MARINARA SAUCE
MELANZANE AL FORNO
PASTA AND GARLIC SAUCE
RANCHERO CHILI
SPINACH CHEESE PIE

SPINACH NOODLE
CASSEROLE
STUFFED CABBAGE
STUFFED TOMATOES
SWEET AND SOUR CHICKEN
TINI LINGUINI
TOMATO SALMON
CASSEROLE
TUNA CASSEROLE SUPREME
TUNA HAAS
TUNA MUFFINS
VEAL SCALLOPINI
ZUCCHINI SQUARES

POTATO RECIPES AND TOPPINGS

BACON, ONION, AND CHIVE
TOPPING
BARBECUE CHICKEN TOPPING
"CHEDDAR" STUFFED
POTATOES
CHICKEN IN WINE SAUCE
TOPPING
COTTAGE FRIES
HOT GERMAN POTATO SALAD
HORSERADISH TOPPING
MARINATED POTATO SALAD
MUSHROOM TOPPING
POTATO CASSEROLE
SNAPPY CHEDDAR TOPPING

The Eat To Win Recipe Book

SALADS AND SALAD DRESSINGS

BEAN AND VEGETABLE SALAD

BROCCOLI AND ONION SALAD

CAESAR SALAD DRESSING

CAULIFLOWER CURRY

CHICKEN SALAD

CREAMY ITALIAN DRESSING

CUCUMBER SALAD

GREEN GODDESS DRESSING

JEFF'S "CREAM" DRESSING

MARINATED VEGETABLES

THOUSAND ISLAND
DRESSING

WALDORF SALAD DELUXE

YOGURT TOMATO DRESSING

SAUCES AND SPREADS

APPLE BUTTER

DILL SAUCE DELUXE

HAAS MAYONNAISE SPREAD

HAAS PEANUT BUTTER

SOUPS

BLACK-EYED PEA SOUP

CHILI BEAN AND RICE SOUP

HOWARD'S ONION SOUP

KIDNEY BEAN SOUP

POTATO SOUP

SWEET POTATO SOUP

BREAKFAST

BUCKWHEAT PANCAKES
Yields 6 pancakes

*1½ cup Aunt Jemima
Buckwheat Pancake
Mix*

*½ cup skim milk
2 egg whites*

1. Spray a nonstick frying pan with Pam. Place on medium heat to warm pan.

2. Mix all ingredients. Pour batter on to hot

pan. Turn when tops are covered with bubbles. Only turn once.

3. Serve with Tree of Life spreads such as apple butter, raspberry spread, strawberry spread, etc.

NUTRITIONAL INFORMATION PER SERVING

Calories . . 267.5   Carbohydrate . . 41.4 g
Protein . . . 15.9 g   Fat . . . . 2.5 g
Sodium . . 761.0 mg   Cholesterol . . . . 3.0 mg

HAAS "SCRAMBLED EGGS AND BACON"
Serves 1

1 piece unsalted matzo
2 egg whites
1 tablespoon bacon chips
1 tablespoon Parmesan cheese
1 tablespoon bran
1 tablespoon evaporated skim milk
1 teaspoon Tamari soy sauce
Dash of pepper
1 to 1½ cups water

1. Bring water to a boil. Break matzo into small pieces and place in water. Turn off heat. Let matzo sit in water.

2. In the meantime mix the rest of the ingredients. Use wire whisk to beat lightly.

3. Drain matzo well. Add to egg mixture.

4. Spray nonstick pan with Pam. Pour mixture into pan. Cook on medium heat mixing with spatula until eggs are set.

NUTRITIONAL INFORMATION PER SERVING

Calories . . 105.8	Carbohydrate . . 9.2 g
Protein . . . 12.3 g	Fat . . . . 2.5 g
Sodium . . 514.9 mg	Cholesterol . . . . 10.0 mg

OATMEAL ROYALE
Serves 2

¼ cup raisins
1 medium apple, peeled
and diced
1 banana, cut in half
and sliced
⅔ cup oatmeal

⅓ cup bran
¼ teaspoon cinnamon
1 tablespoon orange
juice concentrate
1½ cups water

1. Place water, orange juice concentrate, and fruit in saucepan.

2. Bring to a rapid boil. Add oatmeal and bran. Turn off heat immediately. Stir constantly.

3. Add cinnamon and all of the fruit. Leave over heat approximately 1 minute stirring constantly.

4. Remove from heat and pour into bowls. Serve piping hot.

NUTRITION INFORMATION PER SERVING

Calories . . 227.8	Carbohydrate . . 55.7 g
Protein . . . 4.3 g	Fat . . . . 2.3 g
Sodium . . 7.8 mg	Cholesterol . . . . 0.0 mg

SOUPS

BLACK-EYED PEA SOUP
Serves 8 to 10

7 *cups water*
12 *ounces black-eyed*
  peas
2 *medium potaotes,*
  peeled and diced
3 *stalks celery, sliced*
2 *carrots, sliced*
3 *tablespoons Tamari*
  soy sauce

1 *medium onion,*
  chopped
2 *cloves garlic, diced*
¼ *teaspoon pepper*
1 *teaspoon basil*
1 *teaspoon dried dill*
  weed

1. Rinse black-eyed peas well. Place in a large pot and cover with water by 1" (in addition to water listed in ingredients). Soak overnight.

2. Add rest of ingredients. Bring to a boil. Boil 2 minutes.

3. Reduce heat to medium-low. Simmer 1 to 2 hours or until beans are tender. Stir occasionally mashing beans and potatoes against sides of the pot to thicken soup.

NUTRITIONAL INFORMATION PER SERVING

Calories . . 133.9   Carbohydrate . . 25.2 g
Protein . . . 7.8 g   Fat . . . . 0.5 g
Sodium . . 283.2 mg Cholesterol . . . . 0.0 mg

CHILI BEAN AND RICE SOUP
Serves 8 to 10

12-ounce bag pinto
  beans, rinsed
7 cups boiling water
3 to 4 cloves garlic,
  minced
1 medium onion, diced
¼ teaspoon marjoram
¾ cup raw brown rice,
  rinsed

2 28-ounce cans whole
  tomatoes, rinsed and
  chopped
1 bay leaf
¼ teaspoon thyme
3 tablespoons Tamari
  soy sauce
1½ teaspoons hot Mexi-
  can chili powder

1. Soak pinto beans for 1 hour. Drain and empty them into a large pot. Add boiling water, garlic, onion, bay leaf, thyme and marjoram. Boil 5 to 6 minutes. Cover and simmer for 1 to 1½ hours or until pinto beans are tender.

2. Add brown rice, tomatoes, Tamari soy sauce and chili powder. Bring to a boil. Boil for 5 minutes. Reduce heat and simmer 30 to 45 minutes until brown rice is cooked.

NUTRITIONAL INFORMATION PER SERVING

Calories . . 211.4   Carbohydrate . . 39.9 g
Protein . . . 10.1 g   Fat . . . . 0.3 g
Sodium . . 320.4 mg   Cholesterol . . . . 0.0 mg

HOWARD'S ONION SOUP
Serves 4

¼ cup evaporated skim milk

4 to 6 cloves garlic, minced

5 to 6 cups onions, sliced into separate rings

1 teaspoon granulated fructose

1 tablespoon whole wheat flour

5 cups water

½ cup Burgundy

3 tablespoons Tamari soy sauce

2 whole wheat onion bagels, sliced lengthwise

2 tablespoons Parmesan cheese, grated

1. Spray a large stick-free frying pan with Pam. Saute garlic and onion until onion is clear and lightly browned. Add evaporated skim milk. Cook 5 more minutes.

2. Combine water, Burgundy, Tamari soy sauce, flour and fructose in 4-quart saucepan. Bring to a boil stirring to dissolve the fructose and flour. Add onion and garlic. Simmer 20 to 25 minutes.

3. Preheat oven to 425°.

4. Lightly toast bagel. Ladle soup into 4 oven-proof bowls. Place 1 slice of bagel in each bowl. Sprinkle 1 tablespoon of Parmesan cheese in each bowl on top of the bagel slice.

5. Place bowls on flat pan. Bake for 10 minutes or until cheese is golden.

NUTRITIONAL INFORMATION PER SERVING

Calories . . 216.7	Carbohydrate . . 32.7 g
Protein . . . 8.6 g	Fat . . . . 1.5 g
Sodium . . 544.6 mg	Cholesterol . . . . 10.0 mg

KIDNEY BEAN SOUP
Serves 6 to 8

1 pound cooked kidney
   beans
2 cups tomato sauce
3 medium onions,
   coarsely chopped
3 ribs celery, chopped
2 cloves garlic, minced
1 teaspoon thyme

1 teaspoon oregano
1 tablespoon Tamari
   soy sauce
½ teaspoon pepper
1 teaspoon dried dill
   weed
7 cups water

1. Combine all ingredients in a large pot.
2. Simmer for 1 hour.

NUTRITIONAL INFORMATION PER SERVING

Calories . . 79.4	Carbohyrate . . . . 15.7 g
Protein . . . 3.8 g	Fat . . . . 0.3 g
Sodium . . 186.7 mg	Cholesterol . . . . 0.0 mg

POTATO SOUP
Serve 6

4 *medium potatoes,* *peeled and diced*	⅛ *teaspoon pepper*
	⅛ *teaspoon nutmeg*
1 *medium onion, chopped*	1 *teaspoon Tamari*
1 *cup celery, diced*	*soy sauce*
2 *cups water*	2 *teaspoons dried dill*
1 *cube VegeX (vegetable* *bouillon cube)*	*weed*
1½ *cups evaporated* *skim milk*	

1. In a large pot combine water, VegeX, potatoes, onion, and celery.

2. Cover and cook on medium heat 20 minutes or until potatoes are soft.

3. Place in blender or food processor. Purée.

4. Return purée to pot. Add rest of ingredients.

5. Heat soup, but do not boil.

NUTRITIONAL INFORMATION PER SERVING

Calories	..115.6	Carbohydrate	..22.6 g
Protein	... 6.1 g	Fat	.... 0.0 g
Sodium	..289.9 mg	Cholesterol	.... 0.5 mg

SWEET POTATO SOUP
Serves 6

2 large or 3 medium
  sweet potatoes,
  cooked
2¾ cups water
1 cube VegeX (vegetable
  bouillon)
⅓ cup plain low-fat
  yogurt
⅛ teaspoon white pepper

5 tablespoons Parme-
  san cheese, grated
1 tablespoon Tamari
  soy sauce
1 teaspoon dried dill
  weed
½ cup dry cooking
  sherry

1. Scoop out centers of cooked potatoes. Place in a food processor with 1¾ cup water and yogurt. Purée

2. Place purée in saucepan with rest of water, sherry, and VegeX over medium heat. Slowly add cheese, pepper, Tamari soy sauce, and dill weed.

3. Bring to a boil stirring constantly. Reduce heat to medium stirring until soup thickens slightly (10 to 15 minutes).

NUTRITIONAL INFORMATION PER SERVING

Calories . . 141.5	Carbohydrate . . 22.4 g
Protein . . . 3.9 g	Fat . . . . 1.7 g
Sodium . . 317.1 mg	Cholesterol . . . . 9.2 mg

SALADS AND SALAD DRESSINGS

BEAN AND VEGETABLE SALAD
Yields 4 cups

20-ounce can kidney beans (rinse well)
1½ cups corn (rinsed if canned)
½ cup green pepper, chopped
½ cup red pepper, chopped

½ cup celery, sliced
½ cup onion, chopped
¼ cup Bunker Hill Italian Dressing
⅛ cup red wine vinegar
1 teaspoon Italian seasoning

1. Combine and toss gently all ingredients in a large bowl.
2. Chill and serve.

NUTRITIONAL INFORMATION PER SERVING

Calories . . 585.7	Carbohydrate . . 115.4 g
Protein . . . 11.8 g	Fat . . . . 3.2 g
Sodium . . 704.9 mg	Cholesterol . . . . 0.0 mg

BROCCOLI AND ONION SALAD
Serves 4 to 6

1½ pounds fresh broccoli, cut into 1" pieces
1 small red onion, thinly sliced
¼ cup Herb Magic Italian Dressing
¼ cup red wine vinegar

2 tablespoons lemon juice
¼ teaspoon dry mustard
½ teaspoon dried tarragon leaves
⅛ teaspoon freshly ground pepper

250

1. Steam broccoli until tender but firm. Cool.
2. Toss with onion.
3. Mix rest of ingredients. Blend well.
4. Pour over broccoli and onion.
5. Marinate in refrigerator 4 to 8 hours.

NUTRITIONAL INFORMATION PER SERVING

Calories . . 34.2	Carbohydrate . . 6.5 g
Protein . . . 2.8 g	Fat , , ... 0.1 g
Sodium . . 210.2 mg	Cholesterol . . . . 0.0 mg

CAESAR SALAD DRESSING
Serves 2

4 egg whites
3 tablespoons vinegar
4 teaspoons lemon juice
½ teaspoon garlic
  powder (crushed fresh
  garlic optional)
½ teaspoon anchovy
  paste

1 teaspoon Tamari soy
sauce
1 teaspoon Worcester-
shire sauce
1 tablespoon Parmesan
cheese, grated

1. Combine egg whites, vinegar, lemon juice, Tamari, and Worcestershire in rough wooden bowl.

2. Add anchovy paste and mix thoroughly until smooth consistency results.

3. Blend in crushed fresh garlic or garlic powder.

4. Toss with ice cold Romaine lettuce. Sprinkle with Parmesan cheese and retoss. Serve with freshly ground pepper and croutons if desired.

NUTRITIONAL INFORMATION PER SERVING

Calories .. 55.9	Carbohydrate ..2.6 g
Protein ... 8.5 g	Fat ....0.8 g
Sodium ..414.2 mg	Cholesterol ....8.7 mg

CAULIFLOWER CURRY

Serves 4 to 6

1 medium head of cauliflower, cut flowrettes in small pieces	**½ teaspoon Mexican chili powder**
2 onions, finely chopped	**¼ teaspoon turmeric**
½ cup red lentils, rinsed well	**1 teaspoon curry powder**
	Juice of 1 lemon
	Tamari to taste

1. Sauté onions in a small amount of water 4 to 5 minutes.

2. Add cauliflower, lentils, and spices.

3. Add 1 cup water. Cook on low flame covered until cauliflower is tender.

4. Add lemon juice and Tamari soy sauce if needed.

NUTRITIONAL INFORMATION PER SERVING

Calories ..95.3	Carbohydrate ..17.4 g
Protein ... 7.1 g	Fat .... 0.2 g
Sodium ..44.0 mg	Cholesterol .... 0.0 mg

CHICKEN SALAD
Yields 1 cup

1 cup breast of chicken, cooked and cubed
⅓ cup celery, chopped
1 tablespoon onion, chopped
3 tablespoons Haas mayonnaise spread

1 tablespoon plain low-fat yogurt
½ teaspoon Dijon mustard
⅛ teaspoon pepper
½ cup apple, cubed (optional)

1. Combine all ingredients in a bowl.
2. Chill. Serve on a bed of lettuce.

NUTRITIONAL INFORMATION PER SERVING

Calories ..226.9   Carbohydrate ..20.8 g
Protein ... 30.7 g   Fat .... 1.6 g
Sodium ..398.6 mg   Cholesterol ....88.8 mg

CREAMY ITALIAN DRESSING
Yields 1.5 cups
Serving size: 2 tablespoons

1 cup low-fat cottage cheese (1% milk fat)
½ cup plain low-fat yogurt
1 tablespoon lemon juice
1 tablespoon Dijon mustard
2 tablespoons onion, chopped

1 teaspoon Worcestershire sauce
1 teaspoon dried basil
1 teaspoon dried oregano
½ teaspoon dried parsley
¼ teaspoon garlic powder

1. Place all ingredients in a blender or food processor.
2. Blend until smooth. Chill.
3. Serve over a garden fresh salad.

NUTRITIONAL INFORMATION PER SERVING

Calories . . 23.0	Carbohydrate . .1.7 g
Protein . . . 2.9 g	Fat . . . . .0.4 g
Sodium . .106.6 mg	Cholesterol . . . .0.8 mg

CUCUMBER SALAD
Serves 6 to 8

2 cucumbers, peeled and
  thinly sliced
1 medium onion, thinly
  sliced into separate
  rings
1 cup distilled vinegar
1 cup water

2 packets Equal sugar
  substitute
1 teaspoon Tamari
  soy sauce
¼ teaspoon pepper
  (optional)

1. Toss cucumbers and onions.
2. Combine rest of ingredients in quart jar.
3. Add onions and cucumbers.
4. Chill. Best if chilled overnight.

NUTRITIONAL INFORMATION PER SERVING

Calories . .13.0	Carbohydrate . .2.5 g
Protein . . . 0.3 g	Fat . . . . .0.0 g
Sodium . .45.5 mg	Cholesterol . . . .0.0 mg

GREEN GODDESS DRESSING
Yields 1 cup
Serving size: 2 tablespoons

½ cup low-fat cottage cheese (1% milk fat)
¼ cup plain low-fat yogurt
1 teaspoon Dijon mustard
2 tablespoons red wine vinegar
1 tablespoon Tamari soy sauce
Pinch of basil
Pinch of thyme
1 tablespoon parsley flakes
1 clove of garlic, minced
3 scallions, diced, including green portion
¼ cucumber, diced

1. Place all ingredients in a food processor or blender.
2. Mix until smooth.
3. Chill. Serve over salad or as a dip for fresh vegetables.

NUTRITIONAL INFORMATION PER SERVING

Calories .. 20.1	Carbohydrate ..1.9 g
Protein ... 2.3 g	Fat ....0.3 g
Sodium ..126.4 mg	Cholesterol ....0.6 mg

JEFF'S "CREAM" DRESSING
Yields 2 cup
Serving size: 2 tablespoons

1¾ cups low-fat cottage cheese (1% milk fat)
4 tablespoons white vinegar
4 teaspoons chives, chopped
2 teaspoons onion, grated
3 dashes of Tabasco

255

1. Place all ingredients in a blender or food processor.
2. Blend until completely smooth.
3. Chill. Serve over garden fresh salad.

NUTRITIONAL INFORMATION PER SERVING

Calories . . 12.3	Carbohydrate . . 0.6 g
Protein . . . 2.1 g	Fat . . . . 0.2 g
Sodium . . 67.4 mg	Cholesterol . . . . 0.1 mg

MARINATED VEGETABLES
Serves 6 to 8

½ *cup wine vinegar*	2 *cups water*
2 *tablespoons lemon*	1 *cup zucchini, sliced*
juice	1 *cup yellow squash,*
1 *teaspoon coriander*	*sliced*
seed, crushed	1 *cup broccoli, chopped*
3 *cloves garlic, minced*	1 *cup green beans*
½ *teaspoon pepper*	

1. Place first 6 ingredients in a pot. Bring to a boil.
2. Add vegetables. Reduce heat.
3. Simmer until vegetables are crisp (not soggy).
4. Vegetables may be served hot over brown rice or chilled and served as a salad.

NUTRITIONAL INFORMATION PER SERVING

Calories . . 32.4	Carbohydrate . . 7.6 g
Protein . . . 1.2 g	Fat . . . . 0.1 g
Sodium . . 3.1 mg	Cholesterol . . . . 0.0 mg

THOUSAND ISLAND DRESSING
Yields 1½ cups
Serving size: 2 tablespoons

1 cup low-fat cottage
cheese (1% milk fat)
⅓ cup ketchup
2 heaping tablespoons
chopped onion

1 tablespoon lemon
juice
½ cup sweet pickles,
chopped and rinsed
well

1. Combine all ingredients except pickles in a blender.
2. Blend until completely smooth.
3. Stir in pickles. Chill.

NUTRITIONAL INFORMATION PER SERVING

Calories .. 27.9   Carbohydrate ..4.0 g
Protein ... 2.5 g   Fat ....0.3 g
Sodium ..169.4 mg   Cholesterol ....0.1 mg

WALDORF SALAD DELUXE
Serves 4

SALAD

1 cup seedless green
grapes
½ cup celery, chopped
1 medium green apple
(Granny Smith), diced
¼ cup raisins

1 medium red sweet
apple, diced
1 banana, halved and
sliced
½ cup Grape Nuts cereal
Lettuce

SAUCE

1 cup plain low-fat
yogurt
2 tablespoons nonfat
dry milk powder

2 teaspoons orange juice
concentrate
½ cup unsweetened
crushed pineapple

1. Combine all fruit in a large bowl. Toss gently to mix.

2. Place all ingredients for the sauce in a blender or food processor. Blend until smooth.

3. Pour sauce over fruit. Gently toss. Chill for 1 hour or more.

4. Right before serving add Grape Nuts. Toss.

5. Serve in lettuce cups. Sprinkle with paprika.

NUTRITIONAL INFORMATION PER SERVING

Calories . . 293.5   Carbohydrate . . 66.3 g
Protein . . .   6.0 g   Fat . . . .   1.5 g
Sodium . . 178.8 mg   Cholesterol . . . . 5.0 mg

YOGURT TOMATO DRESSING
Yields 2½ cups
Serving size: 2 tablespoons

¾ cup plain low-fat
yogurt
¼ cup low-fat cottage
cheese (1% milk fat)
1 tablespoon lemon
juice
1 teaspoon onion powder
½ teaspoon dried dill
weed

2 tablespoons green
onions, chopped
1 teaspoon Tamari
soy sauce
1 packet Equal sugar
substitute
28-ounce can whole
tomatoes, rinsed and
chopped

1. Place all ingredients in blender or food processor.
2. Blend until smooth. Chill.
3 . Serve over garden fresh salad.

NUTRITIONAL INFORMATION PER SERVING

Calories .. 48.0	Carbohydrate ..7.8 g
Protein ... 3.1 g	Fat ....0.4 g
Sodium ..176.6 mg	Cholesterol ....1.7 mg

POTATO RECIPES AND TOPPINGS

BACON, ONION, AND CHIVE TOPPING
Yields 1 cup
Serving size: 2 tablespoons

½ cup plain low-fat yogurt
⅓ cup low-fat cottage cheese (1% milk fat)
1 tablespoon Parmesan cheese
½ teaspoon Tamari soy sauce

1 tablespoon green onions, chopped, including green portion
1 tablespoon imitation bacon chips
2 teaspoons dried chopped onion

1. Place first 4 ingredients in a food processor or blender. Mix until completely smooth.
2. Stir in the rest of the ingredients. Chill.
3. Serve as a topping for a baked potato or dip for fresh vegetables.

NUTRITIONAL INFORMATION PER SERVING

Calories .. 40.2   Carbohydrate ..2.9 g
Protein ... 5.0 g   Fat ....0.9 g
Sodium ..204.8 mg   Cholesterol ....2.5 mg

BARBECUE CHICKEN TOPPING
Serves 4 to 6

6-ounce can tomato
  paste
¼ cup onion, chopped
¼ cup wine vinegar
¼ cup Worcestershire
  sauce
1 teaspoon dry mustard
4 cloves garlic, minced
2 tablespoons Parmesan
  cheese

1 tablespoon granulated
  fructose
¼ cup skim milk
¼ cup dry sherry
1½ cups boned chicken,
  coarsely chopped
  (white meat only)

1. Combine all ingredients in a saucepan.
2. Simmer for 20 to 25 minutes. Stir occasionally.
3. Serve on top of baked potatoes.

NUTRITIONAL INFORMATION PER SERVING
Calories .. 96.0   Carbohydrate ..12.6 g
Protein ... 4.9 g   Fat .... 0.8 g
Sodium ..157.0 mg   Cholesterol ....11.9 mg

260

"CHEDDAR" STUFFED POTATOES
Serves 4

2 *medium potatoes,*
  baked
4 *tablespoons low-fat*
  cottage cheese (1%
  milk fat)
4 *tablespoons of Kraft's*
  Cheddar flavor Ameri-
  can cheese food,
  grated

4 *tablespoons plain*
  low-fat yogurt
1 *teaspoon dried dill*
  weed
4 *tablespoons green*
  onion, chopped,
  including green portion
Paprika

1. Preheat oven to 350°
2. Cut potatoes in half. Spoon out center of potatoes being careful not to break shells.
3. Blend yogurt, cottage cheese, American cheese and dill weed until smooth but not creamy using an electric mixer or fork. Add green onion.
4. Spoon mixture into potato shells. Sprinkle tops with paprika.
5. Place in oven for 15 to 20 minutes until heated through.

NUTRITIONAL INFORMATION PER SERVING

Calories .. 97.7	Carbohydrate ..12.8 g
Protein ... 5.3 g	Fat .... 2.7 g
Sodium ..120.4 mg	Cholesterol ....16.2 mg

CHICKEN IN WINE SAUCE TOPPING
Yields 2½ cups
Serving size: 2 tablespoons

½ cup low-fat cottage
cheese (1% milk fat)
½ cup plain low-fat
yogurt
2 teaspoons dry sherry
1 tablespoon plus 1
teaspoon Parmesan
cheese

1 teaspoon Tamari soy
sauce
½ cup mushrooms, sliced
½ cup chicken breast,
cooked and cubed
1 tablespoon green
onion, chopped

1. Combine first 5 ingredients in a food processor or blender. Blend until completely smooth.
2. Add mushrooms, chicken, and green onion.
3. Serve on top of baked potato. (May heat and serve over brown rice or pasta).

NUTRITIONAL INFORMATION PER SERVING

Calories .. 39.1	Carbohydrate ..2.7 g
Protein ... 4.6 g	Fat ....0.7 g
Sodium ..137.8 mg	Cholesterol ....8.2 mg

COTTAGE FRIES
Serves 1

2 medium potatoes, raw
Paprika
Black pepper

Garlic powder
3 teaspoons grated
Parmesan cheese

262

1. Slice potatoes into thin "chip" slices and lay on stick-free broiling pan or cookie sheet sprayed with Pam.

2. Sprinkle potatoes with paprika, pepper, and grated Parmesan cheese.

3. Preheat oven on broil. Broil potatoes about 8 minutes on one side and 3 to 5 minutes on the other.

4. Serve plain or with salt and sugar-free ketchup.

NUTRITIONAL INFORMATION PER SERVING

Calories . . 209.7   Carbohydrate . . 42.4 g
Protein . . .   6.1 g Fat . . . .   1.5 g
Sodium . . 101.3 mg Cholesterol . . . . 9.9 mg

HOT GERMAN POTATO SALAD
Serves 6

5 to 6 medium potatoes, peeled, boiled, and diced

3 tablespoons imitation bacon chips

½ cup onion, chopped

2 teaspoons granulated fructose

2 teaspoons Tamari soy sauce

1 teaspoon whole wheat flour

⅛ teaspoon pepper

9 tablespoons red wine vinegar

3 tablespoons Bunker Hill Italian Dressing

½ cup water

263

1. Cook onion in large stick-free frying pan in the Bunker Hill Italian Dressing. Cook on medium heat until onions are clear.

2. Stir in fructose, flour, and pepper. Slowly add Tamari soy sauce, 6 tablespoons of the vinegar and water. Bring to a boil and stir until sauce thickens. Add bacon chips. Toss gently.

3. Add potatoes. Toss potatoes gently to coat with sauce. Make sure potatoes are coated with sauce. Remove from heat and add rest of wine vinegar. Toss. Serve immediately.

NUTRITIONAL INFORMATION PER SERVING

Calories . . 115.0   Carbohydrate . . 25.5 g
Protein . . .   2.8 g   Fat . . . . 0.3 g
Sodium . . 282.0 mg   Cholesterol . . . . 0.0 mg

HORSERADISH TOPPING
Yields 1 cup
Serving size: 2 tablespoons

¾ cup low-fat cottage cheese (1% milk fat)

1 tablespoon uncreamed horseradish sauce

¼ cup plain low-fat yogurt

1 teaspoon Worcestershire sauce

1 tablespoon dried chives

1. Combine first 4 ingredients in food processor or blender. Blend until completely smooth.

2. Add chives. Cool.
3. Serve over baked potato or as a raw vegetable dip.

NUTRITIONAL INFORMATION PER SERVING

Calories . .21.5   Carbohydrate . .1.5 g
Protein . . . 3.1 g   Fat . . . . .0.3 g
Sodium . .99.9 mg   Cholesterol . . . .0.7 mg

MARINATED POTATO SALAD
Serves 6

7 to 8 new potatoes cut up and boiled until tender
1 cup cooked cauliflower
1 cup cooked green peas

¾ cup Herb Magic Italian Dressing
1 teaspoon prepared uncreamed horseradish

1. Mix dressing and horseradish. Pour over vegetables.
2. Chill.

NUTRITIONAL INFORMATION PER SERVING

Calories . .107.4   Carbohydrate . .23.1 g
Protein . . .   3.3 g Fat . . . . 0.0 g
Sodium . .1407.3 mg Cholesterol . . . . 0.0 mg

MUSHROOM TOPPING
Yields 1 cup
Serving size: 1 cup

¾ cup low-fat cottage
cheese (1% milk fat)
¼ cup plain low-fat
yogurt
½ teaspoon garlic
powder

½ teaspoon Tamari
soy sauce
1 cup fresh mush-
rooms sliced

1. Combine first 4 ingredients in food processor or blender. Blend until completely smooth.
2. Add mushrooms. Chill. Serve over baked
potato.

NUTRITIONAL INFORMATION PER SERVING

Calories .. 214.9   Carbohydrate ..16.7 g
Protein ...   27.7 g   Fat .... 3.2 g
Sodium ..1300.4 mg Cholesterol .... 5.2 mg

POTATO CASSEROLE
Serves 4

3 large potatoes, peeled,
cubed, and boiled
¾ cup low-fat cottage
cheese (1% milk fat)
2 green onions, chopped
including green
portion
1 small onion, finely
diced

½ teaspoon dried dill
weed
¾ cup plain low-fat
yogurt
3 cloves garlic, minced
4 dashes hot sauce

266

1. Preheat oven to 350°.
2. Combine all ingredients except potatoes. Blend well.
3. Add potatoes. Spray 1½ quart casserole dish with Pam. Pour potato mixture into casserole dish.
4. Bake 30 to 35 minutes covered.

NUTRITIONAL INFORMATION PER SERVING

Calories . . 154.0	Carbohydrate . . 26.1 g
Protein . . . 9.8 g	Fat . . . . 1.2 g
Sodium . . 208.7 mg	Cholesterol . . . . 3.6 mg

SNAPPY CHEDDAR TOPPING
Yields 1 cup
Serving size: 2 tablespoons

¾ cup low-fat cottage cheese (1% milk fat)
¼ teaspoon Tamari soy sauce

¼ cup plus 1 tablespoon Kraft's sharp Cheddar flavor American cheese food, grated

1. Place all ingredients in blender or food processor.
2. Blend until completely smooth.
3. Chill. Serve over baked potato or as a raw vegetable dip.

NUTRITIONAL INFORMATION PER SERVING

Calories . . 33.1	Carbohydrate . . 0.7 g
Protein . . . 3.7 g	Fat . . . . 1.6 g
Sodium . . 121.8 mg	Cholesterol . . . . 9.4 mg

SAUCES AND SPREADS

APPLE BUTTER
Yields 10 cups
Serving size: 2 tablespoons

8 cups Rome apples,   1 teaspoon cinnamon
  peeled and diced
5 cups unsweetened
  apple cider

1. Cook apples in apple cider until soft.

2. When cooked put the apples through a sieve or a food processor to purée.

3. Return apple purée to saucepan and cook on medium heat until it is thick enough to spread.

4. Add cinnamon. Chill.

NUTRITIONAL INFORMATION PER SERVING

Calories . . 25.0   Carbohydrate . . 6.2 g
Protein . . . 0.1 g   Fat . . . . 0.2 g
Sodium . . 0.7 mg   Cholesterol . . . . 0.0 mg

DILL SAUCE DELUXE
Yields 1 cup
Serving size: 2 tablespoons

¾ cup low-fat cottage
 cheese (1% milk fat)
¼ cup plain low-fat
 yogurt
1 tablespoon lemon
 juice
2 teaspoons Grey Poupon
 mustard

1 teaspoon onion powder
2 teaspoons dried
 parsley flakes
4 teaspoons dried dill
 weed
1 tablespoon Parmesan
 cheese

1. Mix all ingredients in a blender or food processor until smooth.
2. Chill. Serve over fish.

NUTRITIONAL INFORMATION PER SERVING

Calories .. 27.9
Protein ... 3.5 g
Sodium ..121.5 mg

Carbohydrate ..2.0 g
Fat ....0.5 g
Cholesterol ....1.9 mg

HAAS MAYONNAISE SPREAD
Yields ¾ cup
Serving size: 2 tablespoons

1 cup low-fat cottage
 cheese (1% milk fat)
2 teaspoons lemon juice
½ teaspoon Tamari
 soy sauce

1 teaspoon prepared
 mustard

269

1. Combine all ingredients in a food processor or blender. Mix until completely smooth.
2. Chill.

NUTRITIONAL INFORMATION PER SERVING

Calories .. 28.4	Carbohydrate ..1.2 g
Protein ... 4.7 g	Fat ....0.4 g
Sodium ..176.0 mg	Cholesterol ....0.2 mg

HAAS PEANUT BUTTER
Yields ½ cup
Serving size: 1 tablespoon

1 medium ripe banana   **6 tablespoons toasted wheat germ**

1. Place ingredients in food processor or blender.
2. Mix until smooth.
3. Spread on whole wheat bread.

NUTRITIONAL INFORMATION PER SERVING

Calories ..90.3	Carbohydrate ..13.4 g
Protein ... 5.5 g	Fat .... 2.4 g
Sodium .. 0.9 mg	Cholesterol .... 0.0 mg

ENTRÉES

BASIC BROWN RICE AND CHICKEN
Serves 1

1 cup cooked brown rice
*2 ounces breast of
  chicken, cooked*
*1 teaspoon Tamari
  soy sauce*

*1 tablespoon Parmesan
  cheese*
*1 teaspoon lemon
  juice*
Water

1. Spray a stick-free pan with Pam. Place lemon juice, Tamari soy sauce, brown rice and chicken in pan. Cook on medium heat.

2. Cook quickly stirring constantly. You may need to add a little water if it becomes dry in the pan while cooking. Sprinkle with Parmesan cheese. Toss gently to cover rice and chicken. Serve immediately. (Use any fresh vegetables while cooking if desired, e.g., celery, mushrooms, carrots, onions.)

NUTRITIONAL INFORMATION PER SERVING

Calories . . 264.2	Carbohydrate . . 38.8 g
Protein . . . 18.8 g	Fat . . . . 1.8 g
Sodium . . 610.3 mg	Cholesterol . . . . 59.9 mg

BROCCOLI BROWN RICE HOLLANDAISE
Serves 6

3 cups broccoli flower-
ettes, cooked and
chopped
6 egg whites beaten
until stiff
1 cup skim milk
2 cups cooked brown
rice

6 tablespoons Parme-
san cheese, grated
5 dashes hot sauce
½ teaspoon crushed
coriander seed
1 teaspoon thyme
1 tablespoon lemon
juice

1. Preheat oven to 350°.
2. Add milk to beaten egg whites.
3. Gradually add 5 tablespoons Parmesan cheese, hot sauce, coriander seed, thyme, and lemon juice. Beat until smooth.
4. Add broccoli and brown rice.
5. Spray a 2-quart casserole dish with Pam. Pour mixture into dish. Sprinkle with 1 tablespoon of Parmesan cheese.
6. Bake 35 to 40 minutes or until golden brown on top.
7. Cool 10 minutes before serving.

NUTRITIONAL INFORMATION PER SERVING

Calories . . 142.9   Carbohydrate . . 19.4 g
Protein . . . 10.9 g   Fat . . . . 1.6 g
Sodium . . 280.6 mg   Cholesterol . . . . 10.9 mg

BROWN RICE AND COTTAGE CHEESE
Serves 6

3 cups cooked brown
  rice
¼ cup scallions, chopped
1½ cups low-fat cot-
  tage cheese (1% milk
  fat)
1 cup plain low-fat
  yogurt

¼ cup evaporated skim
  milk
Dash of Tabasco
1 teaspoon Tamari
  soy sauce
⅓ cup Parmesan cheese
1 to 2 cloves garlic,
  minced

1. Preheat oven to 350°.
2. Combine all ingredients. Mix well.
3. Spray a 1½-quart casserole dish with Pam.
4. Pour mixture into casserole dish.
5. Bake 25 to 30 minutes.

NUTRITIONAL INFORMATION PER SERVING

Calories . . 198.7	Carbohydrate . . 28.3 g
Protein . . . 13.6 g	Fat . . . . 2.6 g
Sodium . . 538.5 mg	Cholesterol . . . . 12.3 mg

CANNELLINI-STUFFED ZUCCHINI
Serves 6 to 8

2 20-ounce cans can-
nellini, drained and
rinsed

1 teaspoon Tamari
soy sauce

5 tablespoons red
wine vinegar

1½ cups cooked brown
rice

4 green onions, chopped

1 tablespoon parsley,
chopped

2 cloves of garlic,
minced

¼ teaspoon pepper

4 medium zucchini
(about 5" to 6")

¾ cup whole wheat
bread crumbs

½ teaspoon garlic
powder

6 tablespoons Parme-
san cheese

½ teaspoon basil

1 teaspoon oregano

Dash of thyme

Dash of marjoram

Paprika

1. Preheat oven to 350°.

2. Mash 1 can of rinsed beans. Add 2 tablespoons water and the Tamari.

3. Place zucchini in boiling water for 5 minutes.

4. Halve zucchini lengthwise and scoop out
centers leaving about ¼" around sides. Chop
center of zucchini.

5. Add zucchini pulp to mashed beans. Add
remaining beans and rest of ingredients, except
bread crumbs, garlic, and paprika.

6. Mix well. Fill zucchini shells with bean
mixture.

7. Mix garlic powder and bread crumbs. Sprinkle top of each zucchini with mixture. Sprinkle
with paprika.

8. Place in a 9"- × -13" baking dish lined with aluminum foil.

9. Bake 30 to 35 minutes or until golden brown on top.

NUTRITIONAL INFORMATION PER SERVING

Calories . . 600.0	Carbohydrate . . 105.8 g
Protein . . . 34.0 g	Fat . . . . 1.3 g
Sodium . . 232.2 mg	Cholesterol . . . . 7.4 mg

CHICKEN CASSEROLE
Serves 4

6 ounces "No Yolk" thin noodles, cooked according to package directions

1 cup chicken breast, cooked and cubed

2 tablespoons dry cooking sherry

1 cup plain low-fat yogurt

½ cup low-fat cottage cheese (1% milk fat)

4 tablespoons Parmesan cheese

⅓ cup ketchup

Pinch of pepper

Pinch of nutmeg

¼ cup whole wheat bread crumbs

1. Preheat oven to 350°.

2. Combine sherry, yogurt, cottage cheese, Parmesan cheese, ketchup, pepper, and nutmeg in a blender or food processor. Blend until smooth.

3. Mix noodles, chicken, and sauce in a large

bowl. Pour into a 1½-quart casserole dish sprayed with Pam. Top with whole wheat bread crumbs.

4. Bake 25 to 30 minutes.

NUTRITIONAL INFORMATION PER SERVING

Calories . . 212.1	Carbohydrate . . 23.3 g
Protein . . . 17.0 g	Fat . . . . 3.5 g
Sodium . . 509.0 mg	Cholesterol . . . . 36.4 mg

CHICKEN CURRY
Serves 4

8 ounces chicken breast, cubed
Pepper
¼ teaspoon cinnamon
1 tablespoon Tamari soy sauce
¾ cup onion, finely chopped
½ cup celery, chopped
1 teaspoon garlic, minced
1½ tablespoons curry powder

1 bay leaf
1½ cups apples, cubed
⅔ cup banana, finely diced
2 teaspoons tomato paste
1¾ cups chicken broth, defatted
½ cup evaporated skim milk
½ cup raisins
4 cups cooked brown rice

1. Sprinkle chicken cubes with pepper.

2. Place ¼ cup chicken broth and Tamari in a large saucepan. Add chicken and brown.

3. Add onion, celery, and garlic. Cook briefly.

276

Sprinkle with curry powder. Add rest of ingredients except apples and evaporated skim milk.

4. Cover and cook 10 minutes. Add apples and cook 5 more minutes.

5. Add evaporated skim milk. Heat through.

6. Serve over beds of brown rice.

NUTRITIONAL INFORMATION PER SERVING

Calories .. 434.2   Carbohydrate ..83.0 g
Protein ... 22.7 g   Fat .... 1.3 g
Sodium ..1008.2 mg Cholesterol ....51.7 mg

CHIK 'N' CHILI
Serves 6

6-ounce can tomato
   paste
1/4 cup onion, chopped
1/4 cup wine vinegar
1/4 cup Worcestershire
   sauce
1 teaspoon dry mustard
4 cloves garlic, minced
2 tablespoons Parmesan
   cheese

2 tablespoons granu-
   lated fructose
1/2 cup skim milk
1/2 cup breast of
   chicken, cooked and
   cubed
1 cup corn
16-ounce can Heinz
   Vegetarian Beans,
   rinsed

1. Combine all ingredients in large saucepan.
2. Simmer 30 minutes.

NUTRITIONAL INFORMATION PER SERVING

Calories ..179.1   Carbohydrate ..32.7 g
Protein ... 9.2 g   Fat .... 1.9 g
Sodium ..503.3 mg Cholesterol ....11.1 mg

CHILI PIE
Yields 8-slice pie
Serving size: 1 slice

FILLING

2 15-ounce cans kidney
beans, rinsed
1 large onion, coarsely
chopped
1 large green pepper,
coarsely chopped
6-ounce can tomato
paste
¼ cup water

½ cup red wine
vinegar
2 teaspoons Mexican
chili powder
1 tablespoon Tamari
soy sauce
1 cup corn (rinse well
if canned)

1. Sauté onions and green pepper in small amount of water.

2. Add tomato paste, seasonings, beans, corn, and water as needed. Heat through.

CRUST

¾ cup cornmeal
¼ cup whole wheat flour
2 teaspoons baking
powder

½ cup skim milk
1 large egg white

1. Let milk and egg white sit until room temperature and then mix together.

2. Preheat oven to 375°.

3. Combine egg white and milk with dry ingredients. Form a ball with dough. Spray a 10" pie plate with Pam. Place dough in middle of

dish and flatten with fingers. Form to the shape of pie plate.

4. Add filling. Bake for 35 to 45 minutes or until crust is golden brown.

NUTRITIONAL INFORMATION PER SERVING

Calories . . 259.8	Carbohydrate . . 50.6 g
Protein . . . 13.8 g	Fat . . . . 1.3 g
Sodium . . 361.2 mg	Cholesterol . . . . 0.4 mg

COQ AU VIN CASSEROLE
Serves 6

6-ounce package "No Yolk" thin noodles, cooked according to package directions
1 cup breast of chicken, cooked and cubed
½ cup pearl onions
½ cup fresh mushrooms, sliced
¾ cup low-fat cottage cheese (1% milk fat)
1 cup plain low-fat yogurt

1 cup dry cooking sherry
1 teaspoon Tamari soy sauce
¼ teaspoon garlic powder
1 tablespoon dried chopped onion
Pinch of pepper
Pinch of curry powder

1. Preheat oven to 350°.

2. Combine cottage cheese, low-fat yogurt, sherry, soy sauce, garlic powder, dried onion,

pepper, and curry powder in a blender or food processor. Blend until completely smooth.

3. Toss noodles, pearl onion, mushrooms, and chicken gently. Pour sauce over mixture and toss gently.

4. Spray a 2-quart casserole dish with Pam. Pour mixture into dish.

5. Bake for 30 to 35 minutes.

NUTRITIONAL INFORMATION PER SERVING

Calories . . 253.8   Carbohydrate . . 20.4 g
Protein . . . 16.8 g   Fat . . . . 1.7 g
Sodium . . 248.9 mg   Cholesterol . . . . 36.5 mg

CORN AND CHICKEN FRITTATA
Serves 6

½ *pound chicken breast, skinned, cooked and finely diced*
1½ *cups corn*
10 *egg whites, beaten*
1 *tablespoon parsley flakes*
½ *teaspoon Tamari soy sauce*

½ *teaspoon celery seed*
3 *tablespoons Parmesan cheese*
⅓ *cup evaporated skim milk*
Pinch of white pepper

1. Combine all ingredients in a large bowl.

2. Spray a nonstick frying pan with Pam.

3. Pour mixture into pan. Cook on medium heat tossing lightly until egg has set.

NUTRITIONAL INFORMATION PER SERVING

Calories . . 126.2	Carbohydrate . . 10.8 g
Protein . . . 18.0 g	Fat . . . . 1.3 g
Sodium . . 282.1 mg	Cholesterol . . . . 38.4 mg

CRABMEAT AU GRATIN
Serves 4

12 ounces crabmeat,
cooked

4 cups cooked brown
rice

1 cup Parmesan cheese

1 cup plain low-fat
yogurt

1 cup low-fat cottage
cheese (1% milk fat)

4 tablespoons dry
cooking sherry

¼ teaspoon curry
powder

Dash of nutmeg

1. Preheat oven to 350°.

2. Combine all the ingredients except brown rice and crabmeat in a blender or food processor. Blend until completely smooth.

3. Place brown rice in equal portions in four casserole dishes. Arrange crabmeat on top of rice (in equal portions). Pour sauce on top of crabmeat and brown rice.

4. Place in oven for 15 to 20 minutes or until bubbly.

NUTRITIONAL INFORMATION PER SERVING

Calories . . 448.8	Carbohydrate . . 46.0 g
Protein . . . 36.3 g	Fat . . . . 9.2 g
Sodium . . 1836.3 mg	Cholesterol . . . . 160.6 mg

EGGPLANT MOUSSAKA
Serves 4

FILLING

1 pound eggplant,
washed, peeled, and
cubed
¾ cup onion, chopped
3 tablespoons tomato
paste
½ cup dry white wine
1 teaspoon Tamari soy
sauce
¼ teaspoon cinnamon

¼ teaspoon allspice
½ teaspoon oregano
½ pound elbow maca-
roni, cooked according
to package directions
6-ounce container low-
fat cottage cheese
2 cups cheese sauce
(recipe below)

1. Steam eggplant until tender.

2. Combined tomato paste, wine, Tamari soy sauce, cinnamon, allspice, and oregano in a saucepan. Bring to a boil. Add eggplant. Lower heat and simmer 15 minutes.

3. Prepare cheese sauce.

CHEESE SAUCE

5 tablespoons whole
wheat flour
2 cups evaporated skim
milk

3 egg whites
8 tablespoons Parme-
san cheese

1. Combine flour and milk in a saucepan. Heat on medium flame stirring constantly with a whisk. Gradually add 4 tablespoons of the Parmesan cheese. Heat until thick and bubbly.

2. Remove 1 cup of mixture. Set aside.

3. Keep mixture on medium heat and whisk in egg whites. Add remaining half of cheese stirring with whisk until blended and smooth. Add macaroni.

4. Preheat oven to 350°. Spray a 9"-×-9" baking dish with Pam. Place half the macaroni mixture in the bottom of baking dish. Place eggplant mixture on top of this, then the cottage cheese. Add remaining macaroni mixture. Pour the cheese sauce that was set aside over the top. Bake for 1 hour and 20 minutes or until golden brown.

NUTRITIONAL INFORMATION PER SERVING

Calories . . 385.5	Carbohydrate . . 53.6 g
Protein . . . 27.9 g	Fat . . . . 4.3 g
Sodium . . 592.0 mg	Cholesterol . . . . 20.9 mg

FISH AND MUSHROOM MARINADE
Serves 4

1 pound swordfish (or any mild tasting white fish fillets)
1 tablespoon Tamari soy sauce
¾ cup dry cooking sherry

1 teaspoon garlic powder
1 cup mushrooms, rinsed well and sliced

1. Combine sherry, Tamari, and garlic powder. Add mushrooms.

2. Place fillets in a shallow dish. Pour marinade over the fish. Place in refrigerator for several hours turning fillets and spooning marinade over them 3 or 4 times.

3. Set oven on broil. Remove fish and mushrooms from dish. Place on broiling pan about 5 inches from broiler. Broil approximately 8 minutes on one side. Turn and broil 5 minutes on other side. (Broiling time varies according to the thickness of the fillets.)

4. Serve with brown rice and steamed vegetables.

NUTRITIONAL INFORMATION PER SERVING

Calories . . 241.3   Carbohydrate . . 4.4 g
Protein . . . 30.6 g   Fat . . . . 6.4 g
Sodium . . 311.2 mg Cholesterol . . . . 52.5 mg

GLAZED RATATOUILLE
Serves 6 to 8

2 medium zucchini,
   sliced
2 medium eggplant,
   peeled and sliced
1 small onion, thinly
   sliced
2 cups cooked brown
   rice
2 large tomatoes,
   thinly sliced
1 tablespoon Tamari
   soy sauce

1 teaspoon rice syrup
   or liquid fructose
1 teaspoon dried dill
   weed
½ cup boiling water
1 cup plain low-fat
   yogurt
2 egg whites
6 tablespoons Parmesan cheese
1 teaspoon arrowroot
   powder

284

1. Steam zucchini and eggplant until just tender.

2. Combine boiling water with rice syrup or fructose, Tamari soy sauce, and dill weed. Stir until rice syrup or fructose dissolves.

3. Preheat oven to 350°.

4. Add yogurt, egg whites, Parmesan cheese, and arrowroot powder to water mixture. Blend well.

5. Arrange in a 9"-square baking dish sprayed with Pam half of the following ingredients in layers: eggplant, zucchini, tomatoes, onions, and rice.

6. Pour half of the yogurt mixture over the first layer.

7. Repeat the same procedure.

8. Bake 45 to 50 minutes or until glaze sets.

NUTRITIONAL INFORMATION PER SERVING

Calories	158.6	Carbohydrate	26.7 g
Protein	9.2 g	Fat	3.1 g
Sodium	309.8 mg	Cholesterol	17.1 mg

IMAM BAYELDI
Serves 4

2 medium eggplants
(about ½ pound)
¼ cup dry cooking
sherry
2 teaspoons ground
coriander
¼ teaspoon cinnamon
Dash of allspice
6-ounce can tomato
paste

½ cup onion, chopped
½ cup tomato, skinned
and chopped
3 tablespoons seedless
golden raisins
1 clove garlic, minced
2 tablespoons Parmesan
cheese

1. Preheat oven to 375°.
2. Halve eggplants and scoop out centers. Leave ¼" border.
3. Chop eggplant centers. Steam until tender.
4. Combine rest of ingredients. Cook on medium heat about 10 minutes. Add eggplant. Mix well.
5. Place mixture in eggplant shells. Bake 40 to 45 minutes.

NUTRITIONAL INFORMATION PER SERVING
Calories . . 120.8   Carbohydrate . . 23.5 g
Protein . . . 5.2 g   Fat . . . . 1.6 g
Sodium . . 69.5 mg Cholesterol . . . . 4.9 mg

INDIAN VEGETABLE AND RICE CASSEROLE
Serves 4

2 cups cooked brown rice

10-ounce package frozen peas, cooked and drained

1½ cups plain low-fat yogurt

1 cup celery, diced

¼ cup onion, chopped

1 teaspoon curry powder

2 teaspoons Tamari soy sauce

½ teaspoon dry mustard

2 tablespoons Parmesan cheese

1 egg white slightly beaten

1. Preheat oven to 350°.
2. Combine all ingredients. Mix well.
3. Spray a 1½ quart casserole dish with Pam. Pour rice mixture into casserole dish.
4. Bake 25 to 30 minutes.

NUTRITIONAL INFORMATION PER SERVING

Calories . . 195.6   Carbohydrate . . 31.9 g
Protein . . .   9.8 g   Fat . . . . 2.1 g
Sodium . . 377.7 mg   Cholesterol . . . . 11.7 mg

ITALIAN MACARONI AND BEANS
Serves 4 to 6

16-ounce can Heinz
  Vegetarian Beans,
  rinsed
½ cup onions, chopped
1 medium zucchini,
  thinly sliced and
  quartered
¾ cup Health Valley
  tomato sauce
¾ cup water

1 teaspoon Tamari soy
  sauce
½ teaspoon oregano
1 clove garlic, minced
2 to 3 dashes hot sauce
1½ cups macaroni,
  cooked according to
  package directions
4 tablespoons Parmesan
  cheese

1. Preheat oven to 350°.
2. Steam zucchini until just tender.
3. Combine rest of ingredients except 2 table-spoons of Parmesan cheese. Add zucchini.
4. Spray a 2-quart casserole dish with Pam. Pour macaroni and bean mixture into dish. Sprinkle top with 2 tablespoons Parmesan cheese.
5. Bake 30 minutes.

NUTRITIONAL INFORMATION PER SERVING

Calories . . 155.2	Carbohydrate . . 27.0 g
Protein . . . 7.4 g	Fat . . . . 2.3 g
Sodium . . 518.9 mg	Cholesterol . . . . 6.6 mg

ITALIAN STUFFED PEPPERS
Serves 4

⅓ cup Herb Magic Italian
Dressing
4 medium green peppers
1 quart water
1½ cups cooked brown
rice
16-ounce can tomato
sauce (no salt or
sugar added)
1 teaspoon Tamari
soy sauce

½ teaspoon basil
1 clove garlic, minced
⅓ cup onion, chopped
2 15-ounce cans dark red
kidney beans, rinsed
and drained
1 tablespoon parsley,
chopped
4 tablespoons Parmesan
cheese

1. Cut ½" off tops of peppers. Remove seeds
and membranes.

2. Bring water to a boil in a large pot. Add
peppers and boil 3 minutes. Drain upside down
on paper towels.

3. Preheat oven to 350°.

4. Combine rest of ingredients.

4. Place peppers in 8"-square baking dish. Stuff
with rice mixture.

6. Bake 40 minutes.

NUTRITIONAL INFORMATION PER SERVING

Calories .. 445.7   Carbohydrate ..81.5 g
Protein ... 24.8 g   Fat .... 3.0 g
Sodium ..1335.7 mg Cholesterol .... 9.9 mg

ITALIAN VEGETABLE BAKE
Serves 4

1 *medium zucchini,*
   thinly sliced
1 *medium onion, thinly*
   sliced
2 *medium tomatoes,*
   thinly sliced
15-*ounce can tomato*
   sauce

1 *teaspoon basil*
1 *teaspoon oregano*
2 *cloves garlic, minced*
2 *tablespoons Parmesan*
   cheese

1. Preheat oven to 350°.
2. Combine tomato sauce, basil, oregano, and garlic.
3. Spray an 8"- × -8" baking dish with Pam.
4. Arrange vegetables in layers in baking dish as follows: zucchini, onion, tomato, tomato sauce, 1 tablespoon Parmesan cheese. Repeat twice more.
5. Bake 30 to 35 minutes covered. Let cool a few minutes before serving.

NUTRITIONAL INFORMATION PER SERVING

Calories .. 98.1   Carbohydrate ..16.7 g
Protein ... 5.5 g   Fat .... 2.0 g
Sodium ..729.4 mg   Cholesterol .... 9.9 mg

ITALIAN WHITE BEANS
Serves 4

16-ounce can cannellini
(white kidney beans),
rinsed

2 cups tomatoes,
peeled, seeded, chopped

1 tablespoon red wine
vinegar

1 tablespoon garlic,
minced

½ teaspoon sage

Pinch of pepper

½ teaspoon sweet basil

½ teaspoon oregano

1 teaspoon fructose or
rice syrup

2 teaspoons Tamari soy
sauce

6-ounce can tomato
paste

8-ounce package spa-
ghetti, cooked acording
to package directions

1. Combine all ingredients except cannellini
and spaghetti in a saucepan. Mix well. Simmer
for 30 minutes.

2. Add beans. Simmer 10 more minutes.

3. Spoon over spaghetti. Serve immediately.

NUTRITIONAL INFORMATION PER SERVING

Calories . . 414.0   Carbohydrate . . 84.0 g
Protein . . . 15.9 g   Fat . . . . 1.6 g
Sodium . . 228.3 mg   Cholesterol . . . . 0.0 mg

MACARONI AND CHEESE LOMBARDO
Serves 6 to 8

1 cup chicken, cubed and cooked

8 ounces whole wheat pasta shells, macaroni or rigatoni

2 cups low-fat cottage cheese (1% milk fat)

¼ teaspoon dry mustard

⅔ cup Kraft's sharp Cheddar flavor American cheese food, grated

⅓ cup evaporated skim milk

¾ cup whole wheat bread crumbs

1 tablespoon Parmesan cheese

⅛ teaspoon pepper

1. Preheat oven to 350°.
2. Spray a 2-quart casserole dish with Pam.
3. Purée cottage cheese. Slowly add cheese food and dry mustard. Blend in food processor or blender until completely smooth. Set aside.
4. Cook pasta according to package directions. Drain. Toss with chicken and cheese purée. Add evaporated skim milk. Pour into casserole dish.
5. Mix Parmesan cheese with bread crumbs. Sprinkle on top of casserole.
6. Bake 20 to 25 minutes or until hot and bubbly.

NUTRITIONAL INFORMATION PER SERVING

Calories . .279.1	Carbohydrate . .30.3 g
Protein . . . 23.2 g	Fat . . . . 6.2 g
Sodium . .474.3 mg	Cholesterol . . . .57.8 mg

MARINARA SAUCE
Serves 4

28-ounce can of Progresso
  crushed tomatoes
4 cloves garlic, minced
1 tablespoon fresh
  basil

1 tablespoon Tamari
  soy sauce
Parsley

1. Spray a nonstick pan with Pam.
2. Place a small amount of water in frying pan. Sauté garlic.
3. Add crushed tomatoes. Cook for 1 minute.
4. Add basil and Tamari. Add parsley to taste.
5. Heat through. Serve over pasta.

NUTRITIONAL INFORMATION PER SERVING

Calories .. 50.6	Carbohydrate .. 9.7 g
Protein ... 2.5 g	Fat .... 0.0 g
Sodium .. 369.2 mg	Cholesterol .... 0.0 mg

MELANZANE AL FORNO
(BAKED EGGPLANT)
Serves 4 to 6

2½ pounds firm egg-
  plant (small ones if
  possible)
3 cloves garlic, minced
2 cups tomatoes, finely
  chopped
6-ounce can tomato
  paste

¼ cup Parmesan cheese
½ cup whole wheat
  bread crumbs
2 egg whites well beaten
3 tablespoons fresh
  parsley
1 teaspoon basil
Freshly ground pepper

293

1. Wash eggplant and cut in half lengthwise.

2. Cut out all of the inside, leaving a thin layer of eggplant inside the skin.

3. Put shells aside. Chop up eggplant.

4. Place a small amount of water in a saucepan. Add garlic and eggplant. Cood on medium heat until eggplant changes color.

5. Add tomatoes, parsley, basil, and pepper. Simmer on medium heat for 10 minutes.

6. Add cheese, tomato paste, and bread crumbs. The mixture should be moist and thick, not runny.

7. Add more bread crumbs if needed. Stir in egg whites.

8. Spoon mixture in eggplant shells. Preheat oven to 350°. Bake for 30 to 35 minutes.

NUTRITIONAL INFORMATION PER SERVING

Calories . . 103.3		Carbohydrate . . 20.7 g	
Protein . . . 7.0 g		Fat . . . . 1.6 g	
Sodium . . 195.1 mg		Cholesterol . . . . 6.6 mg	

PASTA AND GARLIC SAUCE
Serves 4

2 cups low-fat cottage cheese

4 tablespoons evaporated skim milk

¼ teaspoon white pepper

2 teaspoons dried parsley

6 to 8 cloves garlic, minced

2 teaspoons Tamari soy sauce

8-ounce package of thin spaghetti, cooked according to package directions

1. Place first 6 ingredients in a blender or food processor. Mix until completely smooth.

2. Place in a double boiler on medium heat. Heat until bubbly around edges. Pour over spaghetti and toss gently.

3. Sprinkle with Parmesan cheese (optional). Serve immediately.

NUTRITIONAL INFORMATION PER SERVING

Calories . . 346.7	Carbohydrate . . 56.7 g
Protein . . . 22.3 g	Fat . . . . 2.0 g
Sodium . . 554.4 mg	Cholesterol . . . . 0.6 mg

RANCHERO CHILI
Serves 4 to 6

8 ounces dry pinto beans
2 medium onions, chopped
2 cloves of garlic, minced
4-ounce can whole green chilies, drained and cut into bite-size pieces
1 or 2 jalapeno chilies, diced
1 teaspoon cumin
28-ounce can tomatoes with liquid
½ teaspoon oregano

1. Soak beans overnight. Cook until tender (about 1 hour).

2. Cook onions and garlic in water until tender.

3. Add rest of ingredients and bring to a boil. Add beans.

4. Simmer 1 hour or until sauce reduces.

NUTRITIONAL INFORMATION PER SERVING

Calories . . 189.6	Carbohydrate . . 34.3 g
Protein . . . 10.4 g	Fat . . . . 0.7 g
Sodium . . 166.2 mg	Cholesterol . . . . 0.0 mg

SPINACH CHEESE PIE
Serves 6

10-ounce package frozen chopped spinach, defrosted and drained
1 cup onion, chopped
2½ cups low-fat cottage cheese (1% milk fat)
6 tablespoons Parmesan cheese

1½ teaspoons dried dill weed
⅛ teaspoon pepper
7 egg whites
1 teaspoon Tamari soy sauce
Pinch of nutmeg

1. Preheat oven to 350°. Spray 9″ deep-dish pie plate with Pam.

2. Mix onion and spinach. Place in large bowl.

3. Combine cottage cheese, Parmesan cheese, Tamari soy sauce, dill weed, pepper, nutmeg, and 2 egg whites in a blender or food processor. Blend until completely smooth. Pour over onions and spinach. Mix well.

4. Beat rest of egg whites until stiff. Fold into spinach mixture. Pour into pie plate.

5. Bake 40 to 45 minutes or until lightly browned on top.

NUTRITIONAL INFORMATION PER SERVING

Calories . . 129.6   Carbohydrate . . 6.8 g
Protein . . . 19.4 g   Fat . . . . 2.6 g
Sodium . . 575.0 mg   Cholesterol . . . . 10.2 mg

SPINACH NOODLE CASSEROLE
Serves 4 to 6

1 medium onion, chopped
2 tablespoons Butter
   Buds
¾ cup mushrooms,
   sliced (rinsed well if
   canned)
8-ounce package eggless
   spinach noodles,
   cooked and drained
2 cups low-fat cottage
   cheese (1% milk fat)

½ cup skim milk
½ teaspoon basil
½ teaspoon Tamari
   soy sauce
¼ teaspoon thyme
1 to 2 cloves garlic,
   minced
4 tablespoons Parmesan
   cheese

1. Preheat oven to 350°.

2. Combine all ingredients except noodles in a large bowl. Mix well. Toss with noodles.

3. Spray a 2-quart casserole dish with Pam. Turn mixture into casserole.

4. Bake 30 minutes.

NUTRITIONAL INFORMATION PER SERVING

Calories . . 128.9   Carbohydrate . . 12.4 g
Protein . . . 14.2 g   Fat . . . . 2.0 g
Sodium . . 706.7 mg   Cholesterol . . . . 7.4 mg

STUFFED CABBAGE
Serves 6 to 8

3 cups cooked brown
  rice
1 medium head green
  cabbage
Water
6 tablespoons Parme-
  san cheese
2 15-ounce cans to-
  mato sauce

Tamari soy sauce
Rice syrup or granulated
  fructose
Pepper
½ teaspoon basil
⅛ teaspoon fennel seed
1 small eggplant, cubed
1 medium zucchini, cubed

1. Discard tough green leaves from cabbage and core.

2. Fill an 8-quart Dutch oven ¾ full with water. Bring water to boil. Place cabbage in water cut side up. Gently separate outer leaves as they soften. Remove 12 large leaves. Set aside and drain. Coarsely shred rest of cabbage.

3. Combine brown rice, 1 cup of tomato sauce, 2 teaspoons Tamari, 2 teaspoons rice syrup or 1 teaspoon fructose, and ¼ teaspoon pepper.

4. Place approximately ⅓ cup rice mixture in the middle of each of the cabbage leaves. Roll up two sides of leaves and set aside seam side down.

5. Combine shredded cabbage, 1½ cups water, basil, 4 teaspoons rice syrup or granulated fructose, 1 teaspoon Tamari soy sauce, and remaining tomato sauce in the Dutch oven. Mix well.

6. Place cabbage rolls seam side down in

Dutch oven. Add eggplant and zucchini. Spoon sauce over cabbage and vegetables. Add fennel seed. Mix well.

7. Bring to a boil. Reduce heat, cover and simmer 50 to 60 minutes or until cabbage and vegetables are tender.

NUTRITIONAL INFORMATION PER SERVING

Calories . .121.8	Carbohydrate . .22.7 g
Protein . . . 4.6 g	Fat . . . . 1.2 g
Sodium . .335.7 mg	Cholesterol . . . . 7.4 mg

STUFFED TOMATOES
Serves 4

4 medium tomatoes
2 cups whole wheat
bread crumbs
1½ teaspoons Tamari
soy sauce
1 medium onion,
chopped

4 teaspoons Parmesan
cheese
1 egg white
2 cups corn
1 teaspoon garlic
powder
Pinch of pepper

1. Preheat oven to 350°.

2. Slice ¼ to ½" off top of tomatoes. Hollow out tomatoes and turn upside down to let excess liquid drain.

3. Combine bread crumbs, Parmesan cheese, onion, corn, and garlic powder. Beat egg white until stiff peaks form. Slowly add Tamari soy sauce.

4. Fold egg white into bread crumb mixture. Stuff tomatoes with this mixture.

5. Spray an 8"- × -8" dish with Pam. Place tomatoes in dish. Bake 25 to 30 minutes.

NUTRITIONAL INFORMATION PER SERVING

Calories .. 292.4	Carbohydrate .. 56.4 g
Protein ... 12.1 g	Fat .... 1.9 g
Sodium .. 693.4 mg	Cholesterol .... 6.7 mg

SWEET AND SOUR CHICKEN
Serves 4

1 pound chicken breast, skinned and cut into ½" cubes

½ to 1 cup water

1 tablespoon Tamari soy sauce

⅓ cup liquid fructose

5 tablespoons Tree of Life Cherry Preserves

3 tablespoons cornstarch or arrowroot powder

½ cup vinegar

2 tablespoons Tamari soy sauce

20-ounce can unsweetened pineapple chunks

1 medium green pepper, cut in ½" strips

1 medium onion, cut into quarters and sliced

1. Drain liquid from pineapple chunks. Add enough water to pineapple liquid to equal 2½ cups. Dissolve cornstarch or arrowroot powder in liquid. Place in a large saucepan. Add fructose, cherry preserves, vinegar, and Tamari soy sauce.

2. Bring to a boil stirring constantly until sauce thickens. Add pineapple chunks, green pepper, and onion. Reduce heat to medium. Cook until onion and green pepper are tender but not soggy.

3. Spray a stick-free frying pan with Pam. Place about ½ cup of the water and 1 tablespoon of Tamari soy sauce in pan. Add chicken. Cook on medium heat 15 to 20 minutes or until chicken is cooked through. Add more water if needed.

4. Place equal layers of brown rice, chicken, and sweet and sour sauce in casserole dishes. Serve immediately.

NUTRITIONAL INFORMATION PER SERVING

Calories . . 410.4	Carbohydrate . . 70.6 g
Protein . . . 29.3 g	Fat . . . . 2.0 g
Sodium . . 761.8 mg	Cholesterol . . . . 100.0 mg

TINI LINGUINI
Serves 4

1 cup low-fat cottage cheese (1% milk fat)
½ cup plain low-fat yogurt
½ cup Parmesan cheese
2 tablespoons dried chopped onion
1 teaspoon celery seed
1 cube VegeX (vegetable bouillon)
¼ teaspoon garlic powder
¼ teaspoon curry powder
½ teaspoon anchovy paste
1 cup breast of chicken, cooked and cubed
8-ounce package of spaghetti, cooked according to package directions
Parsley

301

1. Combine first 9 ingredients in a food processor or blender. Mix until completely smooth.

2. Add chicken. Place in double boiler over medium heat. Warm. If sauce thickens too much, add a little skim milk.

3. Spoon sauce over spaghetti. Garnish with fresh parsley.

NUTRITIONAL INFORMATION PER SERVING

Calories . . 416.8 Carbohydrate . . 55.0 g
Protein . . . 33.1g Fat . . . . 5.3 g
Sodium . . 801.3 mg Cholesterol . . . . 74.1 mg

TOMATO SALMON CASSEROLE
Serves 6

7-ounce can salmon, drained
3 cups whole wheat bread crumbs
¼ cup onion, chopped
1 teaspoon Tamari soy sauce
¼ teaspoon pepper
2 cups tomato, chopped
2 egg whites
1 teaspoon Worcestershire sauce
2 teaspoons lemon juice
¼ cup white wine

1. Preheat oven to 350°.
2. Beat egg whites until stiff peaks form.
3. Add rest of ingredients. Blend well.
4. Spray a 1½-quart casserole dish with Pam.
5. Pour mixture into casserole dish.
6. Bake 30 to 35 minutes.

NUTRITIONAL INFORMATION PER SERVING

Calories . . 166.4	Carbohydrate . . 15.6 g
Protein . . . 10.6 g	Fat . . . . 4.6 g
Sodium . . 296.6 mg	Cholesterol . . . . 49.8 mg

TUNA CASSEROLE SUPREME
Serves 6

6 ounces "No Yolk" noodles (medium size), cooked

7-ounce can white tuna packed in spring water, drained

⅔ cup fresh mushrooms, washed and sliced

½ teaspoon garlic powder

½ teaspoon dried dill weed

½ teaspoon celery seed

Pinch of pepper

2 cups plain low-fat yogurt

6 tablespoons Parmesan cheese

¼ cup evaporated skim milk

3 tablespoons dry cooking sherry

½ cup whole wheat bread crumbs

1. Preheat oven to 350°.

2. Gently toss tuna, noodles, and mushrooms.

3. Combine rest of ingredients except whole wheat bread crumbs. Mix until smooth. Pour over tuna and noodles. Mix well.

4. Spray a 2-quart casserole dish with Pam. Turn mixture into dish. Sprinkle top with bread crumbs.

5. Bake covered 30 to 35 minutes or until hot and bubbly.

NUTRITIONAL INFORMATION PER SERVING

Calories . . 212.2   Carbohydrate . . 20.4 g
Protein . . . 18.8 g   Fat . . . . 3.4 g
Sodium . . 288.3 mg Cholesterol . . . . 37.0 mg

TUNA HAAS
Serves 6

7-ounce can chunk white   1 medium stalk of
   tuna packed in   celery, coarsely
   spring water, drained   chopped
2 tablespoons white   Pinch of pepper
   onion, chopped   1 medium tomato,
½ cup plus 2 table-   chopped (optional)
   spoons Haas mayon-
   naise spread

1. Combine first 5 ingredients. Mix well.
2. Spread on whole wheat bread (pita bread). Garnish with chopped tomato.

NUTRITIONAL INFORMATION PER SERVING

Calories . . 80.3   Carbohydrate . . 2.2 g
Protein . . . 13.1 g   Fat . . . . 0.6 g
Sodium . . 165.3 mg Cholesterol . . . . 21.1 mg

304

TUNA MUFFINS
Serves 6

2 cups cooked brown rice

3 tablespoons Parmesan cheese

7-ounce can chunk white tuna packed in spring water, drained and flaked

½ cup celery, chopped

¼ cup plus 1 tablespoon green onion, chopped, including green portion

¼ teaspoon pepper

5 heaping tablespoons low-fat yogurt

1 tablespoon parsley flakes

2 teaspoons Tamari soy sauce

1 tablespoon lemon juice

3 egg whites

1. Preheat oven to 375°.

2. Combine all ingredients except egg whites. Blend.

3. Beat egg whites until stiff. Fold into rest of ingredients.

4. Spray six muffin tins with Pam. Fill with tuna mixture. Make mounds with tuna (should be in the shape of a muffin).

5. Bake 35 to 40 minutes or until golden brown on top. Run knife around edge of each muffin to loosen.

NUTRITIONAL INFORMATION PER SERVING

Calories . . 163.1	Carbohydrate . . 19.2 g
Protein . . . 14.5 g	Fat . . . . 1.2 g
Sodium . . 356.0 mg	Cholesterol . . . . 26.9 mg

VEAL SCALLOPINI
Serves 4

12 thin slices veal
Whole wheat flour
Pepper
1 medium onion,
   coarsely chopped
1 cup fresh mush-
   rooms, sliced
1 cup white Burgundy

3 cups evaporated
   skimmed milk
2 cubes VegeX
2 teaspoons lime juice
4 to 6 tablespoons
   shredded skim milk
   mozzarella cheese

1. Preheat oven to 350°.

2. Sprinkle veal slices with pepper on both sides. Dip in whole wheat flour to lightly coat.

3. Spray a nonstick frying pan with Pam. Brown veal on medium heat. Remove from pan. Spray four casserole dishes with Pam. Arrange veal in dishes.

4. Spray frying pan with Pam again. Cook onions and mushrooms until onion is lightly browned.

5. Dissolve VegeX in evaporated skim milk. Add lime juice. Pour Burgundy over onions and mushrooms. Cook 2 to 3 minutes. Add evaporated skim milk mixture. Cook until bubbly around edges of fry pan.

6. Pour over veal. Sprinkle top with skim mozzarella.

7. Place in oven and heat until cheese is melted.

NUTRITIONAL INFORMATION PER SERVING

Calories . . 431.6	Carbohydrate . . 34.1 g
Protein . . . 40.2 g	Fat . . . . 8.5 g
Sodium . . 945.8 mg	Cholesterol . . . . 96.0 mg

ZUCCHINI SQUARES

Yields 2 to 3 dozen 1" squares
Serving size: 1 square

3 cups zucchini,
   shredded
¾ cup whole wheat
   flour
¼ cup toasted wheat
   germ
½ cup Parmesan cheese
1 teaspoon baking soda
1 package Butter Buds

½ cup onion, finely
   chopped
2 teaspoons dried parsley
1 tablespoon Tamari
   soy sauce
½ teaspoon marjoram
2 dashes hot sauce
2 cloves garlic, minced
6 egg whites

1. Preheat oven to 350°. Spray a 13"-×-9"-×-2"
pan with Pam.

2. Mix Tamari soy sauce, hot sauce, and egg
whites. Beat until stiff peaks form.

3. Mix dry ingredients. Combine all ingredients. Pour into pan.

4. Bake 25 to 30 minutes or until golden
brown.

NUTRITIONAL INFORMATION PER SERVING

Calories . . 26.5	Carbohydrate . . 3.6 g
Protein . . . 2.0 g	Fat . . . . 0.6 g
Sodium . . 84.9 mg	Cholesterol . . . . 2.2 mg

BREADS AND MUFFINS

APPLE BREAD
Yields 20-slice loaf
Serving size: 1 slice

1¾ cup whole wheat
flour
¾ cup toasted wheat
germ
1 teaspoon baking soda
1 teaspoon baking
powder
1 teaspoon cinnamon
½ teaspoon allspice
2 egg whites
½ cup water

12-ounce can frozen
apple juice concentrate
defrosted (no sugar
added)
1½ cups apple,
peeled and finely
diced
½ cup raisins
4 tablespoons granu-
lated fructose

1. Preheat oven to 350°.
2. Mix dry ingredients.
3. Mix liquid ingredients.
4. Combine, mix well, and add the apple and
raisins.
5. Spray an 8"-×-5"-×-3" loaf pan with Pam.
Pour mixture into pan. Bake 50 to 60 minutes or
until a wooden toothpick inserted in the middle
comes out clean.

NUTRITIONAL INFORMATION PER SERVING

Calories . . 107.1	Carbohydrate . . 21.5 g
Protein . . . 4.0 g	Fat . . . . 1.3 g
Sodium . . 49.6 mg	Cholesterol . . . . 0.0 mg

APPLE MUFFINS
Yields 12 muffins

Serving size: 1 muffin

2 cups whole wheat
  flour
¼ cup toasted wheat
  germ
1 tablespoon baking
  powder
2 teaspoons cinnamon
1¼ cup Rome apple,
  coarsely chopped

1 cup raisins
1 egg white, beaten
¾ cup skim milk
¼ cup apple juice
  concentrate
½ cup granulated
  fructose

1. Preheat oven to 400°.

2. Combine all dry ingredients. Add apple and raisins.

3. Combine all liquid ingredients. Add to dry mixture. Blend well.

4. Spray muffin tin with Pam. Fill each tin ⅔ full.

5. Bake 20 to 25 minutes or until golden brown on top.

NUTRITIONAL INFORMATION PER SERVING

Calories . . 184.4   Carbohydrate . . 40.9 g
Protein . . . 5.0 g   Fat . . . . 1.1 g
Sodium . . 95.5 mg Cholesterol . . . . 0.4 mg

BANANA BREAD
Yields 20-slice loaf
Serving size: 1 slice

1¾ cup whole wheat flour

¾ cup toasted wheat germ

1 teaspoon baking powder

1 teaspoon baking soda

1 teaspoon cinnamon

2 egg whites, beaten until stiff

3 cups banana purée (use very ripe bananas)

¼ cup granulated fructose

1½ cups raisins

1. Preheat oven to 325°.

2. Combine dry ingredients.

3. Combine liquid ingredients, including banana purée.

4. Mix the dry and liquid ingredients. Blend well.

5. Add raisins.

6. Spray a 9"-×-5"-×-3" loaf pan with Pam. Pour mixture into pan. Bake 60 to 75 minutes or until wooden toothpick inserted into center of bread comes out clean.

NUTRITIONAL INFORMATION PER SERVING

Calories . . 138.2   Carbohydrate . . 30.0 g
Protein . . .   4.5 g   Fat . . . .   1.2 g
Sodium . . 64.6 mg   Cholesterol . . . .   0.0 mg

BLUEBERRY BRAN MUFFINS
Yields 24 muffins
Serving size: 1 muffin

1¼ cup whole wheat flour

¾ cup toasted wheat germ

1½ cups bran

2 teaspoons baking powder

1 teaspoon baking soda

¼ teaspoon cinnamon

1 cup apple, shredded, including skin

1 cup fresh blueberries

⅓ cup orange juice concentrate

1 cup granulated fructose

¾ cup evaporated skim milk

3 egg whites

1. Preheat oven to 350°.

2. Mix all dry ingredients. Add blueberries and apple.

3. Combine all liquid ingredients. Add to flour mixture and blend well.

4. Spray muffin tin with Pam. Fill each tin two-thirds full.

5. Bake 30 to 35 minutes or until golden brown on top.

NUTRITIONAL INFORMATION PER SERVING

Calories . . 102.2   Carbohydrate . . 21.0 g
Protein . . . 4.0 g   Fat . . . . 1.2 g
Sodium . . 75.1 mg   Cholesterol . . . . 0.1 mg

CORN MUFFINS
Yields 12 muffins
Serving size: 1 muffin

1 cup unrefined yellow
  cornmeal
¾ cup whole wheat
  flour
4 teaspoons baking
  powder
1 teaspoon Tamari soy
  sauce

1½ cups skim milk
2 tablespoons granu-
  lated fructose
3 egg whites, lightly
  beaten
2 cups frozen corn

1. Heat oven to 425°.

2. Mix all the dry ingredients. Combine all the liquid ingredients. Blend liquid and dry together until smooth.

3. Add corn.

4. Spray muffin tin with Pam. Fill tins two-thirds full with mixture.

5. Bake 20 to 25 minutes or until golden brown on top.

NUTRITIONAL INFORMATION PER SERVING

Calories . . 106.6   Carbohydrate . .21.1 g
Protein . . .   4.4 g   Fat . . . . 0.7 g
Sodium . .342.9 mg Cholesterol . . . . 0.8 mg

EARTH BREAD
Yields 2 12-slice loaves
Serving size: 2 slices

2 cups water
¼ cup liquid fructose
1 tablespoon blackstrap molasses
2 tablespoons Tamari soy sauce
½ cup toasted wheat germ
2½ to 3½ cups whole wheat flour
1 tablespoon dry active yeast

1. Warm liquid fructose, Tamari soy sauce, and molasses in a saucepan (about 110 degrees).

2. Remove half of this mixture to a separate bowl. Add yeast and let stand 15 minutes until yeast starts to bubble. Add rest of liquid.

3. Gradually add flour. Knead 2 to 3 minutes. Form a ball. Consistency should be firm and a little sticky to the touch.

4. Place in a bowl sprayed with Pam. Turn dough to coat with Pam.

5. Cover dough and let rise 1 to 2 hours (should be in a warm place, 80°). Let dough double in size.

6. Punch dough down. Knead a few more times.

7. Divide in half and place in 2 bread pans sprayed with Pam. Cover and let rise again until double in size (1 to 2 hours).

8. Preheat oven to 350°.

9. Bake 35 to 40 minutes or until bread has a hollow sound when tapped on top.

NUTRITIONAL INFORMATION PER SERVING

Calories . . 165.9	Carbohydrate . . 33.2 g
Protein . . . 6.8 g	Fat . . . . 1.5 g
Sodium . . 145.6 mg	Cholesterol . . . . 0.0 mg

ORANGE MUFFINS
Yields 12 muffins
Serving size: 1 muffin

1 cup oats
½ cup plus 1 table-
spoon whole wheat
flour
¼ cup plus 3 table-
spoons toasted
wheat germ
3 teaspoons baking
powder
½ teaspoon allspice

½ teaspoon cinnamon
¾ cup raisins
3 tablespoons granu-
lated fructose
3 egg whites
½ cup orange juice
concentrate
½ cup evaporated
skim milk

1. Preheat oven to 400°.

2. Combine all dry ingredients. Add raisins.

3. Combine all liquid ingredients. Add to flour
and raisins. Blend well.

4. Spray muffin tin with Pam. Fill each tin
three-fourths full with mixture.

5. Bake 20 to 25 minutes or until golden
brown.

NUTRITIONAL INFORMATION PER SERVING

Calories .. 131.5   Carbohydrate .. 25.9 g
Protein ...   5.6 g   Fat .... 1.4 g
Sodium .. 102.0 mg   Cholesterol .... 0.1 mg

WHOLE WHEAT BREAD
Yields 2 loaves

*5 to 6 cups whole wheat
  flour*
*2 packages active dry
  yeast*
*2 tablespoons rice syrup
  or liquid fructose*

*3 tablespoons black-
  strap molasses*
2 cups water
¼ cup skim milk

1. Spray 2 loaf pans with Pam.

2. Combine 2 cups whole wheat flour and yeast in a large bowl.

3. Heat rest of ingredients in a saucepan until very warm (120 to 130°).

4. Add warm liquid to flour mixture. Blend at low speed until moistened. Beat 3 minutes on medium speed.

5. Add 2 to 3 more cups of flour by hand (until flour pulls away from sides of bowl). Turn dough onto a floured board and knead ½ to 1 cups more flour. Dough should be slightly sticky to the touch. Spray a large bowl with Pam. Form dough into ball. Place in bowl and turn

once. Cover and let rise in a warm place until dough is double in size (1 to 1½ hours).

6. Punch dough down. Divide in half and form into balls. Allow to rest on counter covered with bowl for 15 minutes.

7. Work with dough. Shape into two loaves. Spray two loaf pans with Pam. Place dough into pans. Cover and let rise in a warm place until dough fills pan (about 1 hour).

8. Preheat oven to 375°. Bake 45 to 55 minutes or until loaves sound hollow when lightly tapped. Remove pans immediately. Cool loaves on wire racks.

NUTRITIONAL INFORMATION PER SERVING

Calories .. 147.1   Carbohydrate ..31.6 g
Protein ...   5.8 g   Fat .... 0.7 g
Sodium ..   5.6 mg   Cholesterol .... 0.1 mg

WHOLE WHEAT RAISIN BREAD
Yields 1 loaf

1¾ cup whole wheat flour
¾ cup toasted wheat germ
1 teaspoon baking soda
1 teaspoon baking powder

1 teaspoon cinnamon
2 egg whites
1 cup evaporated skim milk
4 tablespoons liquid fructose
1 cup raisins

1. Preheat oven to 350°.
2. Combine dry ingredients.
3. Combine liquid ingredients. Add to dry and mix well.
4. Add raisins.
5. Spray a loaf pan with Pam. Pour mixture into pan.
6. Bake 50 to 60 minutes or until well browned on top.

NUTRITIONAL INFORMATION PER SERVING

Calories ..248.2   Carbohydrate ..48.8 g
Protein ... 11.1 g Fat .... 2.5 g
Sodium ..179.9 mg   Cholesterol .... 0.2 mg

DESSERTS

BAKED APPLES
Serves 10

10 medium Rome apples
2½ cups raisins
3 bananas, sliced
1½ teaspoons allspice
2 teaspoons cinnamon
1 teaspoon arrowroot
  powder or cornstarch
Juice from 5 large oranges
  or 1½ cups orange juice

1½ cups water
10 pitted prunes
6 teaspoons imitation
  brandy extract
  (Cointreau may also
  be used)

1. Combine orange juice, water, cinnamon, allspice, cornstarch, and liquor in a large saucepan. Bring to a boil stirring constantly until sauce is slightly thickened.

2. Preheat oven to 375°.

3. Core apples. Place in a baking dish and stuff center with raisins. Place rest of raisins in baking dish.

4. Quarter prunes and lay around apples with raisins. Set aside 10 slices of banana. Place the rest around apples.

5. Pour juice mixture over apples. Pour some in the center over each apple.

6. Top each apple core with a slice of banana.

7. Bake 1 hour, basting every 15 minutes with liquid from dish. Cover while baking.

NUTRITIONAL INFORMATION PER SERVING

Calories . . 269.3	Carbohydrate . . 69.7 g
Protein . . . 1.9 g	Fat . . . . 1.2 g
Sodium . . 12.8 mg	Cholesterol . . . . 0.0 mg

BAKED PLANTAINS
Serves 6

2 large ripe (turning yellow) plantains
12-ounce can unsweetened chunk pineapple
¼ cup prune juice

½ cup unsweetened apple juice
1 teaspoon cinnamon
1 teaspoon nutmeg
½ cup raisins

318

1. Preheat oven to 350°.
2. Mix all juices (including juice from pine-apple chunks).
3. Add cinnamon and nutmeg.
4. Spray an 8"-×-8" baking dish with Pam. Slice plaintains and arrange in baking dish. Add pine-apple chunks and raisins.
5. Pour juice mixture over fruits.
6. Bake 20 to 25 minutes until bubbling.

NUTRITIONAL INFORMATION PER SERVING

Calories . . 187.2	Carbohydrate . .48.7 g
Protein . . . 1.4 g	Fat . . . . 0.5 g
Sodium . . 11.0 mg	Cholesterol . . . . 0.0 mg

BANANA NOODLE CUSTARD
Serves 10

8 ounces "No Yolk"
  wide flat noodles
6 to 7 bananas, peeled
  and sliced
1 cup raisins
4 cups evaporated
  skim milk

7 egg whites
2½ teaspoons vanilla
1 teaspoon cinnamon
3 tablespoons granu-
  lated fructose

1. Cook noodles according to package direc-tions. Drain. Add bananas and raisins. Toss.
2. In a double boiler heat milk until bubbles appear on the side.

3. Beat egg whites and cinnamon lightly. Slowly add milk to egg whites stirring constantly. Return to double boiler. Add fructose and dissolve. Cook, stirring frequently, until mixture coats spoon (15 to 20 minutes).

4. Add vanilla. Remove from heat. Pour mixture over noodles and fruit. Toss gently to mix.

5. Pour into a 9"-×-13" pan. Chill 6 to 12 hours. For best results chill overnight.

NUTRITIONAL INFORMATION PER SERVING

Calories . . 220.1	Carbohydrate . . 43.9 g
Protein . . . 11.7 g	Fat . . . . 0.5 g
Sodium . . 149.8 mg	Cholesterol . . . . 0.8 mg

BROWN RICE FRUIT CUSTARD
Serves 4 to 6

2½ cups evaporated
  skim milk, scalded
4 egg whites, beaten
  until stiff
¼ cup granulated fruc-
  tose or rice syrup
1 teaspoon cinnamon

½ teaspoon nutmeg
½ teaspoon vanilla
½ cup raisins
2 cups cooked brown
  rice
10-ounce can crushed
  pineapple, drained well

1. Preheat oven to 325°.

2. Pour hot milk over rice and stir until smooth.

3. Add rice syrup or fructose, cinnamon, nutmeg, vanilla, and pineapple.

4. Spray 2 8"- × -8"-square baking dishes with Pam. Pour mixture into baking dishes.

5. Bake 50 to 60 minutes.

6. Insert knife into center of dish. If knife is clean after removal custard is done.

NUTRITIONAL INFORMATION PER SERVING

Calories . . 222.8   Carbohydrate . . 43.7 g
Protein . . . 11.4 g   Fat . . . . 0.2 g
Sodium . . 258.3 mg   Cholesterol . . . . 0.8 mg

CRANBERRY RELISH
Yields 5 cups
Serving size: 2 tablespoons

16-ounce package cranberries
1 cup granulated fructose
1⅔ cups water
1 tablespoon grated orange rind

⅓ cup orange juice concentrate
1 cup dark raisins
½ cup golden raisins
2 medium apples, peeled and chopped

1. Place cranberries, fructose, and water in a large saucepan. Bring to a boil.

2. Add orange rind, orange juice concentrate, and raisins. Simmer for 15 minutes.

3. Add apples. Remove from heat. Cover and refrigerate.

NUTRITIONAL INFORMATION PER SERVING

Calories . . 90.7	Carbohydrate . . 23.6 g
Protein . . . 0.7 g	Fat . . . . 0.2 g
Sodium . . 6.1 mg	Cholesterol . . . . 0.0 mg

CRUSTLESS PUMPKIN PIE
Yields 8-slice pie
Serving size: 1 slice

*¾ cup granulated
    fructose*
*½ cup whole wheat
    flour*
*¼ teaspoon baking
    powder*
*¼ teaspoon baking
    soda*
*1 13-ounce can evapo-
    rated skim milk*

1 teaspoon cinnamon
*3 egg whites, beaten
    until stiff peaks
    form*
1 teaspoon allspice
½ teaspoon nutmeg
2 teaspoons vanilla
*16-ounce can of
    pumpkin*

1. Preheat oven to 350°.
2. Spray a 10"-×-1½" pie plate with Pam.
3. Combine all ingredients except egg whites. Blend until smooth. Fold in egg whites.
4. Pour into pie plate. Bake 45 to 50 minutes or until knife inserted in center comes out clean.

NUTRITIONAL INFORMATION PER SERVING

Calories . . 144.7	Carbohydrate . . 28.8 g
Protein . . . 6.5 g	Fat . . . . 0.2 g
Sodium . . 111.2 mg	Cholesterol . . . . 0.4 mg

FRENCH APPLE BAKE
Serves 8 to 10

6 cups apples, thinly
sliced (McIntosh or
Rome)

3 tablespoons arrow-
root powder

1½ teaspoons cinnamon

1 teaspoon allspice

1 tablespoon lemon
juice

2 teaspoons vanilla

⅔ cup granulated fructose

½ cup raisins, plumped
by pouring boiling
water over them

½ cup evaporated skim
milk

5 egg whites

8-ounce package "No
Yolk" wide noodles

1. Preheat oven to 350°.

2. Combine first 6 ingredients plus ⅓ cup of
the granulated fructose in a saucepan over a medium high heat. Stir occasionally to make sure
arrowroot dissolves and sauce thickens slightly.

3. Add raisins. Cook noodles according to
package directions.

4. Beat egg whites until stiff peaks form. Keep
beating egg whites gradually adding remaining
fructose and evaporated skim milk.

5. Toss fruit mixture with noodles. Fold egg
whites. Spray a 9"- × -13" baking dish with Pam.
Pour mixture into pan.

6. Bake 30 to 35 minutes or until golden
brown.

NUTRITIONAL INFORMATION PER SERVING

Calories . . 335.3   Carbohydrate . . 82.5 g
Protein . . . 5.6 g   Fat . . . . 1.1 g
Sodium . . 59.0 mg   Cholesterol . . . . 0.1 mg

HOLIDAY CAKE
Yields 12-slice cake
Serving size: 1 slice

1½ cups cherries
1½ cups crushed
   pineapple
½ cup dates, chopped
½ cup prunes, chopped
1 cup muscat raisins
¾ cup apples, cubed
1 tablespoon orange
   juice concentrate
5 tablespoons brandy
1½ cups granulated
   sugar

½ cup evaporated skim
   milk
2 cups whole wheat
   flour
1½ cups toasted wheat
   germ
3 tablespoons baking
   powder
1½ teaspoons cinnamon
¾ teaspoon nutmeg
4 egg whites, beaten
   until stiff

1. Combine all fruits, brandy, orange juice concentrate, fructose, and spices. Mix well and store in a bell jar for several days.
2. Combine all dry ingredients.
3. Blend with fruit mixture.
4. Fold in egg whites.
5. Spray a 10″ tube pan with Pam.
6. Bake 50 to 60 minutes.

NUTRITIONAL INFORMATION PER SERVING

Calories . . 323.3   Carbohydrate . . 60.7 g
Protein . . . 12.4 g   Fat . . . . 3.7 g
Sodium . . 258.4 mg   Cholesterol . . . . 10.4 mg

NOODLE PUDDING
Serves 10 to 12

½ pound "No Yolk"
eggless wide noodles
5 egg whites
2 cups raisins
16-ounce can crushed
pineapple in natural
juice

¼ cup granulated
fructose
⅔ cup evaporated skim
milk

1. Cook noodles according to package directions. Drain.

2. Preheat oven to 375°.

3. Beat egg whites until stiff. Gradually add fructose and milk.

4. Return drained noodles to pot. Add egg mixture, pineapple with juice, and raisins. Mix.

5. Spray a 9"-×-13" baking pan with Pam. Pour mixture into pan.

6. Bake 45 to 60 minutes or until set and top is golden brown.

NUTRITIONAL INFORMATION PER SERVING

Calories . . 176.3	Carbohydrate . . 39.0 g
Protein . . . 5.1 g	Fat . . . . 0.8 g
Sodium . . 42.8 mg	Cholesterol . . . . 0.1 mg

OATMEAL FRUIT BARS
Serves 4

½ cup plain low-fat
  yogurt
⅔ cup granulated fructose
¼ cup evaporated
  skim milk
1 cup whole wheat
  flour
½ teaspoon baking
  powder

1 cup rolled oats
¼ cup toasted wheat
  germ
2 tablespoons whole
  wheat flour
6-ounce package Sun
  Maid Fruit Bits
½ cup Tree of Life
  Orange Marmalade

1. Preheat oven to 350°.
2. Combine yogurt, fructose, and skim milk.
3. Combine 1 cup of flour, baking powder, oats, and wheat germ. Add to yogurt mixture. Blend well.
4. Sprinkle 2 tablespoons whole wheat flour over fruit bits in a separate bowl. Add orange marmalade. Mix well.
5. Spray an 8"-×-8" baking dish with Pam. Spread half of the yogurt-flour mixture on bottom of dish. Spread fruit mixture on top of flour mixture. Top with second half of flour mixture. Spread evenly (may not completely cover top).
6. Bake 30 to 35 minutes. Let cool before cutting.

NUTRITIONAL INFORMATION PER SERVING

Calories . . 625.1   Carbohydrate . . 135.5 g
Protein . . . 16.8 g   Fat . . . . 4.8 g
Sodium . . 91.1 mg   Cholesterol . . . . 2.4 mg

Bibliography

Ackman, R.G., et al. 1980. "Marine docosenoic acid isomer distribution in the plasma of Greenland Eskimos." *Am. J. Clin. Nutr.* 33:1814.

Adams. M., et al. 1982. "Effect of a supplement on dietary intakes of female collegiate swimmers." *Physic. and Sportsmed.* 10:122.

Adner, M.M., and Castelli, William P., 1980. "Elevated high-density lipoprotein levels in marathon runners." *JAMA* 243:534.

Albrink, M.J., et al. 1979. "Effect of high- and low-fiber diets on plasma lipids and insulin." *Am. J. Clin. Nutr.* 32:1486.

Allen, L., et al. 1978. "Reduction of renal calcium reabsorbation in man by consumption of dietary protein." *Fed. Am. Soc. Exp. Biol.* ——:1345.

Allen, L.H., et al. 1979. "Protein-induced hypercalciuria: a longer term study." *Am. J. Clin. Nutr.* 32:741.

Anderson, B. 1980. "Delayed menarche and amenorrhea in ballet dancers." *N. Eng. J. Med.* 303:1125.

Asmussen, E., et al. 1975. "A follow-up longitudinal study of selected physiologic functions in former physical education students—after forty years." *J. Amer. Ger. Soc.* 23:442.

Baker, E.R., et al. 1982. "Amenorrhea associated with running mileage and age." *Physic. and Sportsmed.* 10:201.

Bang, H.O., et al. 1980. "The composition of the Eskimo food in North-western Greenland. *Am. J. Clin. Nutr.* 33:2657.

Barnes, L. 1980. "Measuring anaerobic threshold simplified." *Physic. and Sportsmed.* 8:15.

————. 1980. "Olympic drug testing: improvements without progress." *Physic. and Sportsmed.* 8:21.

Bass, A., et al. 1975. "Biochemical and histochemical changes in energy supply-enzyme pattern of muscles of the rat during old age." *Gerontologia* 21:31.

Beaudin, P., et al. 1978. "Heart rate response and lactic acid concentration in squash players." *Res. Quart.* 49:406.

Beisel, W., et al. 1981. "Single-nutrient effects on immunologic functions." *JAMA* 245:53.

Benyo, R. 1979. "The heat is on for 1980." *Runner's World* (October):77.

Biss, K., et al. 1971. "Some unique biologic characteristics of the Masai of East Africa." *N. Eng. J. Med.* 284:694.

Blair, S., et al. 1980. "Blood lipid and ECG responses to carbohydrate loading." *Physic. and Sportsmed.* 8:69.

Blake, D., et al. 1981. "The importance of iron in rheumatoid disease." *Lancet*(i):1142.

Blankenship, J.W., et al. 1977. "The effect of diet on the serum cholesterol and triglyceride levels and the red blood cell 2,3-diphosphoglycerate level." *Fed. Proc.* 36:1104.

Bolton, R.P., et al. 1981. "The role of dietary fiber in satiety, glucose, and insulin: studies with fruit and fruit juice." *Am. J. Clin. Nutr.* 34:211.

Bolton, S., et al. 1981. "Caffeine: its effects, uses and abuses." *J. Appl. Nutr.* 33:35.

Borhani, N. 1980. "The case for diet modification to retard atherosclerosis." *J. Card. Med.* (December): 1085.

Bortz, W. 1982. "The runner's high." *Runner's World* 58.

Bray, G., et al. 1981. "Hepatic sodium-potassium-dependent atpase in obesity." *N. Eng. J. Med.* 304:1580.

Bronsgeest-Schoute, D.C., et al. 1979. "Dependence of the effect of dietary cholesterol and experimental conditions on serum lipids in man. I. Effects of dietary cholesterol in a linoleic acid-rich diet." *Am. J. Clin. Nutr.* 32:2183.

———. 1979. "Dependence on the effect of dietary cholesterol and experimental conditions on serum lipids in man. III. The effect on serum cholesterol of removal of eggs from the diet of free-living habitually egg-eating people." *Am. J. Clin. Nutr.* 32:2193.

Bruder, R. 1978. "The traditional carbo-loading

methods are helpful but nature knows best."
Runner's World 50.

Brunzell, J., et al. 1971. "Improved glucose tolerance with high carbohydrate feeding in mild
diabetics." *N. Engl. J. Med.* 284:521.

———. 1980. "Triglycerides and coronary heart
disease." *N. Eng. J. Med.* 303:1060.

Buccola, V.A., and Stone, William J. 1972. "Effects
of jogging and cycling programs on physiological and personality variables in aged men." *Res.
Quart.* 46:135.

Burke, M. 1980. "Cholesterol, triglyceride, and
lipoprotein studies: strategies for clinical use."
Postgrad. Med. 67:263.

Burstyn, P. 1981. "Sodium potassium and blood
pressure." *Lancet* i:328.

Buskirk, E.R. 1977. "Diet and athletic performance."
Postrag. Med. 61:229.

Byrd, R., et al. 1974. "Jogging in middle-aged
men: effect on cardiovascular dynamics." *Arch.
Phys. Med. Rehabil.* 55:301.

Caldwell, F. 1981. "Circuit-running program brings
fitness gains." *Physic. and Sportsmed.* 9:22.

———. 1982. "Menstrual irregularity in athletes:
the unanswered question." *Physic. and Sportsmed.*
10:142.

Calloway, D.H. and Yates-Zezulka, A., 1980.
"Amino acid scores and protein allowances."
Am. J. Clin. Nutr. 33:1319.

———, and Zanni, E. 1980. "Energy requirements
and energy expenditure of elderly men." *Am. J.
Clin. Nutr.* 33:2088.

Carew, T., et al. 1976. "A mechanism by which

high-density lipoproteins may slow the atherogenic process." *Lancet* i:1315.

Carroll, K.K., and Huff, M.W. 1977. "Influence of
dietary fat and protein on plasma cholesterol
levels in the early postnatal period." *Adv. in
Exp. Med. and Biol.* 82:638.

Casdorph, H., and Connor, W. E. 1972. "Nutrition
for endurance competition," *JAMA* 222:1062.

Cerna, O. and Ginter, E. 1978. "Blood lipids and
vitamin-C status." *Lancet* i:1055.

Chapman, E., et al. 1972. "Joint stiffness: effects
of exercise on young and old men." *J. Gerontol.*
27:218.

Chen, L.H. 1981. "An increase in vitamin-E requirement induced by high supplementation of
vitamin-C in rats." *Amer. J. Clin. Nutr.* 34:1036.

Chen, W.L., and Anderson, J.W. 1979. "Effects of
plant fiber in decreasing plasma total cholesterol
and increasing high-density lipoprotein cholesterol (40671)." *Proc. Soc. Exper. Biol. and Med.*
162:310.

————. 1981. "Soluble and insoluble plant fiber in
selected cereals and vegetables." *Amer. J. Clin.
Nutr.* 34:1077.

Choquette, G., and Ferguson, R. 1973. "Blood
pressure reduction in 'borderline' hypertensives
following physical training." *Canad. Med. Assoc.
J.* 108:699.

Clark, H., et al. 1971. "Nitrogen retention of adult
human subjects fed a high protein rice." *Am. J.
Clin. Nutr.* 24:324.

Clausen, J. P. 1977. "Effect of physical training on

cardiovascular adjustments to exercise in man."
Physiol. Revs. 4:779.

Cohen, B.I. 1982. "Safety of phenylpropanolamine."
Lancet ii:96.

Cohen, I.J. 1980. "Unexpected gain from jogging."
Lancet ii:154.

Coleman, E.A. 1981. "Skinfold estimates of body
fat in major league baseball players." *Physic. and
Sportsmed.* 9:77.

————. 1982. "Physiological characteristics of major league baseball players." *Physic. and Sportsmed.*
10:51.

Commentary. 1974. "Vegetarian Diets." *J. Am. Diet.
A.* 65:121

Conley, D.L., et al. 1981. "Training for aerobic
capacity and running economy." *Physic. and
Sportsmed.* 9:107.

Connor. W.E., et al. 1978. "The plasma lipids,
lipoproteins, and diet of the Tarahumara Indi-
ans of Mexico." *Am. J. Clin. Nutr.* 31:1131.

————. 1979. "Too little or too much: the case for
preventive nutrition." *Am. J. Clin. Nutr.* 32:1975.

Corea, L., et al. 1981. "Plasma potassium during
exercise." *Lanet* ii:1292.

Costill, D.L. 1981. "Anaerobic threshold: the metabolic changes that occur between LSD and speed
work." *Runner* 78.

————. 1982. "A racer's edge?" *Runner* 70.

————. 1982. "Physiology." *Runner* 54.

————. 1980. "The right stuff: examining key elements of running talent." *Runner* 84.

————. 1977. "Sweating: its composition and effects on body fluids." *Ann. New York Acad. Sci.* 301:120.

————— et al. 1982. "Dietary potassium and heavy exercise: effects on muscle water and electrolytes." *Am. J. Clin. Nutr.* 36:266.

—————, and Higdon, Hal. 1980. "Get a load of this." *Runner* 68.

—————, and Higdon, Hal. 1981. "If you weigh too much you run the risk of running slower." *Runner* 62.

—————, and Higdon, Hal. 1981. "Fat chance." *Runner* 62.

—————, and Higdon, Hal. 1982. "Feast but not famine." *Runner* 64.

—————, and Higdon, Hal. 1982. "Facts on food." *Runner* 66.

Craig, I.H., et al. 1980. "Effects of modified fat diets on LDL-HDL ratio." *Lancet:* 2:799.

Crapo. P.A., et al. 1980. "Postprandial hormonal responses to different types of complex carbohydrate in individuals with impaired glucose tolerance." *Am. J. Clin. Nutr.* 33:1723.

Crenshaw, J. 1980. "Hypoglycemia—what's causing it?" *Consultant.* (November):163.

Cureton, K., and Sparilin, P. 1980. "Distance running performance and metabolic responses to running in men and women with excess weight experimentally equated." *Med. Sci. Sports Exer.* 12:288.

Dahl, L.K., 1972. "Salt and hypertension." *Am. J. Clin. Nutr.* 25:231.

Demer, L.L., et al. 1981. "Short-term effects of

lacto-ovo-vegetarian diet on plasma lipids and lipoproteins." *Arteriosclerosis.* 1:83.

Detry, J., and Bruce, R. 1971. "Effects of physical training on exertional S-T-segment depression in coronary heart disease." *Circulation* 44:390.

Devries, H.A. 1981. "Tranquilizer effect of exercise: a critical review." *Physic. and Sportsmed.* 9:47.

Dresendorfer, R. H., et al. 1982. "Plasma mineral levels in marathon runners during a 20-day road race." *Physic. and Sportsmed.* 10:113.

————. 1980. "Physiological profile of a master runner." *Physic. and Sportsmed.* 8:49.

Drinkwater, B.L. 1981. "Menstrual changes in athletes." *Physic. and Sportsmed.* 9:99.

Dunn, K. 1981. "Twin studies and sports: estimating the future?" *Physic. and Sportsmed.* 9:131.

Dyerberg, J., and Bang, H.O. 1979. "Haemostatic function and platelet polyunsaturated fatty acids in Eskimos." *Lancet* ii:433.

Dyerberg, J., et al. 1978. "Eicosapentaenoic acid and prevention of thrombosis and atherosclerosis?" *Lancet* ii:117.

Editorial. 1977. "High blood lipid levels can be good or bad—depending on the lipid." *JAMA* 237:1067.

————. 1977. "High density lipoprotein and coronary heart disease." *Scand. J. Clin. Lab. Invest.* 37:191.

Enger, S., et al. 1977. "High density lipoproteins (HDL) and physical activity: the influence of physical exercise, age and smoking on HDL-cholesterol and the HDL-total cholesterol." *Scand. J. Clin. Lab. Invest.* 37:251.

Ermini, M., et al. 1971. "The aging of skeletal (striated) muscle by changes of recovery metabolism." *Gerontologia* 17:300.

Ernst, N., et al. 1980. "Changes in plasma lipids and lipoproteins after a modified fat diet." *Lancet* ii:111.

————, et al. 1980. "The association of plasma high-density lipoprotein cholesterol with dietary intake and alcohol consumption." *Circulation* 62:41.

Fardy, P., et al. 1978. "A comparison of habitual lifestyle, aerobic power and systolic time intervals in former athletes and non-athletes." *J. Sports Med.* 18:287.

Farthing, M.J.G., et al. 1980. "Essential fatty acid deficiency after prolonged treatment with elemental diet." *Lancet* ii:1088.

Feigin, R.D., et al. 1971. "Rhythmicity of plasma amino acids and relation to dietary intake." *Am. J. Clin. Nutr.* 24:329.

Ferstle, J. 1982. "Drinking problems." *Runner* 83.

————. 1981. "Meeting of the minds: the annual gathering of the American College of Sports Medicine." *Runner* 14.

Fisher, H., et al. 1971. "Reassessment of amino acid requirements of young women on low nitrogen diets. II. Leucine, methionine, and valine." *Am. J. Clin. Nutr.* 24:1216.

Flynn, M.A., et al. 1979. "Effect of dietary egg on human serum cholesterol and triglycerides." *Am. J. Clin. Nutr.* 32:1051.

Forgag, M.T. 1979. "Carbohydrate loading—review." *J. Amer. Diet. Assoc.* 75:42.

Fox, E.L., et al. 1975. "Frequency and duration of interval training programs and changes in aerobic power." *J. Appl. Physiol.* 38:481.

Franklin, B.A., and Rubenfire, M. 1980. "Losing weight through exercise." JAMA 244:377.

———, et al. 1981. "Characteristics of national-class race walkers." *Physic. and Sportsmed.* 9:101.

Fujisawa, K. 1974. "Some observations on the skeletal musculature of aged rats. Part 1. Histological aspects." *J. Neuro. Sci.* 22:353.

Gasque. D., and Gasque. P. 1979. "Food for exercise." *Runner's World* (17 December).

Goldberg, I.K. 1980. "L-tyrosine in depression." *Lancet* ii:364.

Goldstein, R. G. 1982, "California breathing." *Runner* 14.

Gonen, B., et al. 1981. "Diet alters HDL metabolism." *Arteriosclerosis* 1:85.

Gonzalez, E. R. 1982. "Premature bone loss found in some nonmenstruating sportswomen." *JAMA* 248:513.

Gordon, T. 1978. "Risk factors and HDL." *Circulation* 57:1032.

———. 1977. "High density lipoprotein as a protective factor against coronary heart disease." *Am. J. Med.* 62:707.

Grundy, S., 1975. "Effects of polyunsaturated fats on lipid metabolism in patients with hypertriglyceridemia." *J. CLin. Invest.* 55:269.

Hagan, R.D., et al. 1981. "Marathon performance

in relation to maximal aerobic power and training indices." *Med. Sci. Sports Exer.* 13:185.

Hage, P. 1982. "Diet and exercise programs for coronary heart disease: better late than never." *Physic and Sportsmed.* 9:121.

————. 1982. "Caffeine, testosterone banned for Olympians." *Physic. and Sportsmed.* 10:15.

Hall, J.A., et al. 1982. "Effects of diet and exercise on peripheral vascular disease." *Physic. and Sportsmed.* 10:90.

Hartung, G. H., et al. 1980. "Relation of diet to high-density-lipoprotein cholesterol in middle-aged marathon runners, joggers, and inactive men." *N. Eng. J. Med.* 302:357.

Haymes, E. M., and Dickinson, A.L. 1980. "Characteristics of elite male and female ski racers." *Med. Sci. Sports Exer.* 12:153.

Heaney, R. P., et al. 1978. "Menopausal changes in calcium balance performance." *J. Lab. Clin. Med.* 92:953.

Hermansen, L., and Wachtlova, M. 1971. "Capillary density of skeletal muscle in well-trained and untrained men." *J. Appl. Physiol.* 30:860.

Hervey, G.R., et al. 1981. "Effects of methandienane on the performance and body composition of men undergoing athletic training." *Clin. Sci.* 60:457.

Hickson, R.C., et al. 1980. "Strength training effects on aerobic power and short-term endurance." *Med. Sci. Sports Exer.* 12:336.

Hirai, A. et al. 1980. "Eicosapentaenoic acid and platelet function in Japanese." *Lancet* ii:1132.

337

Holloszy, J. and Booth, F. 1976. "Biochemical adaptations to endurance exercise in muscle." *Ann. Rev. Pysiol.* 38:273.

Horton. E.S. 1982. "Effects of low energy diets on work performance." *Am. J. Clin. Nutr.* 35:1228.

Howley, E.T. and Gover, M.E. 1974. "The caloric costs of running and walking one mile for men and women." *Med. Sci. Sports Exer.* 6:235.

Hulley, S., et al. 1980. "Epidemiology as a guide to clinical decisions: the association between triglyceride and coronary heart disease." *N. Eng. J. Med.* 302:25.

Ismail, A.H., and Montgomery, D.L. 1979. "The effect of a four month physical fitness program on a young and an old group matched for physical fitness." *Eur. J. Appl. Physiol.* 40:137.

Jackson, R.L., et al. 1978. "The role of dietary polyunsaturated fat in lowering blood cholesterol in man." *Cir. Res.* 42:447.

Jausman, P. 1978. "Effect of dietary cholesterol on serum cholesterol." *Am. J. Clin. Nutr.* 31:1970.

Jenkins, P.J., et al. 1978. "Severity of coronary atherosclerosis related to lipoprotein concentration." *Brit. Med. J.* 5:388.

Jerome, J. 1980. "The last ounce of strength." *Quest* April, 26.

———. 1982. "Don't pity the aging runner." *Running* 26.

Karlsson, J. and Saltin, B. 1971. "Diet, muscle glycogen, and endurance performance." *J. Appl. Physiol.* 31:203.

Kasch, F. W., and Wallace, J. P. 1976. "Physiological variables during 10 years of endurance exercise." *Med. Sci. Sports Exer.* 6:5.

Katch, V.L., et al. 1980. "Muscular development and lean body weight in body builders and weight lifters." *Med. Sci. Sports Exer.* 12:340.

Kavanagh, T. 1977. "The effects of continued training on the aging process." *Ann. New York Acad. Sci.* 301:656.

Keith, R.E., et al. 1980. "Dietary vitamin-C supplementation and plasma vitamin-E levels in humans." *Am. J. Clin. Nutr.* 33:2394.

Kelley. M. 1980. "Physical conditioning and fibrinolysis." *N. Eng. J. Med.* 303:757.

Kelsay, J.L., et al. 1979. "Effect of fiber from fruits and vegetables on metabolic responses of human subjects." *Am. J. Clin. Nutr.* 32:1876.

Keys, A. et al. 1974. "Bias and misrepresentation revisited: perspective on saturated fat." *Am. J. Clin. Nutr.* 27:188.

Kiehm, T.G., et al. 1976. "Beneficial effects of a high carbohydrate, high fiber diet on hyperglycemic diabetic men." *Am. J. Clin. Nutr.* 29:895.

Kiesling, S. 1982. "Souped-up bodies." *Review* 35.

Kiessling, K.H., et al. 1974. "Enzyme activities and morphometry in skeletal muscle of middle-aged men after training." *Scand. J. Clin. Lab. Invest.* 33:63.

Kilbom, A. 1971. "Physical training in women." *Scand. J. Clin. Lab. Invest.* 28 (supp. 119):1.

Knockel, J. P. 1977. "Potassium deficiency during training in the heat." *Ann. New York Acad. Sci.* 301:175.

Koletsky, S., and Puterman, D.I. 1976. "Effect of low calorie diet on the hyperlipidemia, hypertension, and life span of genetically obese rats." *Proc. Soc. Exper. Biol. and Med.* 151:368.

Kramsch, D.M., et al. 1981. "Prevention of primate atherosclerosis by agents not affecting atherogenic serum lipids." *Ateriosclerosis* 1:58.

Kruse, B. 1982. "Blood doping." *Runner's World* 58.

Kummerow, F.A. 1974. "Current studies on relation of fat to health." *JAOCS.* 51:255.

———. 1979. "Nutrition imbalance and angiotoxins as dietary risk factors in coronary heart disease." *Am. J. CLin. Nutr.* 32:58.

———. 1976. "Additive risk factors in atherosclerosis." *Am. J. Clin. Nutr.* 29:579.

———. 1977. "The influence of egg consumption on the serum cholesterol level in human subjects." *Am. J. Clin. Nutr.* 30:664.

Kuntzleman, C.T. 1981. "Aerobic shopping: absolutely everything burns some calories." *Runner* 96.

Lafontaine, T.P., et al. 1981. "The maximal steady state versus selected running events." *Med. Sci. Sports Exer.* 13:190.

Lakin. M. 1980. "Jogger's liver." *N. Eng. J. Med.* 303:589.

Larrson, L., and Karlsson, J. 1978. "Isometric and dynamic endurance as a function of age and skeletal muscle characteristics." *Acta. Physiol. Scand.* 104:129.

———. 1978. "Histochemical and biochemical

changes in human skeletal muscle with age in sedentary males, age 22–65 years." *Acta. Physiol. Scanda.* 103:31.

Larrson, L. 1979. "Muscle strength and speed of movement in relation to age and muscle morphology." *J. Appl. Physiol.* 46:451.

Legwold, G. 1982. "Does aerobic dance offer more fun than fitness?" *Physic. and Sportsmed.* 10:147.

—— ——. 1982. "Do morning exercisers lose more weight?" *Physic. and Sportsmed.* 10:28.

Lemon, P.W.R. and Nagle, F.J. 1981. "Effects of exercise on protein and amino acid metabolism." *Med. Sci. Sports Exer.* 13:141

Leon, A.S., et al. 1979. "Effects of a vigorous walking program on body composition, and carbohydrate and lipid metabolism of obese young men." *Am. J. Clin. Nutr.* 32:1776.

Lewis, S., et al. 1976. "Effects of physical activity on weight reduction on obese middle-aged women." *Am. J. Clin. Nutr.* 29:151.

Linkswiler, H., et al. 1974. "Calcium retention of young adult males as affected by level of protein and of calcium intake." *Trans. N.Y. Acad. Sci.* 36:333.

Lipson, A., and Margolis, S. 1981. "Effects of egg ingestion on serum cholesterol, triglycerides, LDL-and HDL- cholesterol." *Arteriosclerosis.* 1:72.

Lopez, A., et al. 1974. "Effect of exercise and physical fitness on serum lipids and lipoproteins." *Ateriosclerosis.* 20:1.

McBean, L., and Speckmann, E. 1974. "A recognition of the interrelationship of calcium with various dietary components." *Am. J. Clin. Nutr.* June:603.

Macdougall, J.D., et al. 1977. "Biochemical adaptation of human skeletal muscle to heavy resistance training and immobilization." *J. Appl. Physiol.* 43:700.

Makheja, A., et al. 1979. "Inhibition of platelet aggregation and thromboxane synthesis by onion and garlic." *Lancet* ii:781.

Marcus, A. 1978. "The role of lipids in platelet function: with particular reference to the arachidonic acid pathway." *J. Lipid Res.* 19:793.

Margen, S., et al. 1974. "Studies in calcium metabolism. I. The calciuretic effect of dietary protein." *Am. J. Clin. Nutr.* 27:584.

Maron, B., et al. 1980. "Sudden death in young athletes." *Circulation* 62:218.

Maurer, A. 1982. "Aspirin for runner's wall." *Omni* 45.

Memoranda. 1979. "Protein and energy requirements: a joint FAO-WHO memorandum." *Bull. World Health Organ.* 57:65.

Mickelson, O., et al. 1979. "Effects of a high fiber bread diet on weight loss in college-age males." *Am. J. Clin. Nutr.* 32:1703.

Milvy, P. 1977. "The marathon: physiological, medical, epidemiological, and physchological studies." *Ann. New York Acad. Sci.* 301:1.

Mirkin, G. 1981. "Losing weight for good: count miles, not calories." *Runner* 16.

———. 1973. "Carbohydrate loading: a dangerous practice." *JAMA* 223:1511.

Montgomery, D.L. 1981. "Heart rate response to racquetball." *Physic. and Sportsmed.* 9:59.

———. 1982. "The effect of added weight on ice hockey performance." *Physic. and Sportsmed.* 10:91.

More, M. 1981. "Carbohydrate loading: eating through the wall." *Physic. and Sportsmed.* 9:97.

Morganroth, J., et al. 1975. "Comparative left ventricular dimensions in trained athletes." *Ann. Int. Med.* 82:521.

Morris, A.F. 1982. "Sleep disturbances in athletes." *Physic. and Sportsmed.* 10:75.

Multiple Risk Factor Intervention Trial Group. 1978. "The multiple risk factor intervention trial." *Ann. N.Y. Acad. Sci.* 304:293.

Murase, Y., et al. 1981. "Longitudinal study of aerobic power in superior athletes." *Med. Sci. Sports Exer.* 13:180.

Nalin. D. 1976. "Onion, garlic, and atherosclerosis." *Luncet* ii:575.

Needleman, P., et al. 1977. "Coronary tone modulation: formation and actions of prostaglandins, endoperoxides, and thromboxanes." *Science* 195:409.

Nelson, R.A. 1982. "Nutrition and physical performance." *Physic. and Sports Med.* 10:55.

Nikkila, E.A., et al. 1981. "Effect of physical inactivity on plasma lipoproteins: decrease of high-density lipoproteins and apolipoprotein A-1 in immobilized patients." *Arteriosclerosis* 1:89.

Nilsson, B. E., and Westlin, Nils. E. 1971. "Bone density in athletes." *Clin. Ortho.* 77:179.

Norman, James, 1976. "The Tarahumaras: Mexico's long distance runners." *National Geographic* (May): 702.

Nuttall, F.Q. 1980. "Dietary recommendations for individuals with diabetes mellitus, 1979: summary of report from the food and nutrition committee of the American Diabetes Association." *Am. J. Clin. Nutr.* 33:1311.

O'Brien, B.D., and Reiser, R. 1980. "Human plasma lipid responses to red meat, poultry, fish, and eggs." *Am. J. Clin. Nutr.* 33:2573.

O'Brien, J.R., et al. 1976. "Effect of a diet of polyunsaturated fats on some platelet-function tests." *Lancet* ii:995.

————. 1976. "Acute platelet changes after large meals of saturated and unsaturated fats." *Lancet* i:878.

Olsen, E. 1982. "Fitness report from the morgue." *Runner* 57.

————. 1982. "Triathlon fever." *Runner* 54.

————. 1982. "Nutrition." *Runner* 56.

Ostrander, L. D., et al. 1981. "Blood glucose and risk of coronary heart disease." *Arteriosclerosis* 1:33.

Ott, D.B., and Lachance, P.A. 1979. "Retinoic acid—a review." *Am. J. Clin. Nutr.* 32:2522.

Patten, R.L., et al. 1980. "Associations of plasma high-density lipoprotein cholesterol with clinical chemistry data." *Circulation* 62:31.

Permutt, M.A. 1980. "Is it really hypoglycemia? If so, what should you do?" *Med. Times.* 108:35.

Persky, V., et al. 1979. "Uric acid: a risk factor for coronary heart disease?" *Circulation* 59:969.

Peto. R. 1981. "Cancer, cholesterol, carotene, and tocopherol." *Lancet* ii:97.

Plowman, S., et al. 1979. "Age and aerobic power in women: a longitudinal study." *J. Gerontol.* 34:512.

Pollock, M.L., et al. 1976. "Physiologic responses of men 49 to 65 years of age to endurance training." *J. Amer. Ger. Soc.* 24:97.

Porter, M., et al. 1977. "Effect of dietary egg on serum cholesterol and triglyceride of human males." *Am. J. Clin. Nutr.* 30:490.

Posner, J. 1982. "How to live forever." *Playboy* 188.

Quintao, E. et al. 1971. "Effects of dietary cholesterol on the regulation of total body cholesterol in man." *J. Lipid. Res.* 12:233.

Randall, F. 1982. "Getting to the heart of the matter." *Runner* 40.

Ratelle, A., and Fedo, M. 1982. "Cycling and running." *Runner's World* 61.

Redwood, D.R., et al. 1972. "Circulatory and symptomatic effects of physical training in patients with coronary-artery disease and angina pectoris." *N. Engl. J. Med.* 286:959.

Register, U.D., and Sonnenberg, L.M., 1973. "The vegetarian diet." *J. Am. Diet. A.* 62:253.

Reiser, R. 1973. "Saturated fat in the diet and serum cholesterol concentration: a critical examination of the literature." *Am. J. Clin. Nutr.* 26:524.

Reiser, S., et al. 1979. "Isocaloric exchange of dietary starch and sucrose in humans. I. Effects on levels of fasting blood lipids." *Am. J. Clin. Nutr.* 32:1659.

Richardson, D.P., et al. 1979. "Quantitative effect on an isoenergetic exchange of fat for carbohydrate on dietary protein utilization in healthy young men." *Am. J. Clin. Nutr.* 32:2217.

Rickman, F., et al. 1974. "Changes in serum cholesterol during the Stillman diet." *JAMA.* 228:54.

Ross, M.H. 1972. "Length of life and caloric intake." *Am. J. Clin. Nutr.* 25:834.

Roth, M. 1977. "Dietary behavior and longevity." *Nutr. Rev.* 35:257.

Sacks, F. M., et al. 1975. "Plasma lipids and lipoproteins in vegetarians and controls." *N. Eng. J. Med.* (29 May):1148.

―――. 1974. "Blood pressure in vegetarians." *Am. J. Epidemiol.* 100:390.

Sakula, A. et al. 1980. "Vitamin-A and cancer." *Lancet* ii:1029.

Saltin, B., et al. 1974. "Phosphagen and carbohydrate metabolism during exercise in trained middle-aged men." *Scand. J. Clin. Lab. Invest.* 33:71.

Santosham, M., et al. 1980. "Hyperkalemia and glucose-electrolyte solutions." *Lancet* ii:583.

Saris, S., et al. 1982. "Lack of effect of nonsteroidal anti-inflammatory drugs on exercise-induced hyperkalemia." *New Engl. J. Med.* 307:559.

Sawka, M.N., et al. 1980. "Competition is a factor in blood lactate concentration." *Physic. and Sportsmed.* 8:13.

Schaefer, E.F., et al. 1981. "Effects of cholesterol-lowering diets on lipoprotein cholesterol levels." *Arteriosclerosis* 1:90.

Sedwick, A.W., et al. 1974. "The effects of physical training on the day and night long-term heart rates of middle aged men." *Europ. J. Appl. Physiol.* 33:307.

Sheehan, G. 1981. "The moral minority." *Physic. and Sportsmed.* 9:33.

———. 1980. "Running à la mode." *Physic. and Sportsmed.* 8:33.

Shekelle, R., et al. 1981. "Diet, serum cholesterol, and death from coronary heart disease: the Western Electric study." *N. Eng. J. Med.* 304:65.

———. 1981. "Dietary vitamin-A and risk of cancer in the Western Electric study." *Lancet* ii:1185.

Shorey, R. L., et al. 1976. "Efficacy of diet and exercise in the reduction of serum cholesterol and triglyceride in free-living adult males." *Am. J. Clin. Nutr.* 29:512.

Siess, W., et al. 1980. "Platelet-membrane fatty acids, platelet aggregation and thromboxane formation during a mackerel diet." *Lancet* 1:441.

Smith, E. L. 1982. "Exercise for prevention of osteoporosis: a review." *Physic. and Sportsmed.* 10:72.

———, et al. 1981. "Physical activity and calcium modalities for bone mineral increase in aged women." *Med. Sci. Sports Exer.* 13:60.

Smith, M.P., et al. 1982. "Exercise intensity, dietary intake, and high-density lipoprotein cholesterol in young female competitive swimmers." *Am. J. Clin. Nutr.* 36:251.

Solomon, L. 1979. "Bone density in aging Caucasian and African populations." *Lancet* ii:1326.

Spence, D.W., et al. 1980. "Descriptive profiles of highly skilled women volleyball players." *Med. Sci. Sports Exer.* 12:299.

Stewart, L. 1981. "The drink of choice among runners: beer." *Runner's World* 68.

Stewart, P. J., and Posen, G. A. 1980. "Case report: acute renal failure following a marathon." *Physic. and Sportsmed.* 8:61.

Strahinich, J. 1982. "The endorphin puzzle." *Runner* 48.

Suominen. H., et al. 1977. "Effect of eight weeks' physical training of muscle and connective tissue of the M. Vastus lateralis in 69-year-old men and women." *J. Gerontol.* 32:33.

Thaler, P. 1982. "At the races." *Runner* 84.

Thompson, R. G., et al. 1979. "Triglyceride concentrations: the disaccharide effect." *Science* 206:838.

Thompson, W. R., et al. 1982. "Physiological and training profiles of ultramarathoners." *Physic. and Sportsmed.* 10:61.

Thorngren, M., and Gustafson, A. 1981. "Effects of 11-week increase in dietary eicosapentaenoic acid on bleeding time, lipids, and platelet aggregation." *Lancet* ii:1190.

Town, G., et al. 1980. "The effect of rope skipping rate on energy expenditure on males and females." *Med. Sci. Sports. Exer.* 12:295.

Truswell, A.S. 1977. "Dietary fat and heart-disease." *Lancet* ii:1173.

————. 1978. "Diet and plasma lipids—a reappraisal." *Am. J. Clin. Nutr.* 31:977.

Tucker, J. B. 1982. "The rhythms of running." *Runner* 50.

Tzankoff, S.P., et al. 1972. "Physiological adjustments to work in older men as affected by physical training." *J. Appl. Physiol.* 33:346.

Vaccaro. P., et al. 1981. "Physiological characteristics of master female runners." *Physic. and Sportsmed.* 9:105.

————. 1981. "Physiological characteristics of female master swimmers." *Physic. and Sportsmed.* 9:75.

Vahouny, G.V., et al. 1981. "Lymphatic absorption of shellfish sterols and their effect of cholesterol absorption." *Am. J. Clin. Nutr.* 35:507.

Vergroesen, A. 1977. "Physiological effects of dietary linoleic acid." *Nutr. Rev.* 35:1.

Vonlossonczym, T.O., et al. 1978. "The effect of a fish diet on serum lipids in healthy human subjects." *Am. J. Clin. Nutr.* 31:1340.

Wade, J., et al. 1981. "Evidence for a physiological regulation of food selection and nutrient intake in twins." *Am. J. Clin. Nutr.* 34:143.

Wahren, J., et al. 1974. "Influence of age on the local circulatory adaptation to leg exercise." *Scand. J. Clin. Lab. Invest.* 33:79.

Wald, N., et al. 1980. "Vitamin-A and cancer." *Lancet* ii:1144.

Walker, A.R.P. 1972. "The human requirement of calcium: should low intakes be supplemented?" *Am. J. Clin. Nutr.* 25:518.

————. 1972. "The influence of numerous pregnancies and lactations on bone dimensions in South African Bantu and Caucasian mothers." *Clin. Sci.* 42:189.

Walker, R. M., and Linkswiler. H. M. 1972. "Calcium retention in the adult human male as affected by protein intake." *J. Nutr.* 102:1297.

Walker, W. 1977. "Changing United States lifestyle and declining vascular mortality: cause or coincidence?" *N. Eng. J. Med.* 297:163.

Watt, E., et al. 1976. "Effect of dietary control and exercise training on daily food intake and serum lipids in postmyocardial infarction patients." *Am. J. Clin. Nutr.* 29:900.

Weissmann, G. 1972. "Lyosomal mechanisms of tissue injury in arthritis." *N. Eng. J. Med.* 286:141.

Weltman, A., et al. 1980. "Caloric restriction and/or mild exercise: effect on serum lipids and body composition." *Am. J. Clin. Nutr.* 33:1002.

Werth. J. 1980. "A little wine for thy heart's sake." *Lancet* ii:1141.

White, A.J., and Finn, R. 1980. "Meat induced hypercholesterolemia." *Lancet* ii:922.

Williams, M. H. 1981. "Blood doping: an update." *Physic. and Sportsmed.* 9:59.

Williams, M. H., et al. 1981. "The effect of induced erythrocythemia upon 5-mile treadmill run time." *Med. Sci. Sports Exer.* 13:169.

Wilmore, J., and Haskel, W. 1972. "Body composition and endurance capacity of professional football players." *J. Appl. Physiol.* 33:564.

Wintsch, S. 1981. "Beading the heat." *Science* 80.

Wischnia, R. 1980. "DMSO—is it the magic formula or the perfect chemical hoax?" *Runner's World* (November):63.

Wissler, R. W. 1978. "Current status of regression studies." *Athero. Rev.* 3:213.

———. 1979. "Evidence for regression of advanced atherosclerotic plaques." *Arteriosclerosis* 5:398.

———, and Vesselinovitch, D. 1976. "Studies of regression of advanced artherosclerosis in experimental animals and man." *Ann. N.Y. Acad. Sci.* 275:363.

Young, V., et al. 1975. "Total human body protein synthesis in relation to protein requirements at various ages." *Nature* 253:192.

Zilversmit, Donald B., 1979. "Atherogenesis: a postprandial phenomenon." *Circulation.* 60:473.

Zimmerman, B. 1980. "Exercise, diet, and high-density lipoprotein cholesterol." *N. Eng. J. Med* 303:223.

———. 1980. "Brain peptides—new synaptic messengers?" *Lancet* ii:895.

———. 1980. "The link between cholesterol and cancer." *Lancet* ii:243.

———. 1980. "Triglycerides and CHD: new data on a continuing controversy." *Mod. Med.* (15, 30 November):72.

———. 1980. "Fish-oil diet." *Science Digest* (November–December):108.

———. 1976. "The multiple risk factor intervention trial." *JAMA* 235:825.

———. 1981. "High-density lipoprotein." *Lancet* I:478.

————. 1981. "Steroid bust, Plucknett loses his record." *Time* 61.

————. 1980. "Urinary calcium and dietary protein." *Clin. Nutr.* 38:9.

————. 1981. "Thinness, delayed menarche, and irregular cycles." *N. Eng. J. Med.* 305:229.

————. 1979. "Do onions and garlic prevent thrombi?" *Mod. Med.* 23.

————. 1980. "Better running: Bill Rodgers training table, a week in the life of a diet." *Runner* 21.

————. 1980. "Exercise and menstrual function." *Physic. and Sportsmed.* 8:41.

————. 1979. "Cave men ate their veggies." *Sci. Digest Spec.* 98.

————. 1982. "Fight infections with exercise." *Science* 6.

————. 1982. "Drug abuse in sports: denial fuels the problem." *Physic. and Sportsmed.* 10:114.

————. 1982. "Confusion about blood fats and exercise." *Health Letter* 20:5.

————. 1982. "Active women need more vitamin-B2." *Medical Update* 6:3.

————. 1982. "The exercise and heart attack question." *Health Letter* 20:7.

Index

353

Index

357

INDEX

Estrogens, 224
Evert Lloyd, Chris, 98
Exercise, mineral loss during, 103–105

Fast-food restaurants, 95–97
Fasting blood sugar levels, 44–45
Fasting myth, 27–28
Fat loss, 214–21
 and complex carbohydrates, 217–21
Fats, 49, 181–82
 and muscles, 34–35
 restricted on diets, 135–36
 saturated and unsaturated, 48–49
 for sport-specific diets, 174–75
 see also Blood fats; Obesity
Fat tissue, calorie burning of, 111–12
Fawcett, Farrah, 110
Fish, 52, 59, 93, 179
Fish and Mushroom Marinade, 283–84
Fleckenstein, Viki, 21, 182, 233
Food additives, 154–55
Food and Drug Administration, 204, 207
Foods
 antioxidants in, 138–55
 beta carotene in, 143–44
 categories for sport-specific diets, 172–81
 high-energy, 9–10
 high-protein, 32
 and muscles, 32–36
 PABA in, 149–50
 pyridoxine in, 148–49
 selenium in, 152–53
 thiamin in, 147–48
 vitamin C in, 141–43
 vitamin E in, 139–40

 see also Diet; Primary foods; Secondary foods; Supplementary foods
Food Values of Portions Commonly Used (Pennington/Church), 210
Free-radicals, 131
 and aging, 132
 and arthritis, 136
 autocatalytic, 134
Freezing, 67–68
French Apple Bake, 323
French gourmet restaurants, 88
French nouvelle cuisine restaurants, 88
Fresh fruits, 53, 56, 59, 89, 92, 178
Fruit. *See* Dried fruit; Fresh fruits
Fruit juices, 178
Fruit pie, 94

Gerulaitis, Vitas, 129, 145
Ginseng, 207–208
Glazed Ratatouille, 284–85
Glucose, 39–40, 44, 50, 55, 58, 159, 201
 see also Blood sugar
Glycogen, 103
 and muscles, 33–34, 106, 167
 see also Carbohydrates
Golf, diets for, 191–94
Gout, 42, 45, 220
Grains. *See* Whole grains
Grated cheese, 53, 59
Greeks (ancient), 23
Green Goddess Dressing, 255
Green peppers
 Italian Stuffed Peppers, 289

Haas Mayonnaise Spread, 269–70

358

Index

Index

Neuroendocrine hormones, 224
Neuromuscular disorders, 205
Neurotransmitters, 209, 210
Neutrophils, 134
Nonfat dry milk, 237
Noodle Pudding, 325
Noodles
  Banana Noodle Custard, 319–20
  Spinach Noodle Casserole, 297
Norepinephrine, 209, 210
Norris, Bill, 225
Nouvelle cuisine restaurants, 88
No-win eating situations, 97–98

Oatmeal Fruit Bars, 326
Oatmeal Royale, 243
Obesity, and sex, 224–25
Octacosanol, 204–206
Oils, 180–81
  saturated and unsaturated, 48–49
  for sport-specific diets, 174–75
  see also Cooking oils; Vegetable oil
Onions
  Bacon, Onion, and Chive Topping, 259–60
  Broccoli and Onion Salad, 250–51
  Howard's Onion Soup, 246–47
Oral contraceptives, and depression, 125–27
Orange Muffins, 314
Osahwa, George, 219
Osteoporosis, 117, 119
Overweight, 170

PABA, 149–50

"Pac-Man" drugs, 132
Pancakes
  Buckwheat pancakes, 91, 241–42
Pantothenic acid, 151–52
  calcium salt of, 211, 213
Para-aminobenzoic acid. See PABA
Parmesan cheese, 59, 238
Pasta, 55, 58, 61–62, 218
  see also Spaghetti
Pasta and Garlic Sauce, 294–95
Peanut butter, 237
  Haas Peanut Butter, 270
Peanut oil, 175
Peas, 56, 59, 115
  Black-Eyed Pea Soup, 244
Pennington, Jean, 210
Peter, Ed, 89
Phenylalanine, 209–11
Phenylbutazone, 135
Phenylethylamine, 209
Phenylpropanolamine, 196, 211
Physician, role of, 15
Phytic acid, 113
Pie. See Fruit pie
Pizza, 96–97
Plantains
  Baked Plantains, 318–19
Popcorn, 53, 59
Porter, Hilarie, 233
Portion size, in sport-specific diets, 169–70
Postcompetition meal, 162–64
Potassium, 25, 104
Potato Casserole, 266–67
Potatoes, 51, 218
  see also Baked potato
Potato recipes and toppings, 259–67
  Bacon, Onion, and Chive Topping, 259–60
  Barbecue Chicken Topping, 260

361

Index

Water *(continued)*
  availability of, 107–108
  and muscles, 103, 106
  pure, 103
  and skin, 106–107
Wayne, John, 195
Weight, and food portion
    size, 66
Weight lifting, diets for,
    189–91
Weight loss, 11, 216
  and complex carbohydrates,
    217–21
  drastic, 165
  see also Overweight
Weight resistance (machine)
    training, diets for, 189–91
Wendy's, 96
Whole eggs, 237
Whole grain breads, 55, 58
Whole grain cereal, 58, 91
Whole grains, 51
Whole Wheat Bread, 315–16
Whole wheat flour, 113
Whole Wheat Raisin Bread,
    316–17

Women (active), 109–27
  and amenorrhea, 124–25
  calories for, 110–13
  and drugs, 123–24
  iron requirements for,
    112–16
  "mini-meal" program for,
    121–24
  and oral contraceptives,
    125–27
  riboflavin and calcium for,
    116–19
Wrestling, diets for, 184–86

Yogurt
  low-fat, 67, 237
  low-fat frozen, 56
  low-fat plain, 52, 56, 59
Yogurt Tomato Dressing,
    258–59

Zucchini
  Cannellini Stuffed Zucchini,
    274–75
Zucchini Squares, 307

SIGNET Books for Your Reference Shelf

**Buy them at your local
bookstore or use coupon
on last page for ordering.**

Ø
_____

Helpful Titles from SIGNET

(0451)

☐ **FEEDING THE HUNGRY HEART: The Experience of Compulsive Eating by Geneen Roth.** Roth, once a compulsive overeater and self-starver, broke free from the destructive cycle of compulsive eating, and went on to help other women do the same. Those women are all here in this inspiring guide to show others that the battle against a hunger that goes deeper than a need for food *can be won.* "Amid all the diet books there is one—this one—that is different ... offers hope and inspiration." —*West Coast Review of Books* (125649—$3.50)*

☐ **KICKING YOUR STRESS HABITS: A Do-It-Yourself Guide for Coping With Stress by Donald A. Tubesing, Ph.D.** The 10-step program for getting rid of unhealthy stress, including: how to develop stress-managing skills; how to replace anxiety-producing attitudes with positive views; and how to break loose from a stressful lifestyle. (118340—$3.50)

☐ **KICKING IT: The New Way to Stop Smoking—Permanently by Dr. David L. Geisinger.** The unique and powerful program that promises "In five weeks you will smoke your last cigarette and never smoke again!" (131274—$2.50)*

☐ **FEELING GOOD: The New Mood Therapy by David D. Burns, M.D.** Preface by Aaron T. Beck, M.D. The clinically proven, drug-free treatment for depression, from the University of Pennsylvania School of Medicine. (126556—$3.95)*

*Prices slightly higher in Canada

_____

**Buy them at your local
bookstore or use coupon
on last page for ordering.**

Self-Help Books from SIGNET

Buy them at your local
bookstore or use coupon
on next page for ordering.

SIGNET Books by Barbara Kraus

VALERIO MASSIMO MANFREDI

THE IDES OF MARCH

Translated from the Italian by Christine Feddersen-Manfredi

McArthur & Company
Toronto

This paperback edition published in 2010 by
McArthur & Company
322 King Street West, Suite 402
Toronto, Ontario
M5V 1J2
www.mcarthur-co.com

First published in Canada in 2009 by
McArthur & Company

First published in English in the United Kingdom by Macmillan

First published in Italian as *Le Idi di Marzo* by
Arnoldo Mondadori Editore S.p.A., Milano

Library and Archives Canada Cataloguing in Publication

Manfredi, Valerio
        The ides of March / Valerio Massimo Manfredi ; translated
from the Italian by Christine Feddersen-Manfredi.

Translation of: Idi di marzo.
ISBN 978-1-55278-835-6

        1. Caesar, Julius--Fiction. 2. Rome--History--53-44 B.C.--
Fiction. I. Feddersen-Manfredi, Christine II. Title.

PQ4873.A47I3413 2010   853'.914   C2009-907365-X

Typeset by SetSystems Ltd, Saffron Waldon, Essex
Cover illustration by Luca Tarlazzi © 3ntini Service

Printed in Canada by Webcom

10 9 8 7 6 5 4 3 2 1

TO JOHN AND DIANA

Those who are about to die are dead,
and the dead are nothing.

Euripides, *Alcestis*, 527

1

Romae, ante diem VIII Idus Martias, hora prima

Rome, 8 March, six a.m.

THE DAY DAWNED GREY. The winter sky was heavy, leaden, the morning a mere hint of light filtering through the vaporous mass spreading over the horizon. Sounds were muffled as well, as dull and sluggish as the clouds veiling the light. The wind came down the Vicus Jugarius in uncertain puffs, like the laboured breathing of a fugitive.

A magistrate appeared in the square at the south end of the Forum. He walked alone, but the insignia he wore made him recognizable all the same, and he was advancing at a brisk pace towards the Temple of Saturn. He slowed in front of the statue of Lucius Junius Brutus, the hero who had overthrown the monarchy nearly five centuries earlier. At the feet of the frowning bronze effigy, on the pedestal bearing his epitaph, someone had scribbled in red lead: 'Do you slumber, Brutus?'

The magistrate shook his head and continued on his way, adjusting the toga that slipped from his narrow shoulders at every flurry. He walked quickly up the temple steps, past the still-steaming altar, and disappeared into the shadows of the portico.

A WINDOW OPENED on the top floor of the House of the Vestals. The virgins who maintained the sacred fire were busy with their duties, while the others were preparing to rest after their night-long vigil.

The Vestalis Maxima, wrapped all in white, had just left the inner courtyard and turned towards the statue of Vesta, which stood in the centre of the cloister, when the earth began to shake beneath her feet. The goddess's head swayed to the right and then to the left. The moulding behind the fountain cracked and a chunk broke off, falling sharply to the ground, the sound amplified by the surrounding silence.

As the Vestal raised her eyes to the wind and clouds, dull thunder could be heard in the distance. Her eyes filled with foreboding. Why was the earth trembling?

ON THE TIBER ISLAND, headquarters to the Ninth Legion, which was stationed outside the city walls under the command of Marcus Aemilius Lepidus, the last shift was going off guard duty. The soldiers and their centurion saluted the Eagle and returned in double file to their quarters. The Tiber flowed turbulently around the island, her dark, swollen waters rising to wash over the bare branches of the alders that bent at her banks.

A HIGH-PITCHED, broken scream punctured the livid silence of dawn. A scream from the residence of the Pontifex Maximus. The House of the Vestals was practically adjacent and the virgins were thrown into panic. They'd heard the scream before, but each time it was worse.

Another scream and the Vestalis Maxima went to the door. From the threshold she could see the bodyguards, two enormous Celts, flanking the door of the Domus. They were apparently impassive. Perhaps they were accustomed to the screams and knew where they came from. Could they be coming from him? From the Pontifex himself? The sound was distorted and mewling now, like the whine of an animal in pain. Hurried footsteps could be heard as a man approached the door carrying a leather bag and made his way past the two Celts, solid and still as telamons. He slipped into the front hall of the ancient building.

The rumble of distant thunder still sounded from the mountains and a stiff wind bowed the tops of the ash trees on the Quirinal. Three trumpet blasts announced the new day. The Vestalis Maxima closed the door to the sanctuary and gathered herself in prayer before the goddess.

THE DOCTOR was met by Calpurnia, the wife of the Pontifex Maximus. She seemed quite frightened.

'Antistius, at last! Come this way quickly. We haven't been able to calm him down this time. Silius is with him.'

Searching through his bag as he followed her, Antistius pulled out a wooden stick covered with leather and entered the room.

Lying on an unkempt bed and dripping with sweat, his eyes staring at nothing, his mouth drooling while his teeth were clenched tight and bared in a snarl, was the Pontifex Maximus, Dictator Perpetuo, Caius Julius Caesar, in the throes of a seizure. The brawny arms of his adjutant, Silius Salvidienus, held him down.

Calpurnia lowered her eyes so that she wouldn't have to see her husband this way and turned to the wall. Meanwhile, Antistius got on to the bed and worked the wooden stick between his patient's teeth until he could force them apart.

'Keep him still!' he ordered Silius. 'Still!'

He extracted a glass phial from his bag and placed a few drops of dark liquid on Caesar's tongue. In a short while, the seizures began to let up, but Silius didn't release his hold until the doctor signalled that he could ease Caesar back down on to his back. The adjutant then gently covered him with a woollen blanket.

Calpurnia drew closer. She wiped the sweat from Caesar's brow and the drool from his mouth, then wet his lips with a piece of linen soaked in cool water. She turned to Antistius.

'What is this terrible thing?' she asked him. 'Why does it happen?'

Caesar now lay in a state of complete prostration. His eyes were closed and his breathing was laboured and heavy.

'The Greeks call it the "sacred disease", because the ancients believed it was the doing of spirits – demons or the gods. Alexander himself suffered from it, so they say, but in reality no one knows what it is. We recognize the symptoms and can only try to limit the damage. The greatest danger is that the person suffering an attack will bite off his tongue with his own teeth. Some have even been suffocated by their tongues. But I've given him his usual sedative, which fortunately seems quite effective. What worries me is the frequency of the attacks. The last one was only two weeks ago.'

'What can we do?'

'Nothing,' replied Antistius, shaking his head. 'We can't do any more than we've already done.'

Caesar opened his eyes and slowly looked around. He then turned to Silius and Calpurnia.

'Leave me alone with him,' he said, gesturing towards the doctor.

Silius shot a puzzled glance at Antistius.

'You can go,' said Antistius. 'There's no immediate danger. But don't go too far. You never know.'

Silius nodded and left the room with Calpurnia. He had always helped and supported her and was her husband's – his commander's – shadow. Centurion of the legendary Tenth Legion, a veteran with twenty years' service, he had salt and pepper hair, dark, damp eyes, as quick as a child's, and the neck of a bull. He followed Calpurnia out like a puppy.

The doctor put his ear to his patient's chest and listened. Caesar's heartbeat was returning to normal.

'Your condition is improving,' he said.

'That doesn't interest me,' replied Caesar. 'Tell me this instead: what would happen if I had such a fit in public? If I

4

fell to the floor foaming at the mouth in the Senate or at the Rostra?'

Antistius bowed his head.

'You don't have an answer for me, do you?'

'No, Caesar, but I understand you. The fact is that these attacks don't give any warning. Or not that I know of.'

'So they depend on the whims of the gods?'

'You believe in the gods?'

'I am the Pontifex Maximus. What should I tell you?'

'The truth. I'm your doctor and if you want me to help you, I have to understand your mind as well as your body.'

'I believe that we are surrounded by mystery. There's room for anything in mystery, even the gods.'

'Hippocrates said that this illness would only be called the "sacred disease" until its causes were discovered.'

'Hippocrates was right but, unfortunately, the disease continues to be "sacred" today and will remain so, I fear, for some time to come. And yet I cannot afford to give any public display of my weaknesses. You can understand that, can't you?'

'I can. But the only one who can tell when an attack is coming on is you. They say that the sacred disease gives no warning, but that each man reacts differently to it. Have you ever had a sign, something that made you think an attack was about to take place?'

Caesar drew a long breath and remained silent, forcing himself to remember. At length, he replied, 'Perhaps. Not any clear sign, nothing that is identical from one time to the next. But occasionally it happens that I see images from other times, suddenly . . . like flashes.'

'What kind of images?'

'Massacres, fields strewn with dead bodies, clouds galloping, shrieking like Furies from hell.'

'They might be actual memories, or simply nightmares. We all have them. You more than anyone, I imagine. No one else has lived a life like yours.'

5

'No, they're not nightmares. When I say "images", I'm talking about something I actually see in front of me, like I am seeing you now.'

'And are these . . . visions always followed by attacks of this sort?'

'Sometimes they are and sometimes they aren't. I can't say for certain that they are connected to my disease. It's a sly enemy I've made for myself, Antistius, an enemy with no face, who pounces, strikes and slips away like a ghost. I am the most powerful man in the world and yet I'm as helpless in the face of this as the lowest of wretches.'

Antistius sighed. 'If you were anyone else, I would recommend . . .'

'What?'

'That you withdraw into private life. Leave the city, public office, political strife. Others have done so before you: Scipio Africanus, Sulla. Perhaps the disease would let go of you if you let go of your daily battles. But I don't suppose you'd ever follow my advice, would you?'

Caesar raised himself into a sitting position on the side of the bed, then swung his feet to the floor and stood up.

'No. I can't afford to. There are still too many things I must do. I'll live with the risk.'

'Then surround yourself with men you trust. Arrange things so that, if it should happen, someone is there to cover you with a toga and there is a closed litter ready to take you where no one can see you. I will be waiting there for you. When the crisis has passed you will be able to return to what you were doing as if nothing had happened. That's all I can say.'

Caesar nodded. 'It's good advice. You can go now, Antistius. I feel better.'

'I'd rather stay.'

'No. You must have other business to attend to. Send in Silius with my breakfast. I'll have something to eat.'

Antistius nodded. 'As you wish. Along with your breakfast,

Silius will bring you a potion I'll mix for you now. It will help to thin the humours of your spleen. That should provide some relief. Now, lie back and give those stiff limbs a little rest. When you feel stronger, a hot bath and a massage would be in order.'

There was no answer from Caesar and Antistius walked out with a sigh.

HE FOUND Calpurnia in the atrium, sitting in an armchair. She was still wearing her nightgown and she had not bathed or eaten. The signs of strain were evident on her face and in her posture. When she saw Antistius heading for the kitchen, she followed him.

'Well?' she asked. 'What do you think?'

'There's nothing new, but unfortunately I have the impression that the disease has taken hold. For the moment all we can do is seek to limit its effects. However, we can always hope that it will go away as suddenly as it started. Remember that Caesar is a man of great resources.'

'No man can weather so many storms of the body and spirit without suffering lasting damage. The past ten years have been as intense as ten lives and they've taken their toll. Caesar is fifty-six years old, Antistius, and yet he intends to embark on another expedition in the East. Against the Parthians.'

As the doctor was crushing seeds in a mortar and then setting them to boil on the stove, Calpurnia sat down. A maidservant began preparing her usual breakfast, an egg cooked under the embers and some toasted bread.

'And that woman is only making the situation worse.'

Antistius didn't need to ask to whom she was referring. Cleopatra VII, the Queen of Egypt, was living in Caesar's villa on the far side of the Tiber. He fell silent, knowing what would happen if he expressed any opinion at all on the subject. Cleopatra had even brought her child to the villa with her, a boy she'd dared to call Ptolemy Caesar.

'That whore,' Calpurnia continued, realizing that Antistius

was not going to pick up on her invitation to join the conversation. 'I hope she drops dead. I've even had the evil eye put on her, but who knows what antidotes she's found to protect herself, and what philtres she's given my husband to drink to keep him bound to her.'

Antistius couldn't help but speak. 'My lady, any middle-aged man would be flattered to conceive a child with a beautiful woman in the bloom of youth. It makes him feel young, vigorous . . .'

Here his voice dropped off and he bit his tongue: not exactly the most diplomatic of things to tell a woman who had never been able to have children herself.

'Forgive me,' he added hastily. 'This is really no affair of mine. What's more, Caesar doesn't need to feel vigorous. He is vigorous. I've been a doctor my whole life and I've yet to see another man of such a hardy constitution.'

'Never mind. I'm used to hearing such things,' replied Calpurnia. 'What worries me is the enormous burden he is carrying. He can't keep this up much longer and I'm sure there are many men out there who would like nothing better than to see him on his knees. Many of those who feign friendship today would turn into bloodthirsty beasts tomorrow. I trust no one, you understand? Nobody.'

'Yes, my lady, I do,' replied the doctor.

He took his potion off the flame, filtered it and poured it into a cup that he set on the tray where the cook was arranging Caesar's breakfast: fava beans, cheese and flatbread with olive oil.

Silius entered and took only the potion.

'Does he not want breakfast now?' asked Calpurnia.

'No. I've just spoken to him and he's changed his mind. He no longer wants to eat. He's gone out on to the terrace.'

'Your potion, Caesar.'

Caesar had his back to Silius, his hands on the balustrade.

He was facing the Aventine Hill, from where a flock of starlings had risen like a dark cloud flying towards the Tiber.

He turned slowly, as if he'd only just realized that Silius was present. He took the steaming potion and set it on the parapet. After a few moments he lifted it to his lips and took a sip.

'Where is Publius Sextius?' he asked after he'd swallowed.

'Centurion Publius Sextius is in Modena, on your orders, Caesar.'

'Yes, yes, I know that, but according to my calculations he should be heading back by now. Has he sent a message?'

'No, not that I know of.'

'If a letter arrives from him, inform me immediately, at any time of day or night and no matter what I am doing.'

'You're expected shortly at the Temple of Jupiter Optimus Maximus at the Capitol to offer a sacrifice. If you're feeling strong enough, of course.'

Caesar took another sip of the potion and looked Silius in the eye.

'Of course. At times I forget I'm the High Priest of Rome and yet it should be my foremost concern . . . No bath and no massage, then.'

'That depends on you, Caesar,' replied Silius.

'Remember: wake me, even if I'm sleeping.'

'Sorry?'

'If a message from Sextius arrives.'

'Of course. Don't worry.'

'It should be the first of my concerns . . .' he repeated, as if talking to himself.

Silius looked at him with a puzzled expression, trying to follow Caesar's meandering thoughts.

'. . . my priesthood, that is. And yet I've never believed that the gods care a whit about us. Why should they?'

'It's the first time I've heard you say such a thing. What are you thinking of, commander?'

'Don't you know why we burn victims on the altar day after

9

day? It's so that the gods will see the smoke rising from our cities and remember not to trample them when they walk invisibly on the earth. Otherwise they would crush us as easily as we crush an ant.'

'What an interesting analogy, sir,' replied Silius. 'Antistius said to drink it all,' he added, pointing.

Caesar picked up the cup again and downed the potion.

'In fact, there is no smoke so black or so dense as that of scorched flesh. Believe me, I know.'

Silius knew as well. And he knew what his commander was thinking of. Silius had been at his side at Pharsalus and at Alexandria, in Africa and in Spain. Ever since Caesar had crossed the Rubicon, the bodies he'd seen burning had been those not of uncivilized enemies but of citizens like himself. The bodies of Roman citizens. Burned into Silius's memory were images of the battlefield of Pharsalus covered with the corpses of fifteen thousand fellow citizens, including knights, senators, former magistrates. From his horse, Caesar had scanned the field of slaughter with the eyes of a hawk. He had said, 'It's what they asked for,' but in a low voice, as if talking to himself, as if to clear his conscience.

It was Caesar who shook Silius from his thoughts this time, saying, 'Come now. They're waiting for us and I still have to get ready.'

They went down together and Silius helped Caesar to wash and dress.

'Shall I call for the litter?' Silius asked.

'No. We'll go on foot. The stroll will do me good.'

'Then I'll call your guard.'

'No, don't bother. Actually, I'm thinking I should get rid of them.'

'Of your personal guard? Why would you do that?'

'I don't like the idea of going around my own city with bodyguards. That's what tyrants do.'

THE IDES OF MARCH

Silius regarded him with amazement but said nothing. He blamed Caesar's strange attitude and behaviour on his illness. Could the disease be influencing the way he thought?

'After all,' Caesar continued, 'the senators have approved a *senatus consultum* in which they swear to shield me with their own bodies if my person should be threatened. What better defence could I ask for?'

Silius was dumbfounded. He couldn't believe what he was hearing and was already thinking of how to prevent Caesar from taking such a foolhardy decision. He asked to be excused, went down to the ground floor and instructed several of the servants to follow them at a distance with a litter.

THEY WALKED down the Sacred Way, passing in front of the Temple of Vesta and the basilica that Caesar was building with the spoils of his campaign against the Gauls. Although he had dedicated it two years before, driven by a sense of urgency even then, the work had not yet been completed.

It was a magnificent structure nonetheless, clad in precious marble, with a wide central nave and two aisles. The basilica was one of the gifts that Caesar had offered the city, but certainly not the last. Since his return from Alexandria, Rome no longer satisfied him. The city had grown in a disorderly, unharmonious way, building upon building, creating an impression of unseemly clutter. The imposing roads, majestic palaces and extraordinary monuments of Alexandria, which excited the admiration of visitors from every part of the world, were utterly lacking in Rome.

The Forum to their right was beginning to fill up with people, but no one noticed Caesar because he'd pulled his toga over his head and his face wasn't visible. They passed in front of the Temple of Saturn, the god who had ruled during the Age of Gold, back when men were happy with what the soil and their flocks offered them. Back when men lived in simple wooden huts, sleeping soundly after a modest meal shared around the table with their wives and children, before waking to birdsong.

Silius found himself thinking that the age destiny had reserved for him was quite different: an age of ferocity and greed, of incessant conflict, civil strife, the slaughter of Romans by other Romans, citizens banished, exiled, sentenced to death. A violent age, an age of war and betrayal. And hatred between brothers was the fiercest and most implacable hatred of all, Silius mused, as he glanced over at Caesar's face, which was carved by the shadows of the toga that fell at the sides of his head. He wondered whether this man might truly be the founder of a new age. An age in which these seemingly endless hostilities would run their course and open on to an era of peace so lasting that it would make men forget how much blood had been spilled and how tenaciously their rancour had gripped them. He raised his eyes to the grand temple which dominated the city from the top of the Capitol.

The sky was dark.

was built during the age of the Tarquinian kings and dedicated to the Capitoline Triad (Jupiter, Juno and Minerva). It was burned down, restructured and restored numerous times. Its original architecture must have closely resembled an Etruscan temple, with a tufa podium, masonry walls and a wooden roof, decorated with multi-hued terracotta ornaments.

TEMPLE OF SATURN – The oldest temple in Rome, along with the Temple of Jupiter Capitolinus. Construction was begun during the age of the kings and the temple was inaugurated in the fifth century BC. Completely rebuilt by Munatius Plancus three years after Caesar's death.

TEMPLE OF VENUS GENETRIX – Built by Julius Caesar in his forum. The sanctuary was dedicated to the legendary forebear of the *gens Julia* who was believed to have descended from Julus, the son of Aeneas, who was the son of Venus herself. The propagandistic intent was evident: Caesar was the new father of his homeland, following in the steps of Aeneas.

TIBER ISLAND – An alluvial island in the Tiber river, connected to the mainland by two bridges, the Pons Fabricius and the Pons Cestius. In the first century BC, it was given the shape of a ship, achieving an extraordinary monumental and scenic effect. The Temple of Aesculapius, god of medicine, was built on the island in 290 BC, after a great plague broke out in Rome. The island may have been one of the reasons Rome was originally chosen as a settlement site, acting as a natural ford between the north and south banks of the Tiber, thus connecting the north and south of the Italian peninsula.

TULLIANUM PRISON (later Mamertine Prison) – The oldest prison in Rome, excavated in the south-eastern slopes of the Capitoline hill. Notable prisoners included Tiberius Gracchus, Lentulus and Cethegus – Catiline's fellow conspirators – Vercingetorix, Jugurtha the King of Numidia and, according to an early Christian tradition, the apostle Peter.

VIA SACRA – The street that went from the *Velia*, where the *rex sacrorum* lived, to the *Regia*. From here, it continued to the Temple of Saturn where it turned into the *Clivus Capitolinus*.

VICUS JUGARIUS – The street which began at the Tiber river and led to the Forum, passing between the Temple of Saturn and the Basilica Julia.